DATE DUE

JUN 1 0 2006		
NOV 0 9 2006		
MAY 0 4 2015		

ENEMY ALIENS

ALSO BY DAVID COLE

No Equal Justice:
Race and Class in the American Criminal Justice System

Terrorism and the Constitution:
Sacrificing Civil Liberties in the Name of National Security
(with James X. Dempsey)

ENEMY ALIENS

DOUBLE STANDARDS AND CONSTITUTIONAL FREEDOMS IN THE WAR ON TERRORISM

DAVID COLE

THE NEW PRESS

NEW YORK
LONDON

NOV 0 6 2003

Published in the United States by The New Press, New York, 2003
Distributed by W. W. Norton & Company, Inc., New York

LIBRARY OF CONGRESS CATALOGING-IN-PUBLICATION DATA
Cole, David, 1958–
Enemy aliens : double standards and constitutional freedoms in the war
on terrorism / David Cole.
p.   cm.
Includes bibliographical references and index.
ISBN 1-56584-800-4 (hc.)
1. Aliens—United States.   2. Subversive activities—United States.
3. National security—Law and legislation—United States.
4. Terrorism—United States—Prevention.   I. Title.

KF4800.C58   2003
323.3'291'0973—dc21   2003050966

The New Press was established in 1990 as a not-for-profit alternative to the large,
commercial publishing houses currently dominating the book publishing industry.
The New Press operates in the public interest rather than for private gain, and is committed
to publishing, in innovative ways, works of educational, cultural, and community value
that are often deemed insufficiently profitable.

The New Press
38 Greene Street, 4th floor
New York, NY 10013
www.thenewpress.com

In the United Kingdom:
6 Salem Road
London W2 4BU

Composition by dix!

Printed in the United States of America

2   4   6   8   10   9   7   5   3   1

For my parents, Douglas and Virginia Cole,
who taught me that every human being,
regardless of status, deserves equal dignity and respect.

The alien was to be protected, not because he was a member of one's family, clan, religious community; but because he was a human being. In the alien, therefore, man discovered the idea of humanity.

HERMANN COHEN*

* H. Freedman, ed., *Jeremiah, Soncino Books of the Bible* (series ed. A. Cohen) (London: Soncino Books of the Bible, rev. ed. 1985), 52 (quoting Hermann Cohen).

CONTENTS

PART 3—SECURITY

PART 4—THE RIGHT THING TO DO

ACKNOWLEDGMENTS

I began writing this book several months after the attacks of September 11, but in a sense I've been writing it since I became a lawyer nearly twenty years ago, and had my first trial experience in El Paso, Texas, defending Margaret Randall, who faced deportation under "national security" provisions of the immigration law for having advocated "world communism." Since then, I have worked with countless clients, lawyers, activists, and scholars on issues of national security, immigrants' rights, and constitutional freedoms, and I am indebted to all of them for the many lessons they have taught me.

For direct assistance on the book itself, I owe my greatest thanks to my father, Douglas Cole, who spent many hours teaching me to write as I was growing up (much as other fathers teach their sons to throw a baseball), and came out of retirement to read and edit every page of this manuscript. I also owe special gratitude to my editor, Diane Wachtell, the kind of thoughtful but supportive critic with a perfect ear that every writer should be so fortunate to have. Jonathan Greenberg also owes special mention, for urging me to write a book like this long before September 11. And for supporting me as I obsessed over the details, as well as for her good judgment and editing suggestions throughout, I thank my wife, Nina Pillard.

Many individuals provided comments and feedback on various versions and drafts of this book, including: Alex Aleinikoff, Barbara Babcock, Alan Dershowitz, Amitai Etzioni, Oren Gross, Bonnie Honig, Wendy Kaminer, Juliette Kayyem, Steve Legomsky, Mari Matsuda, Hiroshi Motomura, Natsu Saito, Philip Thomas, Laurence Tribe, and Robert Weisberg. I also benefited from presenting the ideas in this book to a wide range of forums and symposia over the course

of the last two years, and received invaluable feedback from participants in each one, including the Georgetown University Law Center
faculty workshop, the University of Pennsylvania Law School faculty
workshop, the Yale Law School Human Rights Workshop, the
Supreme Court Historical Society workshop, the Social Sciences Research Center, Princeton University's Woodrow Wilson School, the
Joint Military Intelligence College, Stanford Law School, the University of Chicago Law School, Amherst College, Wellesley College, and
the Council on Foreign Relations.

The Open Society Institute, the Ford Foundation, and Georgetown
University Law Center each provided very generous financial support
to free me up to concentrate on this project during a period when it
was a challenge to concentrate on anything.

This book is inspired and guided by the many colleagues with
whom I've worked on immigrants' rights issues. Four deserve special
mention, as they have been both mentors and colleagues—Paul Hoffman, Michael Maggio, Michael Ratner, and Marc Van Der Hout. But I
also owe special gratitude to Phyllis Bennis, Lou Bograd, Jeanne Butterfield, Nancy Chang, Regis Fernandez, Kit Gage, Lee Gelernt, Lucas
Guttentag, Joe Hohenstein, Abdeen Jabara, Ira Kurzban, Josh Levy,
Randall Marshall, Jonathan Martel, Albert Mokhiber, Greg Nojeim,
Ashraf Nubani, Judy Rabinovitz, Mark Rosenbaum, Houeida Saad,
Noel Salah, Peter Schey, Martin Schwartz, Carol Sobel, Len Weinglass,
Frank Wilkinson, and Mike Wishnie, all of whom have in one way or
another devoted all or considerable parts of their careers to fighting
for the rights of those without a voice in the political process.

I had prodigious and invaluable research assistance from a stellar
and hard-working group of Georgetown law students: Cira Caroscio,
Kate Didech, Matt Dubeck, Rebecca Hammel, Matt Kilby, Jeff Lea-
sure, Nicole Nice-Peterson and Jihee Suh. I also benefited from remarkably prompt and thorough support from the staff of the
Georgetown University Law Library and from careful copy-editing
and proofreading by Anna Selden.

Finally, and perhaps most profoundly, I owe a debt of thanks to my clients, who have personally fought for their rights and the rights of all foreign nationals, including: Nasser Ahmed, Mazen Al-Najjar, Bashar Amer, Aiad Barakat, Imad Hamad, Khader Hamide, Hany Kiareldeen, Julie Mungai, Amjad Obeid, Ayman Obeid, Fouad Rafeedie, Margaret Randall, Naim Sharif, and Michel Shehadeh. These individuals spent years of their lives, in many instances locked up on secret evidence, fighting not only for the right to remain in this country but for the principles of political freedom, due process, and equal opportunity inscribed in our Constitution but not yet extended fully to all.

Some of the ideas set out here appeared in earlier form in "Enemy Aliens," 54 *Stanford Law Review* 953 (2002), "The New McCarthyism: Repeating History in the War on Terrorism," 38 *Harvard Civil Liberties-Civil Rights Law Review* 1 (2003), and "Their Liberties, Our Security," *Boston Review*, December 2002/January 2003, 4.

ENEMY ALIENS

INTRODUCTION

Come on, let us deal wisely with them; lest they multiply, and it come to pass, that, when there falleth out any war, they join also unto our enemies, and fight against us, and so get them up out of the land.

EXODUS 1:10

To those who pit Americans against immigrants and citizens against non-citizens, to those who scare peace-loving people with phantoms of lost liberty, my message is this: Your tactics only aid terrorists, for they erode our national unity and diminish our resolve. They give ammunition to America's enemies, and pause to America's friends.

U.S. ATTORNEY GENERAL JOHN ASHCROFT,
TESTIFYING TO SENATE JUDICIARY
COMMITTEE, DECEMBER 6, 2001

On January 24, 2002, the United States military transported John Walker Lindh, a young American raised in Marin County, California, and captured with the Taliban on the battlefields of Afghanistan, to Alexandria, Virginia, where he was to be tried in a civilian criminal court for conspiring to kill Americans. White House press secretary Ari Fleischer announced that "the great strength of America is he will now have his day in court."[1] Lindh did indeed have his day in court. He was represented by one of the nation's premier defense attorneys, James Brosnahan, and a highly skilled former federal prosecutor, George Harris. They mounted a vigorous defense, raising serious constitutional challenges under the First, Fourth, Fifth, and Sixth Amendments to the Constitution. Ultimately, the government dropped its most serious charges—conspiring to kill Americans and aiding Al Qaeda—in exchange for Lindh's guilty plea on charges that he violated an economic embargo regulation by offering his services to the Taliban, and that he had carried a firearm while doing so.

At the same time that Lindh was transported to Virginia, the military was holding 158 foreign nationals, allegedly associated with the Taliban or Al Qaeda, in eight-foot-by-eight-foot chain-link cages at a United States military base in Guantánamo Bay, Cuba.[2] A widely circulated photograph (reproduced on this book's cover) depicted the prisoners bound and shackled, their eyes covered with blacked-out goggles and their mouths covered with surgical masks, kneeling on the ground before U.S. soldiers.[3] Unlike Lindh, most of these individuals, whose identities the government still refuses to disclose, will never get a day in court. In January 2002, President George W. Bush announced that he had categorically determined that the Guantánamo detainees were not entitled to the protections accorded prisoners of war under the Geneva Conventions and need not be given any sort of individualized hearing to determine whether they were appropriately detained. Secretary of Defense Donald Rumsfeld dismissed concerns about their treatment with the assertion that "they are being treated vastly better than they treated anybody else over the last several years."[4] As of May 2003, not one of the more than 650 persons who have been held in Guantánamo Bay has had any kind of hearing to determine whether he is in fact a member of Al Qaeda, the Taliban, or an innocent passerby, despite substantial indications that many of them may have been mistakenly identified as combatants.

Two months before the first prisoners arrived at Guantánamo Bay, the president issued a military order providing that noncitizens accused of Al Qaeda membership or terrorist crimes could be tried by military tribunals, in which the military would act as prosecutor, judge, jury, and executioner, without any appeal to a civilian court.[5] Vice President Dick Cheney defended the order at the time by claiming that "somebody who comes into the United States of America illegally, who conducts a terrorist operation killing thousands of innocent Americans—men, women, and children—is not a lawful combatant. . . . They don't deserve the same guarantees and safeguards that would be used for an American citizen going through the normal judicial process."[6]

As Vice President Cheney's comment reflects, the difference between the treatment afforded John Walker Lindh and his fellow Taliban and Al Qaeda prisoners held in Guantánamo Bay was initially justified on the ground that Lindh was, as the press nicknamed him, "the *American* Taliban." When a reporter asked Attorney General John Ashcroft why Lindh was being tried in an ordinary criminal court rather than before a military tribunal, the attorney general explained that as a citizen, Lindh was not subject to the military tribunals created by President Bush's order.[7] As a purely legal matter, the president could have subjected United States citizens to military commissions; citizens have been tried in military tribunals before, and the Supreme Court upheld such treatment as recently as World War II.[8] But the president chose to limit his order to noncitizens, and the vice president's comments sought to reassure U.S. citizens that *their* rights were not at stake.

Five months later, however, when the administration discovered that one of its captives in Guantánamo Bay, Yasser Hamdi, was probably an American citizen—he had been born in Louisiana—it immediately extended the concept of military justice to citizens. On April 5, 2002, the military transferred Hamdi from Guantánamo Bay to a naval brig in Norfolk, Virginia, but continued to assert authority to hold him under the same conditions as the foreign nationals held in Guantánamo Bay: indefinitely, without charges, without trial, without access to a lawyer, and, for all practical purposes, incommunicado.

In June 2002, the administration went still further. Facing a hearing before a federal judge in which it would have had to justify its detention of Jose Padilla, another U.S. citizen, the government sought to bypass the judge altogether by removing Padilla from the civilian justice system and placing him in military custody. Unlike Hamdi, who was allegedly captured on the battlefield in Afghanistan, Padilla was arrested at O'Hare Airport in Chicago. The government has said that Padilla had looked up information on radioactive "dirty bombs" on the Internet, and had then met with Al Qaeda representatives abroad. But the government did not charge Padilla with a crime. Instead, the government claimed that because President Bush had labeled Padilla an "enemy combatant"—or, in the president's own words, "a bad guy"—the military could hold him, like Hamdi, without trial, without charges, and without access to a lawyer or the outside world.[9] When lawyers sought to challenge Padilla's and Hamdi's detentions, the government initially took the position that the courts had no power whatsoever to review the president's decisions to detain them. When the most conservative federal appellate court in the country— the United States Court of Appeals for the Fourth Circuit—rejected that extreme position, the administration retreated, but only slightly. It conceded that American citizens held here have a right to judicial review, but continued to maintain that they have no right to a lawyer and that the courts must defer to the president's designation without questioning whether the underlying factual allegations are true.

In August 2002, the *Wall Street Journal* reported that the Justice Department was considering creating a special prison camp for Americans who might in the future be designated as "enemy combatants." Administration officials reportedly explained that the obstacles prosecutors had faced in the criminal trials of Lindh and Zacarias Moussaoui, the only person in the United States actually charged to date with involvement in the September 11 attacks, had led them to advocate bypassing the criminal route altogether by holding people in military custody as "enemy combatants."[10]

The treatment of Lindh, Hamdi, Padilla, and the hundreds of nameless noncitizens still held in Guantánamo Bay provides a cautionary tale as the nation struggles over how to respond to the terrorist attacks of September 11, 2001. There has been much talk about the need to sacrifice liberty for security. In practice, however, the government has most often at least initially sacrificed *noncitizens'* liberties while retaining basic protections for citizens. This is a politically tempting way to mediate the tension between liberty and security. Citizens need not forgo *their* rights, and the targeted noncitizens have no direct voice in the democratic process by which to register their objections. No one has ever been voted out of office for targeting foreign nationals in times of crisis; to the contrary, crises often inspire the demonization of "aliens" as the nation seeks unity by emphasizing differences between "us" and "them."

But as Hamdi's and Padilla's cases illustrate, what we do to foreign nationals today often paves the way for what will be done to American citizens tomorrow. The line between citizen and foreigner, so natural during wartime, is not only easy to exploit when restrictive measures are introduced, but also easy to breach when the government later finds it convenient to do so. The transition from denying the rights of enemy aliens to infringing those of American citizens was unusually swift with Hamdi and Padilla; more often, the transition takes years to complete. But history suggests that the transition is virtually inevitable, and that therefore in the long term, the rights of all of us are in the balance when the government selectively sacrifices foreign nationals' liberties.

When a democratic society strikes the balance between liberty and security in ways that impose the costs of security measures equally on all, one might be relatively confident that the political process will achieve a proper balance. Since September 11, we have repeatedly done precisely the opposite, sacrificing the rights of a minority group—noncitizens, and especially Arab and Muslim noncitizens— in the name of the majority's security interests. The government has selectively subjected foreign nationals to interviews, registration, automatic detention, and deportation based on their Arab or Muslim national origin; detained thousands of them, here and abroad; tried many of them in secret, and refused to provide any trials or hearings whatsoever to others; interrogated them for months on end under highly coercive, incommunicado conditions and without access to lawyers; authorized their exclusion based on pure speech; made them deportable for wholly innocent political associations with disfavored groups; and authorized their indefinite detention on the attorney general's say-so. These and other measures targeted at noncitizens, and often defended either explicitly or implicitly by noting that they do not affect American citizens, have inspired relatively little protest from the public.

On the other hand, when the administration has proposed initiatives that would affect citizens' liberties directly, the public response has been markedly different. When the Justice Department announced "Operation TIPS"—the Terrorism Information and Prevention System—which involved recruiting utility employees, delivery personnel, and millions of other private individuals to snoop on their fellow citizens and pass on suspicious information to the Justice Department, it was roundly criticized by liberals and conservatives alike, and, at Republican House Majority Leader Richard Armey's initiative, Congress barred its implementation in Homeland Security legislation. The same bill blocked the development of a national identity card, another initiative that would directly affect citizens. And when the Pentagon proposed a sweeping data-mining program, dubbed "Total Information Awareness," designed to conduct massive computer sweeps of private and public computer records in search of suspicious patterns of behavior, Congress promptly blocked its implementation *as applied to U.S. persons.*[11] If the Pentagon wanted to violate foreign visitors' privacy, Congress effectively said, that would be fine, but citizens' privacy was another matter entirely.

Some argue that treating citizens and noncitizens differently makes perfect sense under the circumstances. The attacks of September 11 were perpetrated by nineteen Arab and Muslim noncitizens, and we have reason to believe that other Arab and Muslim noncitizens are associated with the attackers and will seek to attack again. While over 99.9 percent of Arabs and Muslims have nothing to do with terrorism, it is nonetheless true that Al Qaeda members and operatives are more likely to be Arab and Muslim than Mexican or Quaker. Moreover, if citizens and noncitizens were treated identically, citizenship itself might be rendered meaningless. War inevitably involves the drawing of lines in the sand between citizens of our nation and those against whom we are fighting—"enemy aliens." Citizens, it is said, are presumptively loyal; noncitizens are not. Surely in a warlike setting it makes sense to treat foreign nationals differently from citizens.

As reasonable as such arguments may appear at first glance, the central argument of this book is that trading foreign nationals' liberties for citizens' security should be resisted for four reasons. The double standard is (1) illusory in the long run; (2) likely to prove counterproductive as a security matter; (3) a critical factor in the oft-regretted pattern of government overreaction in times of crisis; and (4) most importantly, constitutionally and morally wrong.

Viewed from the vantage point of history, the claim that Americans' freedoms are not at risk when foreign nationals are targeted in the name of national security is false. What we are willing to allow our government to do to immigrants today creates a template for how it will treat citizens tomorrow. In 1798, driven by nativist fears of radical French and Irish immigrants, Congress enacted the Enemy Alien Act. This law, which remains on the books to this day, authorizes the president during wartime to detain, deport, or otherwise restrict the liberties of any person over fourteen years of age who is a citizen of a country with which we are at war, without any individualized showing of disloyalty, criminal conduct, or even suspicion. During World War II, the government extended that logic to intern 110,000 persons of Japanese ancestry, about two-thirds of whom were U.S. citizens. As the Japanese internment demonstrated, alienage discrimination is often closely tied to (and a cover for) racial animus, and is therefore particularly susceptible to being extended to citizens along racial lines.

Similarly, while we customarily think of the McCarthy era as beginning in the late 1940s, its foundations were laid by several decades of targeting foreign nationals for their purportedly subversive political associations. Putting aside the short-lived Alien and Sedition Acts of 1798, the first federal laws penalizing radical associations and subversive speech date back to 1903, and were targeted exclusively at immigrants. In 1919 and 1920, a young J. Edgar Hoover, then head of the Justice Department's "Alien Radical" division, used those laws in the

"Palmer Raids" to round up thousands of foreign nationals for their suspected political associations. At the time, Hoover and Attorney General A. Mitchell Palmer urged Congress to pass a peacetime sedition law that would give the government similar power over citizens, but Congress balked. In the Cold War, however, Hoover got what he had wanted since 1919: legal authority to regulate the political activities, speech, and association of U.S. citizens in much the same way that, in his first job as a young lawyer, he had been able to control the political activities of noncitizens. In the nation's longstanding struggle with Communism, antialien measures were consistently used as a driving wedge to introduce security initiatives later extended to citizens. American history confirms the prescience of James Madison's remark in 1798 in a letter to Thomas Jefferson: "Perhaps it is a universal truth that the loss of liberty is to be charged to provisions against danger, real or pretended, from abroad." [12]

Similar developments have already occurred in today's war on terrorism. Military justice, introduced by President Bush as limited to noncitizens, and expressly defended on that ground by Vice President Cheney, has been extended to U.S. citizens Padilla and Hamdi. Penalizing the provision of material support to terrorist organizations, a notion which first surfaced in the immigration setting in the early 1990s, justified then by claims that noncitizens do not enjoy the same First Amendment rights as citizens, has now been extended to U.S. citizens through the criminal law. The use of secret, undisclosed evidence, long a feature of the immigration law and defended on the ground that noncitizens deserve reduced due process protections, has now been invoked to defend the freezing of U.S. charities' assets and the detention of U.S. citizens as enemy combatants. And a draft of an administration antiterrorism bill leaked to the press in February 2003 would seek to turn even native-born citizens accused of ties with terrorist groups into "aliens" by stripping them of their citizenship. As these developments illustrate, the line between citizen and noncitizen is a fragile one, and government officials, while quick to cite the distinction when introducing new measures of surveillance and control, are also quick to elide the distinction as they grow accustomed to the powers they exercise over foreign nationals. As political scientist Bonnie Honig has put it, we not only "persecute people because they are foreign . . . [but] we almost always make foreign those whom we persecute."[13]

The second reason to resist relying on double standards to mediate the tension between liberty and security is that they are likely to prove counterproductive as a security matter. Employing a double standard with respect to the basic rights accorded citizens and noncitizens undermines our legitimacy at home and abroad. At home, law enforcement is more effective when it works with rather than against communities. If authorities have reason to believe there might be potential terrorists lurking in Arab and Muslim immigrant communities, it would make sense to work with the millions of law-abiding members of those communities to obtain their assistance in identifying potential threats. Instead of building bridges to those communities, however, the Bush administration has alienated them by treating many of their members as suspect because of their ethnicity, national origin, or religion, and by pursuing others under conditions of inordinate secrecy that invite fear and paranoia.

Legitimacy may be even more critical at the international level. As September 11 illustrated, terrorism is a transnational phenomenon and demands a transnational response. We must maintain a broad coalition and obtain genuine collaboration if we are to succeed in our efforts, not only because we need the cooperation of many different nations' intelligence and law enforcement agencies, but also because if we are seen as fighting for our own parochial interests and not for the interests of justice and peace more broadly, we are likely to inspire more people to take up the mantle of terrorism against us. One might have expected sympathy for America to be at an all-time high after the attacks of September 11. The world did extend such sympathy in the immediate aftermath, but that sympathy dissipated quickly, replaced by an alarming rise in anti-Americanism, even among the populations of our staunchest Western allies.[14] The root complaint of this anti-Americanism is that our nation acts as if it need not adhere to the same rules that govern the rest of the world. In the international arena, we have eschewed international agreements on the environment, ballistic weapons, and international criminal justice, and simply bypassed the United Nations Security Council when it became clear that it would reject authorization to invade Iraq.[15] On the domestic front, the government has selectively imposed on foreign nationals burdens and obligations that would not be tolerated if imposed broadly on American citizens. In both arenas, we have employed a double standard: one set of rules and laws for "us," and another set of rules and laws for "them." As illustrated by our allies' critical responses to the military tribunal order, the Guantánamo Bay detentions, and the march to war with Iraq, our credibility on matters of international law and human rights is at a low ebb, and that has greatly hampered our ability to build and maintain the coalitions we need to respond effectively to the threat of terrorism.[16]

Third, striking the balance between liberty and security equitably for all may help counteract our historic tendency to overreact in times of fear. The virtually unanimous judgment of history is that we have always overreacted in times of crisis. During World War I, we imprisoned people merely for speaking out against the war effort.[17] In World War II, we interned more than 110,000 persons solely because of their Japanese ancestry.[18] And over the course of the Cold War, thousands of innocent persons lost their jobs, were subjected to congressional investigations, or were incarcerated for their mere association with the Communist Party.[19] In hindsight, these responses are widely viewed as shameful excesses. But in their day they were carried out over little objection.

The real challenge is to recognize and correct for the overreaction while the crisis is ongoing. Even though there is broad consensus about the judgment of history, invocations of history and restraint are unlikely to temper our responses. The current crisis always feels new and immediate in ways that past resolved crises cannot. Precommitting to treat the fundamental rights of citizens and foreign nationals equally, however, could provide a prophylactic against such excesses. The entire community would have an immediate stake not only in the security side of the balance, but also in the liberty side. Because our overreactions generally depend upon emergency measures selectively targeted at vulnerable minorities, especially noncitizens, insisting that we respect equally foreign nationals' and U.S. citizens' fundamental human rights might hold us to a more calibrated and just response.

As Justice Robert Jackson wrote many years ago, "nothing opens the door to arbitrary action so effectively as to allow [government] officials to pick and choose only a few to whom they will apply legislation and thus escape the political retribution that might be visited upon them if larger numbers were [affected]."[20] By the same token, "there is no more effective practical guaranty against arbitrary and unreasonable government than to require that the principles of law which officials would impose upon a minority must be imposed generally."[21] Foreign nationals are the paradigmatic "other," especially in times of war. As one critic has argued in connection with the current crisis, "The state's ability to label people as terrorists or terrorist sympathizers, no matter how absurd or far-fetched, works to position those so labeled as non-citizens, outside the moral community, to whom human rights have no relevance."[22] If we can resist the temptation to treat foreign nationals as "enemy aliens," and instead treat them as human beings entitled to the same fundamental rights as the citizenry, we may be able to temper the overreactions before it is too late.

Finally, the most important reason for resisting the temptation to trade foreigners' rights for citizens' security is that it is is morally and constitutionally wrong to do so. Under our Constitution, the rights at stake—political and religious freedom, due process, and equal protection of the laws—are not limited to citizens, but apply to all "persons" subject to our laws. These rights are best understood not as special privileges stemming from a specific social contract, but as inherent in what it means to be a free person with human dignity. They are human rights, not privileges of citizenship, and ought to apply whenever the government seeks to impose legal obligations on persons. The only rights the Constitution describes as applying to "citizens" are the right not to be denied the vote on discriminatory grounds, and the right to run for federal elective office. Precisely because noncitizens do not enjoy the franchise, and therefore cannot rely on the political process for their protection, it is all the more crucial that they be accorded basic human rights enforceable in court.

International and constitutional law have long acknowledged that during wartime the government has special power over "enemy aliens"—nationals of the country with which we are fighting. The Court has upheld the constitutionality of the Enemy Alien Act.[23] And in *Johnson v. Eisentrager*,[24] the Court held that enemy aliens captured on the battlefield abroad had no right to seek habeas corpus in a United States court to challenge their subjection to military trial.[25] The Court noted that at common law, an enemy alien had no rights during a time of war,[26] and that the United States "regard[ed] him as part of the enemy resources."[27] But the "enemy alien" rule applies only in a time of *declared war* and only to *citizens of the country with which we are at war.* Some might argue that in the post–9/11 world, as we fight a war against a phenomenon—terrorism—and an international criminal organization—Al Qaeda—rather than a nation, the "enemy alien" concept should be updated and expanded to justify differential treatment of foreign nationals associated with Al Qaeda or terrorism. But the World War II experience raises serious questions about the validity of the entire "enemy alien" authority, an authority that has not been invoked since. And whatever one thinks of the viability of the "enemy alien" concept, it certainly does not justify the government's actions since September 11. The government has selectively imposed a host of special obligations and burdens on foreign nationals from virtually all Arab and Muslim nations, most of which are working with us in the war on terrorism, and only two of which—Afghanistan and Iraq—were involved in active hostilities against us. The Supreme

Court was careful to stress in *Eisentrager* that the power over enemy aliens is "an incident of war and not . . . an incident of alienage."[28] It is critical to honor that distinction, the Court warned, because " '[m]uch of the obscurity which surrounds the rights of aliens has its origin in this confusion of diverse subjects.' "[29]

In the wake of September 11, we plainly need to rethink the balance between liberty and security. The attacks, which killed more than 3,000 people and revealed newfound depths of human cruelty, succeeded beyond their perpetrators' wildest dreams and our worst nightmares in wreaking destruction and spreading fear throughout the nation. The anthrax scare that followed underscored the gravity of the threats we face, vividly demonstrating that scientific and technological advances have made weapons of mass destruction far too accessible. We feel a profound and deeply unfamiliar sense of vulnerability in their wake and make correspondingly urgent demands for security and reassurance. In such a setting, Attorney General John Ashcroft is not alone in arguing that civil liberties must not stand in the way of victory.[30] After all, as Justice Arthur Goldberg famously said, and administration defenders are fond of quoting, the Constitution "is not a suicide pact."[31]

Such statements are easy to make when someone else's rights are on the line. Indeed, precisely because foreign nationals have borne the brunt of the war on terrorism, at home and abroad, many U.S. citizens view the government's tactics thus far without alarm. Apart from the fear occasioned by the attacks themselves and the continuing threat of other attacks, the visible changes in most citizens' lives seem minor, almost trifling—marginally longer waiting times at airports, more metal detectors and identity checks in public buildings. Other changes, in government surveillance, for example, are largely hidden from view by the administration's penchant for secrecy. But the challenge we face as a nation is to recognize, not in hindsight but now, that the character of America's future is at stake. The dilemma was captured perhaps most eloquently by Justice William Douglas: "As night-

PART 1
RESPONDING TO 9/11

1. THEIR LIBERTY, OUR SECURITY: AN OVERVIEW

> First they came for the Muslims, and I didn't speak
> up because I wasn't a Muslim.
> Then they came to detain immigrants indefinitely
> solely upon the certification of the Attorney General,
> and I didn't speak up because I wasn't an immigrant.
> Then they came to eavesdrop on suspects consulting
> with their attorneys, and I didn't speak up because I
> wasn't a suspect.
> Then they came to prosecute non-citizens before
> secret military commissions, and I didn't speak up
> because I wasn't a non-citizen.
> Then they came to enter homes and offices for
> unannounced "sneak and peek" searches, and I didn't
> speak up because I had nothing to hide.
> Then they came to reinstate COINTELPRO and resume
> the infiltration and surveillance of domestic
> religious and political groups, and I didn't speak up
> because I had stopped participating in any groups.
> Then they came for anyone who objected to
> government policy because it aided the terrorists and
> gave ammunition to America's enemies, and I didn't
> speak up because . . . I didn't speak up.
> Then they came for me . . . and by that time no
> one was left to speak up.
>
> STEPHEN ROHDE, PRESIDENT OF THE ACLU
> OF SOUTHERN CALIFORNIA, INSPIRED BY
> REV. MARTIN NIEMOLLER

No one who witnessed the terrorist attacks of September 11, even from the relatively safe vantage point of the television set, will ever forget them. The attacks exposed the nation and the world to a new and profound sense of vulnerability. Polls taken after the attacks reported that Americans facing this newfound threat were more than willing to sacrifice their rights and liberties for greater security.[1] We wanted above all to be safe, and if civil liberties had to go, so be it. But from the standpoint of sacrificing civil liberties, September 11 "changed everything" more dramatically for some than for others. A National Public Radio (NPR) poll taken a year after the attacks found that only 7 percent of Americans felt that they personally had sacrificed any important rights or liberties in the war on terrorism.[2]

Yet with the exception of the right to bear arms, one would be hard-pressed to name a constitutional liberty that the Bush administration has not overridden in the name of protecting our freedom. Privacy has given way to secret searches without probable cause, FBI spying on religious services, and "Total Information Awareness." The effort to stem funding for terrorists has resurrected guilt by association and official blacklists prepared in secret. Physical liberty and habeas corpus survive only until the president decides someone is an enemy combatant. Assets have been frozen without notice, without a hearing, without any violation of law, and on the basis of secret evidence. Equal protection has fallen prey to ethnic profiling. Conversations with a lawyer may be monitored without a warrant or denied altogether when the military finds that they might impair the persuasiveness of its incommunicado interrogation methods. The right to a public hearing upon arrest exists only at the attorney general's sufferance. And the right to know what our government is doing has been overridden because in order to keep Al Qaeda ignorant, the government says it must keep all of us in the dark as well.

How, then, does one explain the NPR poll reporting that no important rights or liberties have been given up? The answer lies in whose rights are actually at stake. For the most part, the government's measures have been targeted not at Americans, but at foreign nationals, both here and abroad. For them, especially those living here, September 11 has indeed "changed everything." Consider, for example, Ali Al-Maqtari, a twenty-eight-year-old Yemeni national married to a U.S. citizen, who was locked up for two months on the charge that he had been out of status for ten days while transferring his status from tourist to permanent resident. He was arrested on September 15 as he accompanied his wife, Tiffinay Hughes, to Fort Campbell, Kentucky, where she was reporting for army basic training. Apparently the couple had aroused suspicion at their local army induction center in Springfield, Massachusetts, two days earlier, because Tiffinay was wearing the traditional Muslim head covering, a *hijab*, and the couple were overheard speaking to each other in French. When they arrived at the Kentucky army base, their car was searched, and officials found pictures of New York City and two box cutters they had used in their prior jobs.

They were locked in separate rooms and interrogated for more than twelve hours. Agents lied to Al-Maqtari, telling him that the Springfield office had been bombed twenty minutes after he and his wife had left it, accusing him repeatedly of abusing his wife, and claiming they had a statement from her complaining of his abuse. One official threatened Al-Maqtari, telling him he would beat him all the way back to Yemen for mistreating his wife. The authorities took Al-Maqtari first to Nashville, and then to Mason, Tennessee. He passed a lie detector test, but was kept in custody, where guards repeatedly accused him of being a terrorist. Tiffinay, meanwhile, was freed after her interrogation, but three officers followed her constantly during her first two weeks of basic training, and she was eventually driven to take an honorable discharge.

The mere fact that the Immigration and Naturalization Service (INS) has charged a foreign national as deportable does not generally authorize his detention, unless the individual poses a danger to the community or risk of flight.[3] Most persons placed in deportation proceedings remain free while their proceedings are pending. When Al-Maqtari sought release on bond, the government opposed his release, but presented no evidence showing that he was either dangerous or a flight risk. It relied exclusively on an affidavit from an FBI agent, Michael Rolince, reportedly submitted in many post–September 11 immigration cases, and consisting almost entirely of boilerplate assertions about the September 11 investigation. The first four pages of the affidavit recited the facts of the September 11 attacks and the FBI's investigation, without offering any information specific to Al-Maqtari. The only paragraph in the affidavit specific to Al-Maqtari stated:

> ... the FBI continues to download the hard drive of a computer. (The computer was found in a car belonging to Al-Maqtari's wife). When interviewed by the FBI, Al-Maqtari said he had not used the laptop but purchased it for $250 from a customer at the convenience store where he works. Al-Maqtari said the customer obtained the computer from a third party. At present, the download of the hard drive is still running. Once this process is completed the FBI will need several days to review the information obtained.[4]

Needless to say, the fact that an individual bought a used computer does not establish that he is a threat to the community or a risk of flight. But returning to the boilerplate used in other September 11 detention cases, the Rolince affidavit goes on to assert that "the business of counterterrorism intelligence gathering in the United States is akin to the construction of a mosaic":

> At this stage of the investigation, the FBI is gathering and processing thousands of bits and pieces of information that may seem innocuous at first glance. We must analyze all that information, however, to see if it can be fit into a picture that will reveal how the unseen whole operates. . . . What may seem trivial to some may appear of great moment to those within the FBI or the intelligence community who have a broader context within which to consider a questioned item or isolated piece of information. At the present stage of this vast investigation, the FBI is gathering and culling information that may corroborate or diminish our current suspicions of the individuals who have been detained. . . . In the meantime, the FBI has been unable to rule out the possibility that respondent is somehow linked to, or possesses knowledge of, the terrorist attacks on the World Trade Center and the Pentagon. To protect the public the FBI must exhaust all avenues of investigation while ensuring that critical information does not evaporate pending further investigation.[5]

This "mosaic" argument essentially claims that immigration judges should presume danger even where the government offers only "innocuous" information about an individual, as in Al-Maqtari's case, because it is always possible that at the end of the investigation, the innocuous may turn out to be inculpating—the precise inverse of the presumption of innocence that lies at the heart of the American justice system. When coupled with the claim that Al Qaeda "sleepers" live quiet, law-abiding lives until they receive the call to strike, the "mosaic" theory could justify the detention of virtually anyone. The Justice Department's own inspector general reported that the INS filed eighty-nine such form affidavits to oppose bond in cases where individuals challenged their detention, under an official policy of opposing release on bond even where the government lacked any reason to believe an individual was dangerous or a flight risk.[6] In hearings identified by the attorney general as so sensitive that they had to be conducted in secret and could not even be listed on the public docket, most immigration judges simply rubber-stamped the INS's requests for detention without bond. Al-Maqtari was eventually released on a bond of $10,000, but not before he had spent two months behind bars. In September 2002, an immigration judge granted Al-Maqtari's application for permanent resident status. A week later, Tiffinay gave birth to the couple's first child, Ahmed.[7]

For the most part, the government has not asked American citizens to sacrifice their liberty for Operation Enduring Freedom. Instead, it has asked those, like Al-Maqtari, who are not in a position to decline the offer because they have no voice in the democratic process. As the rest of Part I will demonstrate, the government has repeatedly targeted noncitizens, selectively denying them liberties that citizens rightfully insist upon for themselves. This is not to say that citizens have been completely spared. But where the government has extended law enforcement measures to U.S. citizens, it has generally done so only after first using those powers selectively against foreign nationals, or by exploiting some foreign connection of the citizens in question. On those rare occasions where the government has proposed or adopted measures that would broadly affect citizens' rights, Congress has stepped in and blocked their implementation. The war on terrorism has been waged largely through anti-immigrant measures.

2. THE DISAPPEARED

[O]ur anti-terrorism offensive has arrested or detained nearly 1,000 individuals as part of the September 11 terrorism investigation. Those who violated the law remain in custody. Taking suspected terrorists in violation of the law off the streets and keeping them locked up is our clear strategy to prevent terrorism within our borders.

JOHN ASHCROFT, OCTOBER 25, 2001[1]

With these words, delivered to the U.S. Conference of Mayors six weeks after September 11, the attorney general defended the centerpiece of the Justice Department's initial response to the attacks of that day: mass preventive detention. The detentions, Ashcroft explained, are designed to prevent the next atrocity from occurring. Invoking a hero from the other side of the aisle, Ashcroft noted that when Robert Kennedy was attorney general, it was said that he would arrest mobsters for "spitting on the sidewalk." Ashcroft updated the warning, telling "terrorists" that if they overstayed their visas—"even by one day"—they would be arrested and detained.[2]

On October 31, 2001, Ashcroft announced the creation of a Foreign Terrorist Tracking Force (FTTF) to institutionalize this strategy. The explicit purpose of the FTTF, Ashcroft explained, was "to enhance our ability to protect the United States from the threat of terrorist *aliens*."[3] A year later, in October 2002, Ashcroft instructed U.S. attorneys at their national conference to continue this strategy full force. He told his prosecutors that he wanted to "burn three lessons in your consciousness," one of which was that they should "neutralize potential terrorist threats by getting violators off the street by any lawful means possible, as quickly as possible. Detain individuals who pose a national security risk for any violations of criminal or immigration laws."[4]

Ashcroft's avowed goal was and is to use immigration law and criminal law as a pretext to lock people up who might commit terrorism in the future. But absent the psychic's ability to predict future crimes featured in Steven Spielberg's science fiction film *Minority Report,* preventive law enforcement is notoriously risky. For that reason, criminal law generally punishes people for what they have done, not what they might do. Individuals may be arrested or searched only where there is probable cause to believe that they have committed an infraction or possess evidence of crime, and can be punished only when found guilty beyond a reasonable doubt of specific criminal conduct. This does not mean that law enforcement officials must wait until the bomb goes off to arrest or charge a suspect. The law of "conspiracy" and "attempts" allows the government to punish people for planning to commit crimes, as long as the defendants have taken some overt act in furtherance of their plan—such as purchasing materials, recruiting participants, or casing a target. Egyptian Sheikh Omar Abdel Rahman, for example, is currently serving multiple life sentences in federal prison for having conspired to blow up the tunnels and bridges around Manhattan.[5] He and his co-conspirators were captured and put away before they could commit the crimes they had planned.

Without evidence of an "overt act" in furtherance of a conspiracy, however, the criminal law does not permit the government to punish people for potential future crimes. Nor does immigration law generally permit the government to detain or deport people for what it thinks they might do (although it can deny admission in the first place based on concerns about future behavior). While "civil commitment" of mentally ill dangerous persons is permitted in limited circumstances, the Supreme Court has ruled that the Constitution prohibits detaining a person based on fear that he will do something dangerous in the future unless the government can also demonstrate that he has a mental defect that renders him incapable of controlling his dangerous behavior.[6] Absent such a mental defect or a pending criminal or immigration proceeding, the Constitution prohibits detaining people on grounds of future dangerousness.

For these reasons, Ashcroft could not directly impose preventive detention on those he feared might engage in terrorism. He resorted instead to *indirect* methods—pretextual law enforcement. Having identified someone as suspicious, for whatever set of reasons, government agents arrested the suspect and often only *then* searched for some legal violation with which they could charge him, irrespective of its relation to terrorism. The government would use the pretextual charge to justify detaining the individual, so that it could interrogate him in custody and interrupt terrorist plots before they could be carried out.

That the attorney general created a *Foreign* Terrorist Tracking Force to carry out this program rather than a Terrorist Tracking Force was no accident. Terrorists may of course be home-grown—before September 11, the single most deadly act of terrorism on American soil was Timothy McVeigh's 1995 bombing of the Murrah Building in Oklahoma City. And although all nineteen September 11 hijackers were noncitizens, the majority of those the government has actually charged with terrorism crimes since September 11 have been U.S. citizens. As of May 2003, the government had charged seventeen U.S. citizens and nine foreign nationals with terrorist-related crimes allegedly related to Al Qaeda.[7] So it cannot be said that foreigners are the only threat we face. Yet both the attorney general's rhetoric and his preventive detention campaign have focused almost exclusively on noncitizens, and immigration law has been his pretext of choice.

In part, this is because the immigration law is such a useful pretext; it imposes a wide range of technical obligations on all foreign nationals. Because our economy literally depends on illegal immigration, we have long tolerated the presence of literally millions of noncitizens who have violated some immigration rule. This means the attorney general has extremely broad discretion in how and when to enforce immigration obligations; any immigrant community he targets will inevitably include many persons here in violation of their visas. In this sense, the immigration law functions largely as does the traffic law for drug law enforcement; it affords a convenient pretext for targeting millions of individuals. And just as the traffic laws facilitate "driving while black" enforcement, so the immigration law has permitted ethnic profiling. In the wake of September 11, Ashcroft targeted the Arab and Muslim immigrant community, and stretched, twisted, exploited, altered and in many instances, violated immigration law to achieve his preventive detention goal.

Much about the preventive detention program remains shrouded in mystery. The government has refused to provide even the most basic information, beginning with how many people it has locked up. During the first two months of the campaign, the government regularly announced a cumulative tally of persons detained in the September 11 investigation, as if to assure the public that it was aggressively doing something. Ashcroft's statement quoted at the opening of this chapter is a typical instance. But as the number of detainees rose, and as critics began pointing out that not one had actually been charged with terrorism, the Justice Department suddenly halted its practice of announcing a cumulative tally. The last publicly acknowledged total, on November 5, 2001, was 1,182.[8] The Justice Department has refused to give a total number of detainees ever since. The official story is that it is too difficult to keep an accurate count,[9] but the Department found the counting too difficult only when the announcements seemed to harm its public image.

Some estimates can nonetheless be made. As noted, the government admits that there were 1,182 detentions in the first seven weeks of the campaign. As of May 2003, it had also detained some 1,100 more foreign nationals under the Absconder Apprehension Initiative, which expressly targets for prioritized deportation the 6,000 Arabs and Muslims among the more than 300,000 foreign nationals living here with outstanding deportation orders.[10] As of May 2003, another 2,747 noncitizens had been detained in connection with a Special Registration program also directed at Arab and Muslim noncitizens.[11] A conservative estimate would therefore place the number of domestic detentions in the war on terrorism as of May 2003 at over 5,000.

Sadly, this program has been a colossal failure at finding terrorists. Of the more than 5,000 persons subjected to preventive detention as of May 2003, not one has been charged with any involvement in the crimes of September 11. The only person actually charged with the September 11 attacks, Zacarias Moussaoui, was arrested before September 11, and therefore is not part of the roundup. Only five detainees (three noncitizens from the initial wave and two citizens picked up later as material witnesses) have been charged with any terrorist-related crime. Of those five, one has been convicted of conspiracy to support terrorism; two were acquitted on all terrorism charges; the government dropped all terrorism charges against the fourth when he pleaded guilty to a minor infraction; and the fifth is awaiting trial.[12] Government officials reportedly claimed in November 2001 that ten or eleven of the detainees at that point might be members of Al Qaeda, but they never backed up that assertion with any formal charges.[13] One month later, *Newsweek* reported that Justice Department officials had "acknowledged privately" that the department had "no evidence that any of the immigration detainees are members of Al Qaeda."[14] By late 2002, the FBI had affirmatively cleared nearly all the initial immigration detainees of any ties to criminal or terrorist conduct.[15] The Department of Homeland Security in March 2003 claimed that the Special Registration program had identified eight "suspected terrorists," but none has been charged with terrorist crimes.[16] Thus, by the government's own account, nearly all the thousands it has detained in the war on terrorism have turned out to have nothing to do with terrorism.

IMMIGRATION DETAINEES

Immigration law has been the centerpiece of the preventive detention campaign. At every opportunity since September 11, Ashcroft has turned immigration law from an administrative mechanism for controlling entry and exit of foreign nationals into an excuse for holding suspicious persons without meeting the constitutional requirements that ordinarily apply to preventive detention.[17]

From the beginning, the Justice Department determined that secrecy was critical to its preventive detention campaign. Ten days after the attacks of September 11, Chief Immigration Judge Michael Creppy, a Justice Department official, circulated a memorandum to all immigration judges, relaying an extraordinary order from the attorney general that every immigration case that his office designated as of "special interest" to the September 11 investigation must be conducted entirely in secret. No one other than the noncitizen and his attorney would be permitted to attend the proceedings—no press, no public, no legal observers, no family. The memo prohibited listing any such case on the public docket, and instructed immigration judges hearing the cases to refuse to confirm or deny that the cases existed if asked.[18] The government maintained that the privacy interests of the detainees and national security required this unprecedented secrecy.

There were good reasons to be skeptical about the government's claims. The order mandated secret proceedings no matter how routine the hearing in question, without regard to whether any information of a confidential nature would be presented, and even with respect to those detainees whose identities were already widely known. As of May 29, 2002, the government stated that it had subjected 611 noncitizens to such secret hearings.[19] Yet the INS reportedly did not rely on classified information in any of these proceedings, and has imposed few protective orders on the detainees or their attorneys that would bar them from disclosing everything that happened in the hearing.[20] In other words, the government itself did not take precautions one would fully expect it to take were disclosure of the information presented at the hearings truly a threat to national security.

Pastor Rabih Haddad's case illustrates the Justice Department's insistence on secrecy even where none of its purported ends would be jeopardized by a public hearing. In December 2001, Pastor Haddad, a prominent Muslim cleric from Ann Arbor, Michigan, was arrested and detained as a special interest case, and denied release on bond after a closed hearing. Shortly thereafter, the law firm of Arnold and Porter, the Center for Constitutional Rights, immigration lawyer Ashraf Nubani, and I filed a constitutional challenge to the closure of his proceedings. We maintained that due process required a public trial unless the government could make an individualized showing that there was a need for confidentiality in Haddad's case. The government's principal argument for closing Pastor Haddad's hearing, as with the other special interest immigration hearings, was that it did not want to reveal the identity of the detainees, both to keep Al Qaeda ignorant of who was detained, and to protect the privacy of the detainees. But the cat was already out of the bag: Pastor Haddad's arrest had been widely reported in Detroit and national newspapers within days of his detention.[21] And Pastor Haddad did not object to having his name publicly disclosed. Thus, neither secrecy nor privacy interests were served by closing Haddad's hearing.

The district court judge ruled that closing the hearings violated both Pastor Haddad's due process rights and the First Amendment rights of access of the media and public. She acknowledged that closed immigration hearings could be justified in individual cases by case-specific showings of need, but found that the government's across-the-board assertion that it could close every special interest hearing without any individualized showing was unacceptably broad.[22] On appeal, the U.S. Court of Appeals for the Sixth Circuit unanimously upheld that decision, declaring that "[d]emocracies die behind closed doors."[23]

Meanwhile, a group of newspapers filed a second suit challenging closed hearings in New Jersey, where many of the September 11 detainees were being held and tried. Once again, a federal district judge ruled the closures unconstitutional.[24] The government appealed again, but this time, in September 2002, the U.S. Court of Appeals for the Third Circuit reversed by a two to one vote. Over a strong dissent, the court reasoned that there was no right of public access to special interest deportation hearings, and that therefore they could be held in secret without any individualized showing that there was a need for closure.[25] The newspapers sought Supreme Court review, but in May 2003, the Supreme Court denied review, after the government said it was reconsidering its policy. As a legal matter, however, the Court's decision not to hear the case, while not upholding the policy, leaves the government free to try foreign citizens in secret as long as it chooses to hold them within the confines of the Third Circuit (New Jersey, Pennsylvania, or Delaware).

While these cases were proceeding, several human rights organizations sought to uncover information about the detentions through another route, the Freedom of Information Act (FOIA). In August 2002, a federal district court ruled that the government was legally obligated to disclose the names of the detainees and their attorneys.[26] As in the closed hearings cases, the government argued that revealing the information would compromise the investigation by allowing Al Qaeda to map out what the government knew, by discouraging potential witnesses, and by creating the possibility for terrorist organizations to tamper with evidence and witnesses in identified cases. The court rejected each argument. The judge found it implausible that Al Qaeda did not already know about detentions of its members and supporters, particularly as the government had not barred the detainees from informing others of their detentions. She found the concern about discouraging witnesses factually unfounded because the government had made no showing that any of the detainees in fact had any relevant knowledge or were involved in any way with terrorism. Indeed, she pointed out, the government had affirmatively cleared hundreds of the detainees. And she found no basis for the government's speculation that disclosing the identities of the detainees would lead to tampering with evidence. "Secret arrests," the judge wrote, "are a concept odious to a democratic society," and while she acknowledged the government's interest in security, she insisted that "the first priority of the judicial branch must be to ensure that our Government always operates within the statutory and constitutional constraints which distinguish a democracy from a dictatorship."[27] The judge consequently ordered release of the names, unless the government could show that individual detainees objected or that a court order barred disclosure in a specific case.

Again, however, the government appealed, and obtained a stay of the order to disclose names.[28] As of May 2003, the appeals court had not ruled, the stay remains in effect, and the detainees' identities remain a secret. Thus, despite the fact that most of the judges who have reviewed the government's secrecy policy have declared it unlawful, much about the government's detention campaign remains unknown.

The weakness of the government's arguments for secrecy, coupled with its failure to take its own interests sufficiently seriously to block detainees or their lawyers from broadcasting the facts of their cases, suggests that something else may have driven the government's penchant for secrecy. If the press and the public had been made aware of the specifics of a sufficient number of cases, it would have quickly become clear that the Justice Department was often locking people up with no good reason for suspecting terrorism. The real concern, in other words, may have been not that *Al Qaeda* would find out what was going on, but that the American public would find out. Public disclosure not only might have increased objections to the government's measures, but, given that the widely cast net came up empty, would almost certainly have impaired confidence in the job our government was doing to protect us.

In June 2003, the inspector general of the Justice Department issued a scathing report on the post-September 11 immigration detainees that confirmed that the government indeed had something to hide. The report revealed that in connection with the September 11 investigation, the government detained 738 foreign nationals on immigration charges from September 11, 2001 until August 2002. Of these, not a single one was charged with any terrorist crime, and virtually all were cleared of any connection to terrorism by the FBI. The report notes that they were arrested and linked to the September 11 investigation for the flimsiest of reasons—because of an anonymous tip that "too many" Muslims worked at a convenience store, or that a Muslim neighbor kept odd hours, or simply because investigators happened upon an Arab or Muslim immigrant in a place the investigators visited. All the detainees were presumptively treated as terrorists, denied bond even where the government had no evidence that they posed a danger or flight risk, and held for months while the FBI satisfied itself that they were in fact unconnected to terrorism. Many were held in

maximum-security conditions, under 23-hour lockdown, and subjected to physical and verbal abuse. The government imposed an
initial communications blackout, barring the detainees from communicating with each other, lawyers, or the outside world. And after the
blackout ended, the detainees were limited to one call a week, often
making it difficult if not impossible to consult with a lawyer.[29]

Many immigration detainees were initially arrested on no charges
at all. Nine days after the September 11 attacks, the attorney general
changed the rules governing immigration arrests. The old rule had
required the INS either to file charges or to release a foreign national
within twenty-four hours of his arrest. The new regulation authorizes detention without charges for an unspecified "reasonable" period in times of emergency.[30] The government immediately took
advantage of the new rule; documents disclosed in the FOIA lawsuit show that, as of December 2002, 317 detainees had been held
for more than forty-eight hours (the constitutional limit) before
being charged, 136 detainees had been held for more than one week
without charges, and 35 had been held for one to three months before
being charged.[31]

As the Al-Maqtari case discussed above illustrates, once charges
were filed, they were often highly technical and merely a pretext to continue detention. The government's express but secret policy was to
deny bond even where it had no evidence that the individual actually
posed a threat that would warrant detention.[32] For example, Thar Ab-
deljaber, a Palestinian and a lawful permanent resident, was stopped in
Raleigh, North Carolina, in March 2002 for driving four miles per hour
over the speed limit. He was taken into custody, interrogated by FBI
agents, and charged criminally for having failed to file a change-of-
address form with the INS when he moved from Florida to Virginia in
1999. He pleaded guilty to that oversight and was sentenced to twenty-
five days in jail. The INS kept him in custody after he completed his sentence, now charging that he should also be deported for his failure to
report the address change. He ultimately spent four months behind
bars.[33] In July 2002, Ashcroft announced that the INS would vigorously

enforce the change-of-address requirement, rarely if ever enforced before September 11. Many believe he did so primarily to create still more legal pretexts on which to arrest and hold noncitizens.[34]

Mohammed Qayyum, a fifty-eight-year-old Pakistani citizen, was arrested in mid-November 2001 at the mosque where he was living.[35] He was not told why he was detained, and was not charged with any offense, immigration or otherwise. After he had been detained for nineteen days, the INS charged him with overstaying his visa. Qayyum sought release on bond, but the immigration judge refused even to hold a bond hearing, stating that without an FBI clearance, bond would be denied. When the immigration judge subsequently learned that Qayyum's attorneys had filed a habeas corpus petition in federal court requesting a bond hearing, the judge granted a summary hearing, but then denied bond, finding that Qayyum was dangerous, based not on any objective indications of dangerousness, but solely on the FBI's failure to clear him. In May 2002, six months into his incarceration, the FBI finally determined that he had no connections to terrorism. Once Qayyum was cleared, the immigration judge released him on bond, but he had spent nearly half a year in prison. His immigration proceedings were subsequently dismissed because the INS could not justify its nineteen-day delay in charging him. As these cases illustrate and the Inspector General's report found, the government's policy was to lock up first, ask questions later, and presume that a foreign national was dangerous even where there was no basis for that suspicion.

When some immigration judges refused to accept government arguments that the "mosaic" theory justified detention without bond and ordered detainees released, Ashcroft responded by changing the rules. Before September 11, if an immigration judge concluded that there was insufficient evidence to hold an individual pending his immigration proceedings, he would be released, unless the government could convince an appellate immigration court that it had a sufficiently strong appeal that release should be delayed. But in October 2001, the Justice Department changed the rule to permit the district director—the INS prosecutor—to override immigration judges' re-

lease orders. Under the new rule, INS prosecutors can keep noncitizens locked up even after a judicial release order simply by filing a slip
of paper stating that they are appealing. The prosecutor need not
make any showing that the appeal is likely to succeed.[36] Appeals of immigration custody decisions routinely take months and often more
than a year to decide. Two federal courts have declared this regulation
unconstitutional, reasoning that to lock up a person who has been
found to pose no danger or flight risk violates due process.[37]

One limitation on using immigration law as a pretext for preventive detention is that it depends on the individual opposing his deportation. As soon as a noncitizen agrees to leave, there is no longer any
justification for continuing to detain him. Many immigration cases
are routinely resolved through grants of "voluntary departure"—permission to leave the country without adverse consequences—or deportation orders that are not appealed because the noncitizen agrees
to leave. The government ordinarily could not be happier when an individual in deportation proceedings agrees to leave; it gets what it
wants—removal—without the expense and delay of further immigration proceedings. But if the government's real goal is not to remove, but to detain, as was the case with the September 11 detainees,
individuals who agree to leave pose a problem. The INS solved it by
adopting a policy of refusing to let special interest detainees leave
until the FBI had completed its investigation and cleared them of any
criminal, much less terrorist, conduct or ties. The Inspector General
found that the FBI investigations—and therefore the detentions—
took an average of 80 days, and as long as 244 days, to complete.[38]

Ibrahim Turkmen, a citizen of Turkey, was arrested on October 13,
2001, and was granted voluntary departure on October 31. A grant of
voluntary departure requires a finding that the noncitizen has not engaged in terrorist activities.[39] The INS did not appeal that decision.
When Turkmen inquired about release on bond, the immigration
judge assured him that there was no point to pursuing it as he would be
out of the country in days. Two days later, a friend purchased an airline
ticket to Turkey for him and brought it to the INS office. Yet the INS

kept Turkmen in custody for nearly four more months, until the FBI cleared him.[40] The *New York Times* reported that as of February 18, 2002, the Justice Department was blocking the departures of eighty-seven foreign citizens who had either agreed to leave or had been ordered deported.[41] The government was continuing to hold them simply because it had not yet satisfied itself that they were innocent.

These detentions are plainly illegal. Where detention is necessary to effectuate deportation, the Supreme Court has permitted the INS to employ preventive detention until removal can be effectuated.[42] But the INS cannot impose detention for punishment,[43] nor does it have any authority to detain persons "for investigation."[44] Yet the INS did just that with these detainees, holding them on immigration charges long after those charges were resolved and the noncitizens were willing to leave.[45]

Immigration law was Ashcroft's preferred method of preventive detention for several reasons. First, immigration law is expansive, authorizing deportation for a wide range of highly technical infractions, and therefore can be selectively trained on any given immigrant community. A year after the attacks, Ashcroft boasted that his campaign had resulted in nearly 500 deportations. But given the widespread underenforcement of immigration law, the government likely could have achieved the same number of deportations no matter which immigrant community it had targeted.

Second, by employing immigration procedures, the Justice Department was able to avoid those constitutional rights and safeguards that accompany the criminal process but that do not apply in the immigration setting. Had it used criminal charges as a basis for arrest and detention, the government would have had to provide suspects with prompt access to independent federal courts and the assistance of lawyers. The Constitution requires all criminal arrestees to be brought before a judge for a "probable cause" hearing within forty-eight hours of arrest, at which a lawyer is appointed if the arrestee does not already have one.[46] Yet as shown above, the INS now detains foreign nationals for an unspecified "reasonable" period without filing any charges at all; and even after charges are filed, immigration detainees are not guaranteed a lawyer or prompt access to a judge. Eighty percent of immigration detainees are unrepresented.[47] Under criminal law, the government must provide a public trial; yet every special interest immigration detainee was tried in secret. Criminal suspects cannot be held simply because the government entertains vague suspicions about them and has not yet convinced itself that they are innocent. They can be detained without bond only if properly charged, and only if the government proves that they pose a threat to the community or a risk of flight.[48] Even then, the "speedy trial" requirement means that unless a criminal defendant agrees to an extension of time, preventive detention is limited to a matter of weeks.[49] If a judge rules that a criminal suspect should be released on bail pending trial, the prosecutor cannot keep him in jail simply by filing an appeal. In short, Ashcroft could not have carried out the preventive detention campaign on anything like the scale he did without exploiting immigration law for purposes it was not designed to serve.

MATERIAL WITNESSES

As expansive as the immigration law is, not everyone whom the FBI suspects can be charged with an immigration violation. Where the authorities were able to drum up a criminal charge, they used that as a pretext instead. These charges often relied on bootstrapping; in some instances, individuals were suspected, detained, interrogated, and only then charged criminally for having lied to the agents who interrogated them. Two Somali immigrants reported for "suspicious" activity when seen praying in a Texas parking lot were confronted, searched, and arrested for carrying an altered driver's license and a knife one-quarter inch longer than that permitted by Texas law.[50] An Egyptian national was arrested for "trespassing" in the Maryland motel where he was staying.[51] Sometimes the criminal charges seem retaliatory. When Canadian citizen Shakir Baloch brought a lawsuit challenging his extended detention on immigration charges, the Justice Department responded by filing a criminal charge against him for illegal reentry, the very conduct for which he had been held on immigration charges until he filed suit.[52]

The hardest cases, from the government's perspective, are those individuals whom it suspects but cannot charge with either an immigration or a criminal infraction. The American legal system does not permit the government to arrest and hold people on vague suspicions or for mere investigation. So what was the FBI to do about Osama Awadallah? Investigators had found his first name and an old phone number scribbled on a slip of paper in one of the hijackers' cars at Dulles Airport. But Awadallah was a lawful permanent resident, and authorities could find no evidence that he had participated in the attacks or otherwise violated any law.

On September 20, 2001, FBI agents confronted Awadallah in the parking lot at his apartment complex in San Diego, searched his apartment and cars, and interrogated him for six hours at FBI headquarters, all without probable cause of any criminal activity. He admitted recognizing two of the hijackers, but initially claimed he did not know the name of one of them. When the interrogation concluded at 11:00 P.M., the FBI agents allowed him to go home but asked him to return the next morning for a polygraph. He did so, but when he failed two questions on the polygraph, they took him into custody, charging him not with any crime, but as a "material witness."

Federal law generally requires witnesses or suspected witnesses to crime to testify when asked, unless they are entitled to invoke the privilege against self-incrimination. In general, investigators prefer witnesses who freely cooperate, although reluctant witnesses can be ordered to appear by a subpoena, and defiance of the subpoena can lead to incarceration. But federal law also authorizes detention of witnesses in advance of testimony where the government can show a court that an individual has testimony that is material to a criminal proceeding, and that the individual is likely to flee if asked to testify or served with a subpoena.[53] This is an extraordinary power, used only sparingly before September 11, because it authorizes the incarceration of persons who are charged with no crime, based solely on a *prediction* about their reluctance to testify.[54] Since September 11, however, the Justice Department has aggressively exploited the material witness law, not for its legitimate purpose of ensuring that reluctant witnesses are available for trial, but for preventive detention of persons who could not otherwise be held. As Ashcroft himself admitted at an October 31, 2001, press conference, "Aggressive detention of lawbreakers and material witnesses is vital to preventing, disrupting, or delaying new attacks. It is difficult for a person in jail or under detention to murder innocent people or to aid or abet in terrorism."[55] The government has locked up people as material witnesses without ever bringing them before a grand jury or a criminal trial to testify, has held them under harsh conditions more befitting a suspect than a witness, and has interrogated them at length in custody.[56] A study by the *Washington Post* identified forty-four people who had been held as material witnesses in the first fourteen months of the September 11 investigation, almost half of whom had not testified in any proceeding.[57]

Ashcroft discovered that the material witness authority could serve as an end run around the Fourth Amendment rule barring arrest and detention without probable cause of criminal activity. To detain on material witness grounds, the government need not show probable cause that an individual has engaged in criminal activity, but only that the individual has material information and might flee if served with a subpoena. The open-ended nature of grand jury inquiries permits the government to claim that a wide range of potential testimony might be material to such proceedings. The government plainly had some basis for suspecting that Awadallah might have material evidence; the phone number in the hijacker's car and his personal knowledge of two of the hijackers certainly warranted investigation. But there was no reason to believe that Awadallah would flee. He had cooperated in the investigation, had substantial family ties in San Diego, and had engaged in no criminal conduct. The government nonetheless claimed that Awadallah was likely to flee and should be detained because he had ties abroad, knew two of the hijackers, and might have feared that his "prior conduct" could provide a basis for his prosecution. On that basis, a federal judge granted the warrant, and Awadallah was taken into custody.

Awadallah ultimately spent eighty-three days in prison. He was held in solitary confinement, shackled, strip-searched repeatedly, and interrogated at length. He was later charged criminally for denying to a grand jury that he knew the name of one of the September 11 hijackers, even though he identified him by appearance and admitted that he had met him, and had identified another of the hijackers by name. In April 2002, a federal judge dismissed all charges, finding that the government had lied to obtain the material witness warrant, misused the material witness law, and illegally arrested Awadallah.[58]

The material witness law is designed to be used only for reluctant witnesses, and ordinarily a prosecutor would incarcerate a witness only as a last resort, as that treatment could well turn the witness into an adversary. But after September 11, the government used this law to detain and interrogate even witnesses who, like Awadallah, had been fully cooperative, and indeed even witnesses who *voluntarily* came forward to provide information.[59]

In one of the preventive detention campaign's most extraordinary cases, the government invoked all three of its detention authorities—immigration, criminal, and material witness—to hold a man unconnected to terrorism for 422 days. Agents first arrested Tony Oulai on September 14, 2001, because his checked luggage included two storage boxes that contained a stun gun, flight instruction books, and what federal agents thought were "Arabic materials." In an affidavit, officials described Oulai as Arabic. In fact, he was a Roman Catholic from the Ivory Coast. The manuals and gun were in boxes that had been in his brother's storage for years; and the boxes contained no Arabic materials. Oulai was initially held on immigration charges, and on November 15, 2001, he was ordered deported for overstaying his student visa. He accepted the deportation order and agreed to go home.

Instead of deporting him, however, the government held him as a material witness for three more months. In February 2002, a federal judge dismissed the material witness warrant when the government admitted that Oulai was not a suspect and had no information related to terrorism. Yet at the same time, federal authorities charged Oulai with lying to federal agents when he told them in initial interviews that he was living here legally. There seemed little reason for the charge (other than face-saving for the government), as Oulai had already served more time than he could possibly have been sentenced for the charged crime. He was convicted and sentenced to time served. But he was still not allowed to leave the country until November 11, 2002, 422 days after he was first arrested.[60]

The material witness law, like the pretextual use of criminal charges, may be employed against U.S. citizen and foreign national alike. Yet the vast majority of those detained on this authority have been noncitizens. The *Washington Post* reported that only seven of the forty-four material witnesses it identified were U.S. citizens. And while a majority of those charged with actual terrorist-related crimes since September 11 have been U.S. citizens, virtually all those subjected to pretextual criminal charges unrelated to terrorism have been foreign nationals.

ENEMY COMBATANTS

The ultimate move in the government's preventive detention arsenal is to label an individual an "enemy combatant." Attaching that label takes an individual out of the civilian justice system altogether and places him in military custody, potentially for the duration of the "war on terrorism." The government claims that this power authorizes it to arrest and hold anyone, foreign national or U.S. citizen, for an indefinite period, without charges, without a hearing, without access to a lawyer, and, for all practical purposes, incommunicado, simply on the assertion that he is an "enemy combatant." As of March 2003, the government had used this authority to hold over 650 foreign nationals in Guantánamo Bay, and two U.S. citizens in naval brigs off the Atlantic coast.

At least initially, the government suggested that it would apply such "military justice" only to noncitizens. As noted in the Introduction, President Bush's order creating military tribunals limited their jurisdiction to noncitizens, and Vice President Cheney defended the order by distinguishing the rights of American citizens from those of foreign nationals.[61] Politics, not law, exempted citizens from the tribunals, because the Constitution permits trial by military tribunal of U.S. citizens fighting for the enemy. That the Bush administration's political calculation was accurate is demonstrated by the starkly different public reactions to the military's detention of foreign nationals and U.S. citizens as "enemy combatants." The military's indefinite incommunicado detention of over 650 foreign nationals in Guantánamo Bay has sparked substantial criticism from abroad, but not at home. A British court, for example, hearing a claim on behalf of a British national held in Guantánamo Bay, found that "in apparent contravention of fundamental principles recognised by both jurisdictions and by international law, Mr. Abbasi is at present arbitrarily detained in a 'legal black-hole.' "[62] By contrast, the Guantánamo detentions have generated very little attention, much less protest, within the United States. When the administration abandoned Vice President Cheney's distinction, however, and imposed military custody on U.S. citizens Yasser Hamdi and Jose Padilla, the public reaction could not have been more different, as commentators, the press, and courts all questioned the executive's assertion of an unchecked authority to incarcerate citizens without charges or trial.[63]

The military's power to capture and hold people fighting for the enemy during wartime—"enemy combatants"—is well established. The Geneva Conventions, however, adopted after World War II, establish certain minimal legal requirements for such detentions. They authorize wartime detention of "combatants," but require that all combatants be treated presumptively as "privileged," and held as "prisoners of war." The underlying rationale is that it is not illegal to fight a war, and therefore enemy soldiers are "privileged combatants" and should not be tried for their combat actions. They may be held in humane conditions until the war ends in order to stop them from rejoining hostile forces.[64] Those who violate the laws of war—by, for example, targeting civilians, or failing to wear a uniform that distinguishes them from civilians—may be classified as "unprivileged" combatants.[65] Unprivileged combatants may be tried and punished by special military tribunals for their war crimes. Where there is any doubt about an individual's status—privileged combatant, unprivileged combatant, or not a combatant at all—the Geneva Conventions require the military to provide a hearing before a "competent tribunal" to determine the individual's status.[66]

The application of these principles in the current conflict is complicated by the novel character of the war on terrorism. Unlike the war with Iraq, the war on terrorism finds no nation on the other side, but only an international criminal organization and those who "harbor" it. Moreover, the Bush administration (if not Congress) has defined the war on terrorism as being directed against not only Al Qaeda, the perpetrator of the September 11 attacks, but all terrorist organizations of global reach.[67] So defined, the war on terrorism has infinite enemies and no discernible endpoint. All groups today have potentially global reach, and we will almost certainly cure both cancer and the common cold before politically motivated violence directed at civilians is extirpated from the face of the earth. Thus, while the power to capture combatants is ordinarily confined to the armed forces of an enemy nation or nations, a group relatively easy to identify, in this war anyone of any nationality could be an "enemy combatant." Identification will always be difficult and frequently contested. And whereas the length of wartime detention is generally thought to be limited in scope, today's detentions are potentially life sentences.

These differences make the authority asserted by the Bush administration effectively unlimited. Because literally anyone could be an "enemy combatant," and the war is both permanent and global, this authority can be applied for all practical purposes to detain any human being on the face of the earth. The Bush administration has already detained over 650 "enemy combatants" in Guantánamo Bay without any charges or hearings. Most of them were captured on the battlefield in Afghanistan and then transferred to Guantánamo beginning in January 2002. Some, however, were not captured on the battlefield at all, but arrested elsewhere, and sent to Guantánamo rather than extradited through normal legal channels.[68]

The Bush administration has declared all the detainees to be "unprivileged combatants," without affording a hearing to any. It reasons that Al Qaeda is not a state, and that the Taliban did not abide by the laws of war, and that therefore fighters for neither group are entitled to the protected status of "privileged combatants" or "prisoners of war." But even if those categorical determinations are defensible—and the treatment of the Taliban is especially questionable—the administration's position fails to entertain the very real possibility that some of the detainees *may not have been involved in combat at all.* During the Gulf War, the military held nearly 1,200 hearings to assess the status of captured persons, and about two-thirds of those captured were determined not to be combatants at all.[69] Surely it is possible, indeed likely, that in the chaos of the Afghanistan battlefield, the military picked up some individuals who were not combatants. Yet there is absolutely no process for those individuals to assert such claims.

For all practical purposes, the detainees have been held incommunicado.[70] No one has been permitted to consult a lawyer or make a phone call, and correspondence by mail is heavily censored. When the first individuals were dropped at Guantánamo Bay, blindfolded and heavily shackled, President Bush called them "killers," and Vice President Cheney called them "the worst of a very bad lot," "devoted to killing millions of Americans."[71] Today, government officials concede that they have no "big fish" at Guantánamo Bay, and that some of the detainees may not have been combatants. Some are juveniles, as young as thirteen years old.[72] The *Los Angeles Times* reported in December 2002 that intelligence officers had identified fifty-nine Guantánamo detainees, about 10 percent of the total, who had no meaningful connection to either Al Qaeda or the Taliban. Some were taxi drivers, cobblers, or farmers. The military has released thirty-six detainees, presumably having determined that they were not in fact "devoted to killing millions of Americans." But as of May 2003, most of the detainees, including the juveniles, were still there.[73] They remain in legal limbo, stripped of all rights, with no idea how long they will be confined there. Not a single hearing to consider a claim of innocence has been held, and the government has successfully resisted all efforts of the detainees to obtain judicial review. Nineteen Guantánamo detainees have attempted to commit suicide.[74]

As described in the Introduction, this "enemy combatant" treatment has now been extended to two U.S. citizens: Yasser Hamdi, captured on the Afghanistan battlefield while allegedly fighting for the Taliban, and Jose Padilla, arrested at Chicago's O'Hare Airport. Because Padilla was arrested not on the battlefield but inside the United States, and is not alleged to be a member of either Al Qaeda or the Taliban, his case represents the furthest extension of the enemy-combatant detention authority thus far. A Brooklyn native, Chicago gang member, and prison convert to Islam, Padilla was arrested on May 8, 2002. Federal officials had been tailing him for several months, and suspected that he was planning to detonate a radioactive "dirty bomb" on behalf of Al Qaeda. But Padilla has not been charged with any crime.

The government initially detained Padilla as a material witness. On June 9, 2002, however, two days before federal authorities were scheduled to appear in court to answer Padilla's request for release, the government swept him out of the civilian justice system altogether and transferred him to military custody. President Bush had designated him an enemy combatant. While Padilla was a material witness, the court had appointed him a lawyer, as required under the material witness statute. But once Padilla was in military custody, the government held him incommunicado and barred his lawyer, Donna Newman, from communicating with him in any manner whatsoever. She nonetheless independently pursued a legal challenge to his detention on his behalf. In response, the government claimed that it can exercise the same authority over Padilla that it is exercising over the Guantánamo Bay detainees—holding him incommunicado, indefinitely, without a lawyer, and without a hearing or trial.

All of the enemy-combatant detentions have been challenged in court. The legal process has been somewhat surreal, however, because the government has barred the detainees from any communications with the lawyers who purport to represent their interests. Thus, for all the detainees know, the cases do not exist, and for all the lawyers know, the detainees do not even want to challenge their detention. The courts have uniformly refused even to consider the merits of the foreign nationals' claims, ruling either that they have no jurisdiction to hear the claims of foreign nationals held in Guantánamo Bay, technically outside U.S. jurisdiction, or that those purporting to sue on the detainees' behalf lack "standing," or legal authority, to do so.[75] The Bush administration initially argued that U.S. citizens also had no right to seek court review—their detention, it maintained, was entirely a matter of executive discretion. As the U.S. Court of Appeals for the Fourth Circuit put it, the government contended that "with no meaningful judicial review, any American citizen alleged to be an enemy combatant could be detained indefinitely without charges or counsel on the government's say-so."[76] When the Fourth Circuit rejected that "sweeping proposition,"[77] the government argued that even if citizens have a right to habeas corpus review, they have no right to present evidence or otherwise participate in that review, and the courts have no authority to question the facts underlying a detainee's designation as an enemy combatant.

In January 2003, the Fourth Circuit effectively adopted the government's revised view, ruling that at least as to persons captured on the battlefield, the courts may not question the government's factual assertion—in Hamdi's case, a two-page conclusory declaration filed by a government functionary with no direct knowledge of the facts—that an individual is an enemy combatant.[78] The court rested its decision on what it called an "undisputed" fact, namely that Hamdi had been captured on the battlefield.[79] But the court did not explain how that fact could be disputed or undisputed, when his lawyers were never permitted to ask Hamdi whether it was true. Without asking Hamdi, neither his lawyers nor the court had any basis for taking a position one way or the other on that fact. Yasser Hamdi could be entirely innocent, but under the court's analysis he has no forum in which to present that argument.

District Court Judge Michael Mukasey in New York reached an only marginally less deferential result in Jose Padilla's case. He ruled that the president has the power to detain as enemy combatants U.S. citizens arrested on U.S. soil, and that the court's role is only to assess whether there is "some evidence" to support the president's determination. As he put it, "the commission of a judge . . . does not run to deciding *de novo* whether Padilla is associated with al Qaeda and whether he should therefore be detained as an enemy combatant," but only to asking whether "the President had some evidence supporting his finding." [80]

Judge Mukasey did order the government to allow Padilla access to his attorney, however, for the limited purpose of challenging the factual sufficiency of the government's case against him. The government objected even to that limited access, and moved for reconsideration. It argued that its "robust" interrogation of Padilla was predicated on the development of "a relationship of trust and dependency." According to the government, the detainee must come to perceive "that he is reliant on his interrogators for his basic needs and desires." [81] At that point, Padilla had already been held incommunicado and subjected to intensive interrogation for seven months, yet the government maintained that allowing him to speak to a lawyer in any way would interfere with the "trust and dependency" the interrogators sought to foster. The government submitted an expert declaration that maintained that Padilla must be made to believe that he has no hope. [82]

This is a truly extraordinary argument. The government contends that even though someone in its custody has a right to seek judicial review, he has no right to consult with the lawyer pursuing that review because the consultation might interfere with interrogation methods that in any other setting would plainly be unconstitutional. The Supreme Court has long held that confessions obtained against an individual's free will violate due process, and that interrogating an individual even for thirty-six hours straight is a *per se* violation of due process because information obtained after such an ordeal is presumptively coerced.[83] If thirty-six hours straight violates due process, a seven-month incommunicado interrogation certainly does. Yet in Padilla's case the government effectively sought to defend one constitutional violation (keeping a detained man from his lawyer) in order to commit another constitutional violation (coercing information from him against his free will). In March 2003, the district court denied the motion for reconsideration, but the government has appealed.[84]

Short of execution, the power to lock up a human being is the most serious authority the government exercises. In ordinary times, it is generally limited to persons who have been found guilty beyond a reasonable doubt of violating the criminal law. Preventive detention is permitted, but apart from persons with severe and dangerous mental disabilities, it is acceptable only where the individual has been charged with violating some sort of law *and* is a demonstrated danger to the community or flight risk. As the Supreme Court has said, "[i]n our society liberty is the norm and detention prior to trial or without trial is the carefully limited exception."[85]

Since September 11, detention without trial has become, if not the norm, a huge exception. Thousands of people *not* involved in any terrorist activity have been locked up, many in secret, on pretextual charges or no charges at all, and effectively precluded from obtaining their release. The administration has exploited and abused immigration law, criminal law, the material witness law, and the law of war to obtain this result. And it has been able to accomplish it largely because its targets have been, with a few notable exceptions, foreign nationals. The few exceptions—Lindh, Padilla, and Hamdi—have drawn highly disproportionate criticism, even though the charges and the evidence of Al Qaeda and Taliban ties appear to be stronger with respect to them than with respect to many of the foreign national detainees. Thus far, the citizenry seems willing to tolerate preventive detention, as long as it is directed at someone other than themselves.

3. ETHNIC PROFILING

On New Year's Eve, 2001, Edgardo Cureg, a thirty-four-year-old from the Philippines working on his Ph.D. in mathematics at the University of South Florida, was flying home from London to Tampa. Changing planes in Newark, he ran into one of his professors, a Sri Lankan national. They sat together on the plane to Tampa. Sitting near them was Michael Dasrath, a thirty-two-year-old Wall Street financial analyst, born in Guyana but a United States citizen. All three men had successfully cleared security without any problems. Their problems began only after they took their seats.

As Dasrath recounts, another passenger began glaring at the three of them, called over the captain, and said, "Those brown-skinned men are behaving suspiciously." The next thing they knew, the captain had ordered all three men off the plane, without explanation. They were put on a different flight later that day to Orlando, Florida, where the airline provided a car to take them to Tampa.

Dasrath and Cureg were two of five men who filed discrimination lawsuits against several airlines in June 2002 for denying them passage because of discomfort expressed by fellow passengers, discomfort apparently based on nothing more than the color of their skin. In each case, the travelers had been cleared by security officials; in several cases, the airlines left their checked luggage on the planes they were forced to get off; and in all cases, the travelers were put on later flights the same day. In other words, the men were not treated as bona fide security risks.

These men were far from alone. By January 2002, just four months after the attacks of September 11, the Council on American-Islamic Relations had already received 1,658 reports of discrimination, profiling, harassment, and physical assaults against persons appearing Arab or Muslim, a three-fold increase over the prior year.[1] The reports included beatings, death threats, abusive police practices, and employment and airline-related discrimination.

The anti-Muslim and anti-Arab prejudice that lay at the root of these incidents was also reflected in opinion polls after September 11. The attacks of that day prompted a dramatic reversal in public thinking about racial and ethnic profiling as a law enforcement tool. Before September 11, about 80 percent of the American public disapproved of racial profiling—the use of racial generalizations as a factor in determining whom to stop or search.[2] State legislatures, local police departments, and President Bill Clinton had condemned the practice and ordered data collection on the racial patterns of stops and searches.[3] The U.S. Customs Service, sued for racial profiling, had instituted measures to counter racial and ethnic profiling at the borders.[4] Even Attorney General John Ashcroft, no pioneer on civil rights issues, had spoken out against the practice, testifying in his nomination hearings that racial profiling "is wrong and unconstitutional no matter what the context."[5] A federal law banning racial profiling seemed likely.[6]

After September 11, polls reported that nearly 60 percent of the American public favored ethnic profiling, at least as long as it was directed at Arabs and Muslims.[7] The fact that all the perpetrators were male Arab immigrants and that the attack was orchestrated by Al Qaeda, a group consisting largely of Arab Muslims, has led many to believe that it is only common sense to pay closer attention to Arab-looking men boarding airplanes and elsewhere. Commentators argue that the high stakes make the case for profiling stronger here than in routine drug interdiction stops on highways. Thus, Stuart Taylor, a columnist for *Newsweek,* the *National Journal,* and *Legal Times,* before September 11 a harsh critic of racial profiling, wrote shortly after the attacks in favor of ethnic profiling of Arab men on airplanes.[8] Press accounts made clear that, whether as a matter of official policy or not, law enforcement officials were paying closer attention to those who appeared to be Arabs or Muslims.[9]

The Bush administration has repeatedly said that it will not engage in racial or ethnic profiling. Just two days after the attacks, John Ashcroft stated: "We must not descend to the level of those who perpetrated Tuesday's violence by targeting individuals based on their race, their religion, or their national origin."[10] In the first week after the attacks, President Bush condemned those who had lashed out at Arab Americans, insisting that people should be treated as individuals, not tarred by guilt by ethnic association.[11] Several weeks later, Michael Chertoff, who heads the Justice Department's Criminal Division and has played a lead role in coordinating the domestic war on terrorism, told Congress that "We have emphatically rejected ethnic profiling."[12]

But actions speak louder than words, and the Bush administration has sent a very different message through its law enforcement policies. As noted in Chapter 2, virtually all of the men detained as "suspected terrorists" in the first seven weeks of the September 11 investigation were ultimately cleared of any terrorist conduct by the FBI, leading to the strong suspicion that the government was far too quick to equate Arab or Muslim male with "terrorist." And since that time, the Justice Department has confirmed that suspicion by adopting a string of antiterrorism measures explicitly directed at men from Arab and Muslim countries. In the winter of 2001–02, the Justice Department officially selected 5,000 young immigrant men for interviews, based not on any objective information that they were involved in or had knowledge of terrorism, but solely on the basis of their age, date of arrival, and the country from which they came.[13] The countries singled out were said to be those where support for Al Qaeda was believed to exist, but apparently did not include Great Britain, France, Spain, or Germany, even though Al Qaeda suspects from each of these countries have been captured. Virtually all of those interviewed were Arabs or Muslims. Several police departments around the country refused to participate in the interviews on the ground that the practice appeared to constitute ethnic profiling.[14] Notwithstanding substantial objections, the Justice Department announced in March 2002 that it would seek to interview 3,000 more men, again based on their age, date of entry, and Arab or Muslim country of origin.[15]

In November 2001, the State Department also imposed a new

twenty-day waiting period for visas for men between the ages of sixteen and forty-five applying to enter the United States from certain select countries, again nearly all Arab or Muslim.[16] In January 2002, the
Justice Department launched a program to prioritize the deportation
of 6,000 noncitizens, selected from more than 300,000 foreign nationals who have remained in the country after being ordered deported.
The basis for their selection? Once again, nothing more than the fact
that they were young men from countries where Al Qaeda support is
thought to exist, i.e., Arab and Muslim countries.[17]

On September 11, 2002, the Justice Department launched a program requiring foreign nationals from selected countries—again, virtually all Arab or Muslim—to register and submit to fingerprinting
and photographs at entry, thirty days after entry, at one-year intervals
thereafter, and at exit. Failure to satisfy any of the reporting requirements is a crime. The Justice Department subsequently applied similar
requirements to male foreign nationals over sixteen years of age (excluding permanent residents) already living in the United States from
twenty-five countries, again virtually all Arab or Muslim. In the first
week of the registration program, the government detained hundreds
of Muslims and Arabs in California alone.[18] As of May 2003, it had detained 2,797 persons, yet none had been charged with terrorism.[19]

In January 2003, *Newsweek* reported that the FBI had directed its
field offices to count the number of mosques in their regions for a de-
mographic profile to be used as a benchmark for assessing whether
the field offices had conducted a sufficient number of terrorism investigations and national security wiretaps. As a top FBI official explained, the move was "justified by concern about undetected 'sleeper
cells' and troublesome evidence that mosques may be serving as cover
for terrorist activity."[20] After news of the initiative was leaked, the FBI
sought to recharacterize the program, explaining that mosques were
being counted only because "in the past [they] have been targeted for
violence."[21]

In March 2003, as the war with Iraq began, the administration announced yet another program targeted at foreign nationals from Arab

and Muslim nations. All foreigners from thirty-three countries who sought political asylum would henceforth be automatically detained upon entering the United States, and would stay locked up until their asylum cases were resolved, a process that generally takes a minimum of six months. The administration refused formally to identify the countries, describing them only as countries where Al Qaeda or other terrorist groups are known to operate, but civil rights groups obtained the list from government officials informally, and it was once again the usual suspects.[22] Under this program, even where there was absolutely no reason why an individual needed to be detained pending adjudication of her asylum application, because she was neither dangerous nor a flight risk, she would be automatically locked up. In other words, the policy mandated, at least in some cases, wholly unnecessary and therefore arbitrary detention of Arab and Muslim foreign nationals. This program lasted only a month, and was terminated on April 17, 2003.[23]

When Michael Chertoff testified that the Justice Department "emphatically rejected" ethnic profiling, he immediately qualified that statement with the following sentence: "What we have looked to are characteristics like country of passport."[24] There is a technical legal difference between distinctions based on ethnicity and those based on country of passport. Holders of French passports, for example, may be Arab, African, Asian, or European in ethnicity. The immigration law, moreover, has long drawn distinctions based on nationality. From at least 1882, when Congress barred all immigration from China, until 1965, when Congress finally abandoned a forty-year practice of imposing national origin quotas, the immigration law expressly excluded people on the basis of nationality. Today, Cubans get favored treatment under the immigration law, as do certain Central Americans. Thus, the conventional wisdom, as immigration scholar Gerald Neuman has noted, is that "distinctions in federal law among aliens on the basis of their country of current nationality are not constitutionally suspect."[25]

But there are good reasons to question that conventional wisdom.

First, in practice, the vast majority of passport holders from Arab nations will of course also be of Arab ethnicity. The distinction Chertoff invoked may well survive in a court of law, but it is far less clear whether it is a meaningful distinction in the field. The Justice Department rules for selectively targeting interviews, deportations, special registration, and asylum detentions look like what a clever young lawyer would come up with if directed by his superiors to "develop a program for targeting Arabs and Muslims but make sure we can deny that it is ethnic profiling." As Supreme Court Justice William Brennan recognized, "The line between discrimination based on 'ancestry or ethnic characteristics' and discrimination based on 'place or nation of . . . origin,' is not a bright one." [26]

Second, as the above history suggests, and as will be explored in more detail in Chapter 7, the history of nationality distinctions in immigration law is inextricably linked to racism. The first national exclusion laws were directed at Asian immigrants and were accompanied by vicious anti-Asian prejudice. The national origin quotas were expressly designed to favor immigrants from Northern and Western Europe over those considered less "white." And these laws had spillover effects on U.S. residents from the disfavored countries of origin. Until the 1940s and 1950s, Chinese and Japanese nationals were ineligible for naturalization, a benefit expressly limited to white and black persons. Many states in turn barred persons "ineligible for citizenship" from owning property. As the Japanese internment illustrated, even U.S. citizens of Japanese descent were treated as presumptively disloyal "aliens" subject to long-term mass incarceration. Similar attitudes abound today about persons of Arab descent, who are treated as "foreign," presumptively disloyal, and potentially terrorist, regardless of their citizenship status. [27] As Professor Neuman has noted, "alienage labels provide a code in which ethnically specific appeals can be couched." [28]

Third, even if the federal government's profiling is expressly limited to foreign nationals, its actions send a message to private employers, airlines, and local police that Arab and Muslim identity is a central, perhaps *the* central, factor for suspicion of terrorism. That message in turn encourages private discrimination of the type suffered by Edgardo Cureg, Michael Dasrath, and countless others who are or appear to be Arab or Muslim. Because people do not wear their passports on their sleeves, on-the-spot judgments about nationality inevitably rely on ethnic appearance. Thus, what starts as nationality-based profiling swiftly becomes a national campaign of ethnic profiling.

In the immediate aftermath of the September 11 attacks, a reasonable argument could be made that the use of ethnic and immigrant identity as factors in the investigation of those attacks did not constitute ethnic profiling. Authorities had reason to believe that the hijackers, all Arab and Muslim immigrants, were associated with Al Qaeda; that others in Al Qaeda were involved in the plot; that Al Qaeda consisted largely if not exclusively of Arab and Muslim members; and that Al Qaeda had the capability and intent to strike again. In that circumstance, the use of ethnic identity as a factor in seeking out the perpetrators comes close to using racial identity to focus an investigation of a bank robbery where eyewitnesses report that the robbers were two white males of Italian descent in their twenties. The use of race or ethnicity as an identifying criterion in the search for a specific perpetrator is generally not considered racial profiling. Profiling, by contrast, involves reliance on a *generalization* about people of a particular group, such as the widely held presumption that young black men are more likely to deal drugs than elderly white women, or indeed young white men.[29]

Thus, if authorities are specifically looking for perpetrators of a particular crime, such as the attacks of September 11, and have specific identifying information that the perpetrators are Arab or Muslim rather than black Christians, they are permitted to rely on that information in choosing whom to investigate and question. On the other hand, if authorities rely on Arab or Muslim identity because they believe as a general matter that Arabs and Muslims are more likely to be terrorists, they are relying on an ethnic- or religious-based generalization that is generally impermissible under the Equal Protection

Clause. As Professors Samuel Gross and Debra Livingston have pointed out, the problem is that in particular contexts it may be quite difficult to untangle these motivations, and therefore to determine whether the use of race or ethnicity is permissible.[30] That was never more true than in the immediate wake of September 11.

But as the September 11 investigation turned into a more general war on terrorism of indefinite (and potentially infinite) duration, encompassing not a specific locality but the whole nation and indeed the entire world, and not a specific group but all "terrorists of global reach," the Justice Department's reliance on Arab and Muslim identity has come to look more and more like the Army's use of Japanese ancestry as a proxy for suspicion during World War II. As Professor Natsu Saito has argued, "Just as Asian Americans have been 'raced' as foreign, and from there as presumptively disloyal, Arab Americans and Muslims thave been 'raced' as 'terrorists': foreign, disloyal, and imminently threatening."[31] Or as Ibrahim Hooper of the Council on American-Islamic Relations put it, "The common stereotypes [of Muslims] are that we're all Arabs, we're all violent and we're all conducting a holy war."[32] The argument that it is common sense to equate suspicion with ethnicity is precisely the argument used first to impose curfews on, and then to intern, 110,000 persons of Japanese ancestry during World War II. The federal government is now using the same rationale to interview, register, deport, and detain Arab and Muslim foreign nationals.

Precisely because of the pernicious history of racial discrimination in this country, the Equal Protection Clause presumptively forbids government authorities from relying on racial or ethnic categories. Such actions trigger "strict scrutiny," which requires the government to show that its reliance on race or ethnicity is "narrowly tailored" to further a "compelling government interest."[33] There is no question that protecting citizens from terrorism is a compelling government interest, but so too is drug interdiction—in fact, all criminal law enforcement is likely a compelling government interest. The real question from a constitutional perspective is whether reliance on ethnic identity or appearance as a proxy for suspicion is narrowly tailored to further that interest. It is highly unlikely that profiling could satisfy that scrutiny.

First, the vast majority of persons who appear Arab or Muslim—probably well over 99.9 percent—have no involvement with terrorism. There are 1.3 billion Muslims in the world, and 6.5 million Muslims in the United States; there are 280 million persons of Arab ancestry in the world, and 1.2 million in the United States alone.[34] There are reportedly somewhere between 200 and 2,000 actual members of Al Qaeda, and the highest estimates of those who have attended an Al Qaeda training camp are about 10,000.[35] Arab and Muslim appearance, in other words, are grossly inaccurate proxies. In the sex discrimination context, where the Supreme Court applies less stringent scrutiny than it does to ethnic or racial discrimination, the Court has held that statistics showing that 2 percent of young men between the ages of eighteen and twenty-one had been arrested for drunk driving did not justify denying all men of that age the right to purchase an alcoholic beverage.[36] Surely the percentage of terrorists among men of Arab appearance is far smaller than the percentage of drunk drivers among college-age men.

Second, the use of ethnic stereotypes, far from being necessary for effective law enforcement, is likely to be ineffective. When one treats a whole group of people as presumptively suspicious, it means that agents are more likely to miss dangerous persons who do not fit the profile, such as Richard Reid, the British citizen who boarded a plane in Paris headed for Miami with a bomb in his shoe.[37] For that reason, the federal government distributed a memo shortly after September 11, written by five intelligence specialists with the federal government's leading law enforcement agencies, warning against ethnic profiling, and urging law enforcement officers to focus on behavior rather than ethnic identity, not out of equality concerns, but for reasons of security.[38] The fact that nearly all of those targeted on the basis of their Arab or Muslim appearance will prove to be innocent not only means that profiling will squander valuable resources, but is also likely to cause agents to let their guards down, as the false positives lull them into inattention.[39] And as will be explored in more detail in Chapter 13, the Arab and Muslim communities are much more likely to be able to help us identify the Al Qaeda needles in the haystack than are broad-brush programs treating these communities as a whole (or at least their young men) as suspect. Yet because profiling alienates the communities it targets, it makes cooperation from those communities far less likely.

The fact that the federal government's profiling is expressly targeted at foreign nationals not only gives the government a better legal defense in court, but also makes profiling more politically acceptable from the citizenry's standpoint. In practice, profiling deeply affects all those Americans whose ethnic appearance might suggest that they are nationals of the suspected Arab or Muslim countries. Yet the administration defends these practices, like the immigration measures discussed above, on the ground that they are ostensibly limited to foreign nationals.

4. PATRIOTS AND ENEMIES: REDEFINING TERRORISM

Six weeks after September 11, President Bush signed into law a 342-page omnibus bill, awkwardly titled the Uniting and Strengthening America by Providing Appropriate Tools Required to Intercept and Obstruct Terrorism Act, so that its acronym, USA PATRIOT, would send the message that to oppose it was unpatriotic.[1] The PATRIOT Act made many changes to criminal, immigration, banking, and intelligence law. Some of these changes sensibly updated criminal law to reflect changing technologies. For example, the advent of cell phones justified the PATRIOT Act's authorization of so-called "roving wiretaps," which permit wiretapping of any phones that a target may reasonably use, rather than only specified phone numbers, and nationwide warrants, which permit taps to follow an individual even if he travels outside the jurisdiction of a particular federal district. Other provisions removed barriers to the sharing of information between foreign intelligence officials and law enforcement officials in international terrorism investigations, on the reasonable ground that international terrorism is simultaneously a matter of foreign intelligence *and* criminal law enforcement. We certainly want law enforcement authorities with knowledge of Al Qaeda's activities abroad talking to those with knowledge of Al Qaeda's stateside activities. The PATRIOT Act's extensive money laundering provisions seek to respond to new methods of money laundering, and while the financial community has questioned whether the changes will have any effect on terrorism, these provisions do not raise significant civil liberties objections.

But the PATRIOT Act also includes provisions that make less sense, and that do raise substantial concerns about respect for basic human rights and civil liberties. Characteristically, these provisions are principally directed at noncitizens. The act's double standard begins with the very definition of terrorism. For purposes of regulating the citizenry, the PATRIOT Act defines "domestic terrorism" as "acts dangerous to human life that are a violation of the criminal laws . . . [and] that appear to be intended . . . to influence the policy of a government by intimidation or coercion." But for purposes of regulating immigration, "terrorist activity" is defined much more expansively, to include support of the otherwise lawful and nonviolent activities of virtually any group that has used violence, and any use or threat to use a weapon against person or property ("other than for mere personal monetary gain").[2] Thus, for citizens, terrorism has a limited definition that roughly corresponds to common understandings of the phenomenon, whereas for foreign nationals, Congress has labeled as "terrorist" wholly nonviolent activity and ordinary crimes of violence.

Neither Congress nor the executive branch made any attempt to explain why the same act should be "terrorist" when committed by a foreign national but not when committed by a U.S. citizen. This differential treatment runs throughout the PATRIOT Act, which reserves its most severe measures for noncitizens. It makes foreign nationals deportable for wholly innocent associational activity, excludable for pure speech, and subject to incarceration on the attorney general's say-so, without a finding that they pose a danger or a flight risk. A provision that applies largely but not exclusively to foreign nationals authorizes secret searches in criminal investigations without probable cause of criminal activity, the constitutional minimum for criminal searches. With a stroke of the pen, in other words, President Bush denied foreign nationals basic rights of political association, political speech, due process, and privacy.

GUILT BY ASSOCIATION

The centerpiece of the PATRIOT Act's immigration provisions renders noncitizens deportable for their associations with disfavored political organizations.[3] As will be shown in Part 2, this is hardly unprecedented. For much of the twentieth century, immigration law authorized the expulsion of foreigners for their political associations. But as the Cold War waned, those provisions fell into disfavor, and in 1990 Congress repealed them, repudiating guilt by association.[4] The PATRIOT Act ignores the lessons of history and revives this ignoble practice.

Guilt by association is a common response in times of fear. When government authorities are pressed to prevent crimes from occurring, they often seek to expand the substantive grounds for arresting people. If the law makes it illegal merely to associate with or support suspect groups, law enforcement becomes much easier. The government need establish only membership or association, not actual involvement in crime.

Guilt by association facilitates preventive law enforcement, but by the same token it also facilitates the punishment of innocents and the repression of political dissent. By targeting people for their associations, the government contends, it can disrupt the organizations and movements that might someday lead to criminal activity, and thereby prevent crime before it happens. But it can also crush dissident groups that never engage in illegal activity, and punish moral innocents who have no intention of furthering any illegal activity. When fear is high, the government is likely to err on the side of security by targeting groups and individuals even where it has very little basis for predicting criminal conduct. The Communist Party of the United States, for example, while an advocate of revolutionary overthrow of capitalism, was never shown to have taken any concrete steps toward overthrowing the United States government by force or violence. Nonetheless, through guilt by association, the government during the Cold War effectively destroyed the party, as well as many other organizations accused of Communist sympathies.

The excesses of the Cold War taught us the infirmities of guilt by association. In a series of cases beginning as the Cold War was winding down, the Supreme Court reflected that lesson by prohibiting guilt by association, ultimately declaring it to be "alien to the traditions of a free society and to the First Amendment itself."[5] As the Court said in 1961:

> In our jurisprudence guilt is personal, and when the imposition of punish-
> ment on a status or on conduct can only be justified by reference to the re-
> lationship of that status or conduct to other concededly criminal activity
> . . . that relationship must be sufficiently substantial to satisfy the concept
> of personal guilt in order to withstand attack under the Due Process
> Clause of the Fifth Amendment.[6]

Guilt by association also violates the First Amendment right of association, the Court added, because it penalizes individuals who support
only a group's lawful ends.[7] Driven by these dual constitutional concerns, the Court has repeatedly ruled that the Constitution prohibits
punishment for association absent proof that an individual specifically intended to further the *unlawful* ends of the group.

The constitutional prohibition on guilt by association, however,
has not ended the desire for preventive law enforcement in times of
crisis. Government officials pressed by the public to prevent the next
terrorist attack, but barred by history and the Constitution from targeting people for their speech or associations, have sought other ways
of implementing preventive law enforcement. Instead of penalizing
membership, the government has penalized "material support" to terrorist groups in the name of cutting off funds for terrorism.

Like so much else in the war on terrorism, the targeting of "material support" had its genesis in immigration law, although it has since
spread beyond immigration to criminal law provisions that affect citizens as well. When Congress repealed the Cold War–era immigration
law provisions that authorized deportation for mere membership in
groups advocating Communism and other proscribed ideas, it substituted provisions making foreign nationals deportable for engaging in
terrorist activities. The INS immediately interpreted this new law,
however, to make noncitizens deportable not merely for engaging in
or supporting terrorist *activity,* but for providing any material support to a terrorist *organization,* without regard to the purpose or effect of the support.[8] In 1996, Congress extended that concept to the

criminal law in the Antiterrorism and Effective Death Penalty Act, which made it a crime to provide "material support" to any foreign organization designated as terrorist by the secretary of state.[9]

The PATRIOT Act takes immigration law still further. Like the criminal "material support" law, it prohibits wholly innocent associational support of a "terrorist organization," whether or not there is any connection between the noncitizen's support and any act of violence, much less terrorism.[10] The new provision has even more expansive reach, because it defines "terrorist organization" as any group of two or more persons that has used or threatened to use a weapon, literally encompassing every organization that has ever been involved in a civil war or a crime of violence, from a pro-life group that once threatened workers at an abortion clinic, to the African National Congress (ANC), the Irish Republican Army (IRA), or the Northern Alliance in Afghanistan. In addition, the law gives the attorney general unchecked power to blacklist "terrorist organizations" without any process or judicial review.

Under this law, the thousands of noncitizens who supported the ANC's lawful, nonviolent antiapartheid activity could now be deported as terrorists. The ANC used military as well as nonviolent means in its struggle against apartheid, and the State Department routinely designated it as a terrorist organization before it came to power in the 1990s.[11] The law extends even to those who seek to support a group for the purpose of *countering* terrorism. Thus, a noncitizen who offered to train IRA representatives in peace negotiations in the hope of furthering the peace process in Great Britain and forestalling further violence could be deported as a terrorist.

The government has argued that the threat from terrorist organizations abroad and the fungibility of money require adjustments to the constitutional prohibition on guilt by association, permitting the punishment of "material support" where one could not punish mere membership.[12] But the prohibition on guilt by association was developed in the crucible of a battle against an even more formidable foe—the Communist Party, an organization that Congress found to be, and the Supreme Court accepted as, a foreign-dominated organization that used sabotage and terrorism for the purpose of overthrowing the United States by force and violence, and that was backed by the world's other superpower, with thousands of nuclear weapons trained on our cities.[13] If association with the Communist Party deserved protection, surely association with much less powerful groups that have merely used or threatened to use a weapon at some point deserves similar protection.

The fungibility argument is flawed as a factual and a legal matter. It maintains that because money is fungible, even a donation of blankets to a hospital will ultimately support terrorism, by freeing up resources that will then be devoted to terrorism. But this argument assumes that a group engaged in a political struggle that uses both legal and illegal means will divert legal donations to its illegal means. On this assumption, every dollar donated to the ANC for its nonviolent opposition to apartheid freed up a dollar that the ANC then spent on violent, terrorist ends. While some groups (including Al Qaeda) may be so committed to violence that all other activities are merely a front for terrorism, for many and probably most groups that use violence, the violence is but one means to a political end. This is not to excuse the violence, but to insist that one can often meaningfully distinguish between a group's lawful and unlawful activities, just as the Supreme Court insisted was required with respect to the Communist Party.

The fungibility argument also proves too much as a legal matter. The Supreme Court has repeatedly struck down or narrowly construed laws that penalized association with the Communist Party absent proof that the individual specifically intended to further the group's illegal ends.[14] The government insists that money is different, but the Supreme Court has also repeatedly recognized that the rights of speech and association would mean little without the right to raise and spend money for those purposes, and accordingly has protected fundraising and donations as acts of association and speech.[15] As the Court has said, "[t]he right to join together 'for the advancement of beliefs and ideas' . . . is diluted if it does not include the right to pool money through contributions, for funds are often essential if 'advocacy' is to be truly or optimally 'effective.' " [16] If the provision of material support to a group were somehow constitutionally different from membership, all of the anti-Communist measures declared invalid by the Supreme Court could have simply been rewritten to make punishment contingent on the payment of dues, the volunteering of time, or any of the other material manifestations of political association. The right of association would be left a meaningless formality.

Some organizations undoubtedly use legitimate activities as fronts for illegal terrorism. But where a group's "legitimate" activities are a cover for its illegal activities, action against its legitimate enterprises would be justified without relying on guilt by association, just as federal law allows the government to seize legitimate businesses from organized crime groups where it can show that they are fronts for criminal activity.[17] Moreover, intent to further illegal ends can be inferred from the circumstances of a donation; it need not require an outright admission. Short of such showings, however, the law can and should distinguish between lawful and unlawful activities. We could not constitutionally criminalize everyone who leaves a tip at a Mafia-run restaurant or brings a gift to a Mafia don's wedding; nor should we treat as terrorist the provision of genuine humanitarian aid to disfavored "terrorist organizations."

Where organizations do not have lawful activities but are almost entirely committed to terrorism, as appears to be the case with Al Qaeda, guilt by association is also unnecessary. Where a group engages exclusively or predominantly in terrorism, a jury could reasonably infer that an individual's knowing support to that group was specifically intended to further its illegal ends. In those cases the traditional test requiring specific intent need not be jettisoned, for it should easily be satisfied. Where, by contrast, groups genuinely pursue both legal and illegal ends and activities, to punish a person for supporting only the legal ends without intent to further its illegal goals punishes moral innocents, chills legitimate political activity, and empowers the government to selectively target any organization that has ever engaged in illegal activity.

In short, penalizing material support for terrorist groups resurrects guilt by association under a different label. It is no coincidence that its genesis was in immigration laws directed exclusively at foreign nationals, and that the PATRIOT Act has now extended the concept to its limit through the immigration law.

IDEOLOGICAL EXCLUSION

The PATRIOT Act also resurrects another immigration practice thought to be put to rest in 1990—ideological exclusion. Under Cold War laws, the United States denied admission to hundreds of individuals for their political views, including Nino Pasti, a former NATO general, who was intending to speak out against placing nuclear cruise missiles in Europe; Tomas Borges, a leader of the Nicaraguan Sandinistas; and such writers as Graham Greene and Carlos Fuentes.[18] The McCarran-Walter Act authorized federal officials to deny visas to those who had advocated various proscribed political views, including Communism. It survived long after the demise of McCarthyism, and long past the end of the Cold War, but in later years its every invocation sparked widespread criticism that its use clashed with our nation's commitment to the free exchange of ideas.

With much fanfare about our commitment to freedom of expression, Congress in 1990 finally repealed these ideological exclusion provisions.[19] The Soviet Union had fallen, the Berlin Wall was down, and Communism was no longer any real threat. We could afford to be tolerant of others' views. But that history was quickly forgotten in the wake of September 11. The PATRIOT Act denies admission to noncitizens who "endorse or espouse terrorist activity," or who "persuade others to support terrorist activity or a terrorist organization," in ways that the secretary of state determines hamper U.S. efforts to combat terrorism.[20] It also excludes noncitizens who are representatives of groups that "endorse acts of terrorist activity." Because of the breadth of the definitions of "terrorist activity" and "terrorist organizations," this authority would empower the government to deny entry to any noncitizen who advocated support for the ANC, the Contras during the war against the Sandinistas, or opposition forces in Afghanistan and Iran today.

Citizens have a constitutional right to endorse terrorist organizations or terrorist activity, so long as their speech is not intended and likely to produce imminent lawless action.[21] While the Supreme Court has long ruled that noncitizens outside our borders—in contrast to those living among us—have limited constitutional rights,[22] barring them from entry for their expressed or presumed views should nonetheless raise constitutional concerns.[23] The First Amendment, the Supreme Court has said, is designed to protect a robust public debate, and if the government can keep out persons who espouse disfavored ideas, our opportunity to hear and consider those ideas through direct personal exchange will be diminished. More broadly, excluding people for their ideas is contrary to the spirit of political freedom for which the United States stands. We are a strong enough country, and our opposition to terrorism is sufficiently resolute, to make such censorship unnecessary. Yet Congress has now returned to the much-criticized ways of the McCarran-Walter Act, targeting noncitizens not for their acts, not even for what we fear they might do upon entering, but solely for their words, and for words that would be constitutionally protected if uttered by United States citizens.

UNILATERAL EXECUTIVE DETENTION

As Attorney General Ashcroft's preventive detention campaign has illustrated, the government's power to incarcerate foreign nationals using immigration law was capacious even before the PATRIOT Act. Yet the PATRIOT Act gave the attorney general still broader powers to incarcerate noncitizens. He need only certify that he has "reasonable grounds to believe" that a person is "described in" the antiterrorism provisions of the immigration law, and the individual is then subject to potentially indefinite detention.[24] As noted above, the PATRIOT Act's definition of "terrorism" for immigration purposes sweeps in nonviolent humanitarian assistance to disfavored groups and garden-variety crimes, such as brandishing a kitchen knife in a domestic dispute, or threatening another person with a bottle in a barroom brawl. While no one condones threats of violence, surely every noncitizen who gets into a bar fight with a weapon does not warrant unilateral executive detention, particularly as our law does not authorize such detention even for the most hardened, recidivist criminal citizens. While there is no reason to believe that the attorney general will invoke this authority in run-of-the-mill cases, the law's breadth leaves that entirely to his discretion.

Preventive detention is constitutional only in very limited circumstances, where there is a demonstrated need for the detention—because of current dangerousness or risk of flight.[25] Where an individual does not pose a threat to the community or a risk of flight, there is no justification for preventive detention, for there is literally nothing to prevent. Detention in such circumstances violates substantive due process. Yet it is authorized under the PATRIOT Act.

In addition, the PATRIOT Act appears to permit indefinite detention of noncitizens even where they have *prevailed* in their removal proceedings. It provides that detention shall be maintained "irrespective of . . . any relief from removal granted the noncitizen, until the Attorney General determines that the noncitizen is no longer a noncitizen who may be certified [as a suspected terrorist]."[26] But a noncitizen who has been granted relief from removal is lawfully here. Keeping him locked up at that point is akin to keeping a person in prison after he has been pardoned. If the INS cannot remove an individual, it has no basis for detaining him.[27]

SECRET SEARCHES WITHOUT PROBABLE CAUSE

The PATRIOT Act's most controversial intelligence-gathering amendment potentially affects citizens and foreign nationals alike, although its principal targets are likely to be foreigners, and—at least initially—Arab and Muslim immigrants. It authorizes secret searches and wiretaps in criminal investigations without probable cause to believe that the target is engaged in criminal conduct or that evidence of a crime will be found.[28] The constitutional protection of privacy found in the Fourth Amendment generally forbids searches or wiretaps unless the government has probable cause. In addition, federal law generally requires notification of the targets of searches and wiretaps, either before or after the search or tap. The PATRIOT Act allows the government to evade these requirements in criminal investigations wherever it also has a significant "foreign intelligence" purpose.

It accomplishes this by amending the Foreign Intelligence Surveillance Act (FISA).[29] FISA authorizes wiretaps and searches, based not on the usual showing of probable criminal conduct or evidence, but on the much easier showing that the target of the intrusion is an "agent of a foreign power," defined broadly to include any officer or employee of a foreign-based political organization. An employee or board member of Amnesty International could be subjected to a FISA wiretap as a "foreign agent" under this law, even if he or she has never violated a criminal law.[30] If the "agent" is a U.S. citizen or permanent resident alien, the government may not base its warrant on activities protected by the First Amendment, but that restriction does not apply to foreign nationals here on work, student, or visitor visas. At bottom, for citizens and noncitizens alike, the law does not require probable cause of criminal activity.[31]

Searches and wiretaps under FISA may be kept secret from the target, in many cases forever. A person is notified that he was subjected to FISA surveillance only if the government later seeks to use the evidence obtained in a legal proceeding. Even then, individuals have no meaningful opportunity to challenge the validity of the search, because they have no right to see the affidavit that served as the basis for the surveillance.[32] Thus, the legality of FISA surveillance is never subject to adversarial testing in the courts.

The extraordinary authority provided by FISA was initially justified on the ground that foreign intelligence gathering is different from criminal law enforcement, and that the intelligence power would not be used for the purpose of investigating crime. In order to obtain a FISA warrant, the primary purpose of the investigation had to be the collection of foreign intelligence, *not* criminal law enforcement. The PATRIOT Act, however, eliminated the "primary purpose" requirement, amending FISA to allow wiretaps and physical searches without probable cause in criminal investigations so long as "a significant purpose" of the intrusion is to collect foreign intelligence, a showing that should be easy to make whenever the government's target is a foreign national with political ties overseas.[33] Government officials argued that the "primary purpose" test erected an artificial wall between criminal law enforcement and foreign intelligence gathering that hindered investigation of international terrorism. But the PATRIOT Act loophole is not limited to terrorism investigations, but applies to criminal investigations wholly unconnected to terrorism. In effect, it denies the Fourth Amendment's most basic protection to any person who might qualify as a foreign agent—predominantly but not exclusively foreign nationals.

Concerns that FISA's looser standards might impermissibly infect criminal investigations led a special court of the federal judges who rule on FISA applications to issue a rare opinion in May 2002 rebuking the Justice Department for its interpretation of its newly expanded powers under the PATRIOT Act. In general, the FISA court judges have not been a major obstacle for the government; they have reportedly never turned down a request for electronic surveillance over the statute's twenty-five year history, and have only once rejected a warrant application of any kind.[34] This time, however, the FISA court, attempting to mimimize end runs around the probable cause requirement, interpreted the statute to prohibit criminal law enforcement officials from supervising foreign intelligence warrant applications.[35]

The Justice Department immediately appealed the FISA court's decision. (FISA authorizes appeals only by the government). A special appellate court that had never before met—because the government had never before had any reason to appeal—heard argument in secret and only from the government (represented by the solicitor general himself, who ordinarily argues only in the Supreme Court). The American Civil Liberties Union (ACLU) and the National Association of Criminal Defense Lawyers (NACDL) submitted amicus briefs, but the appellate court heard argument before those briefs were even filed.

On November 18, 2002, the appeals court issued its opinion, and, not surprisingly given the one-sided process, the government won.[36] The appeals court rejected the lower court's requirement, and further opined that the PATRIOT Act amendments were consistent with the Constitution, even though that issue was neither decided by the lower court nor presented on appeal. The ACLU and the NACDL objected to the decision and asked the Supreme Court to review it, but the government was the only party authorized to appeal, and the Supreme Court predictably denied review.

PATRIOT II: DOMESTIC SECURITY ENHANCEMENT ACT

Apparently, even these sweeping powers are not sufficient for the Bush administration. In February 2003, the Center for Public Integrity disclosed a leaked draft of the the Domestic Security Enhancement Act (DSEA). The draft legislation, stamped "Confidential" and dated January 9, 2003, appeared to be in final form, but had not yet been introduced in Congress. Still, it provides a glimpse into where the Justice Department would like to go.[37]

If the PATRIOT Act was so named to imply that those who questioned its sweeping new government powers were traitors, the DSEA takes that theme one giant step further. It provides that anyone who supports even the lawful activities of an organization the executive branch deems terrorist is presumptively stripped of his or her citizenship. Dramatically crossing the citizen-noncitizen line, the DSEA would literally turn citizens who are associated with "terrorist" groups into "aliens."

They would then be subject to the deportation power, which the

DSEA would expand to give the attorney general authority to deport any noncitizen—even lawful permanent residents or expatriated U.S. citizens—whose presence he deems inconsistent with our "national defense, foreign policy, or economic interests." One federal court of appeals has already ruled that that standard, borrowed from a pre-existing statute, is not susceptible to judicial review.[38] So this provision would effectively resurrect the sweeping but short-lived Alien Act of 1798, by giving the executive branch unreviewable authority to deport any noncitizen it chooses, without any need to show that the individual has violated criminal or immigration law.[39]

A U.S. citizen stripped of his citizenship and then ordered deported would presumably have difficulty finding a country to take him in. But still another provision authorizes the attorney general to deport persons "to any country or region regardless of whether the country or region has a government." And failing deportation to Somalia, the Justice Department has taken the position that it can detain indefinitely suspected terrorists who are ordered deported but cannot be removed.[40]

Other DSEA provisions are designed to further insulate the war on terrorism from public and judicial scrutiny. The bill would authorize secret arrests, a practice common to some other regimes but never before affirmatively authorized in the United States. Because the provision permits secrecy until an indictment or information is filed—the formal initiation of criminal proceedings—it would have its most dramatic effect on foreign nationals picked up on immigration charges, as immigration proceedings do not require the filing of an information or indictment. The DSEA would also automatically terminate all consent decrees (court orders entered into by parties settling a lawsuit) barring illegal police spying issued before September 11, 2001, without regard to whether continuing judicial supervision was necessary. When Congress has authorized the use of force, the bill would allow the government to conduct secret wiretaps and searches without obtaining a warrant from the Foreign Intelligence Surveillance Court. And it would give the government the same access to credit reports that private companies have. Historically, we have imposed both a higher threshold and judicial oversight on government access to such private information because government has the motive and the wherewithal to abuse the information in ways that private companies generally do not.

The future trajectory of the war on terrorism may be best illustrated by an obscure provision that would eliminate the distinction between "domestic terrorism" and "international terrorism" for a host of investigatory purposes. The administration's argument sounds reasonable enough: terrorism is terrorism, whether it takes place entirely within the United States or has an international component. But in the PATRIOT Act debates, the administration argued that it should be afforded broader surveillance powers over "international terrorism" precisely because such acts are simultaneously a matter of domestic law enforcement and foreign intelligence. Because foreign intelligence gathering has traditionally been subject to looser standards than criminal law enforcement, the government argued, the looser standards should extend to "international terrorism." It now proposes to extend the same relaxed standards to wholly domestic law enforcement.

The DSEA's treatment of expatriation and domestic terrorism are harbingers of what is to come in the war on terrorism. Thus far, much of the campaign has been targeted at foreign nationals, and sold to the American public on that ground. Americans' rights are not at stake, the argument goes, because we are concerned with "international" crime committed mostly by "aliens." With the DSEA, however, the Bush administration seeks to transgress both the alien-citizen line, by turning citizens into aliens for disfavored political ties, and the domestic-international line, extending to wholly domestic criminal law enforcement tools previously reserved for international terrorism investigations.

5. TARGETING CITIZENS

While the principal gambit in the trade-off between liberty and security has been to sacrifice the liberty of foreign nationals for the security of the citizenry, citizens have not been entirely spared. Some measures, such as new surveillance powers, the strengthening of laws against domestic terrorism, and the easing of restrictions on FBI spying, affect citizens as well as noncitizens, although in the short term their principal targets will likely be foreign nationals. The response to these measures confirms the double standard at work: where citizen's rights are directly affected, the political process has been much more sensitive to civil liberties concerns.

DON'T TAKE OUR RIGHTS AND LIBERTIES

Security proposals that would directly affect us all have received much closer attention, and often a far more skeptical reception, than initiatives directed at immigrants. The proposal to create a national identity card, on the table since September 12, has gone nowhere. Even though most of us already have drivers' licenses that effectively function as identity cards, the notion that there would be a centralized card that everyone would be expected or required to carry is apparently unacceptable. At House Majority Leader Richard Armey's insistence, the Homeland Security Act expressly forbids the development of a national identity card.[1]

Similarly, airport screening, which affects everyone who flies (although, as described above, some more acutely than others) has been the subject of careful attention. Government officials and the airline industry have spent a great deal of time negotiating ways of increasing security without unduly hampering the convenience of airline travel. Initially, Washington's Ronald Reagan National Airport was closed altogether, curbside check-in was prohibited, and security lines were long and slow. But within a year, airline travel had returned to something approximating normal, with only minor and occasional inconveniences relating to security.

Operation "Terrorist Information and Protection System," or TIPS, is another example. This program, devised by the Justice Department, was slated to recruit 11 million private citizens to spy on their neighbors. The volunteer spies were to be drawn primarily from the ranks of delivery personnel, meter readers, and others who find themselves out on the roads or with access to people's homes. On one view, the program would merely have institutionalized an existing informal process; concerned citizens have always been permitted and encouraged to report suspicious activity to law enforcement agencies. But the proposal to formalize that relationship with a "volunteer corps" elicited widespread consternation across the political spectrum, from Phyllis Schlafly to the ACLU. As with national identity cards, Richard Armey ensured that the Homeland Security Act expressly prohibited any expenditure of funds on Operation TIPS.[2]

Perhaps the best example of the public reaction to a proposal affecting everyone's rights is the response to "Total Information Awareness" (TIA), a project of the Pentagon's research arm, Defense Advance Research Projects Agency (DARPA). The project aims to develop technology to collect and search all the computer-accessible information about individuals that currently exists in the public and private sectors. Virtually everything we do in the modern world leaves a computer trace, including our credit card and banking transactions; our library borrowing records; our e-mail, Internet, and phone traffic; and our travel plans. At present, however, while many distinct entities have select portions of this information for their own legitimate purposes, the government lacks the capacity to collect and search it on a mass scale for law enforcement ends. There is generally no constitutional barrier to the government obtaining such information, because the Supreme Court has ruled that the Fourth Amendment's probable cause and warrant requirements do not apply to any information we share with a third party. In effect, the Court has reasoned, when we share such information with a third party, we assume the risk that the third party will share it with the government, and therefore we have no "reasonable expectation of privacy" in that information.[3] But the government has not previously sought to collect and mine all this data.

Notwithstanding the Supreme Court's reasoning, it is one thing to share one's private transactions with the credit card company as a necessary incident to obtaining credit, but another matter entirely to share them with the U.S. government, much less the military. The TIA program generated broad opposition, from the Cato Institute and the *New York Times*'s William Safire to the American Civil Liberties Union and the Electronic Privacy Information Center.[4] (The Pentagon did not help its cause by assigning John Poindexter, who was convicted of lying to Congress in connection with the Iran-Contra affair, to head the program, or by creating a trademark for the program that consists of a pyramid topped by a large eye, a variant on the official seal, with the words "Knowledge is Power" emblazoned across the top; the only thing it did not do was name the program "Big Brother.")[5] In February 2003, Congress voted to block the program until the Defense Department provides Congress with information and receives affirmative statutory authorization to proceed.[6] But as noted in the Introduction, Congress tellingly blocked the program only as applied to U.S. persons, leaving the Pentagon free to deploy it against most foreign nationals.

Judicial decisions to date in the war on terrorism also reflect the double standard. While federal courts have ruled certain aspects of the Justice Department's detention campaign illegal, for example, they have done so for the most part at the behest of citizens, not immigrants. As discussed above, several judges have ruled that the blanket closure of immigration hearings violates the Constitution, but the principal basis for those rulings has been the First Amendment rights of U.S. citizens and the press to attend the deportation hearings. Similarly, the federal court that ordered disclosure of the detainees' names did so to vindicate U.S. citizens' rights to know under the Freedom of Information Act. And as noted above, while the courts have insisted upon some (albeit limited) judicial review of the detention of U.S. citizens as enemy combatants, they have declined even to address the merits of detaining foreign nationals as enemy combatants. Where citizens' rights are directly at stake, in other words, both the legal and the political processes have proven much more rights-sensitive. Where only foreign nationals' rights appear to be at risk, the system hardly blinks.

FIRST THEY CAME FOR THE ALIENS

As the enemy combatant and ethnic profiling discussions above illustrate, citizens' rights have already suffered spillover effects from measures initially targeted at foreign nationals. Other examples abound. One provision of the PATRIOT Act, for example, authorizes investigators to obtain the records of literally *any* business—whether a credit-card company, the telephone company, a college or university, a bookstore, or an employer—for *any* person simply by certifying that the records are "relevant" to an "international terrorism" investigation. Entities subject to such requests may not inform their patrons or customers that they have turned over their records. Prior to the PATRIOT Act, that authority was limited to records of foreign agents themselves, who were largely, although not exclusively, foreign nationals.[7]

This provision also applies to records of nonprofit entities, including libraries, and has prompted some libraries to warn their patrons that their borrowing records are susceptible to FBI review. It has generated substantial opposition from librarians and booksellers in particular, and in March 2003 Representative Bernie Sanders introduced a bill to exempt bookstores and libraries from its ambit.[8]

Similarly, the criminal prohibition on providing material support to "terrorist organizations"—the centerpiece of the Justice Department's criminal war on terrorism—marks an extension to citizens of an authority that the government has asserted against foreign nationals in the immigration setting since 1990.[9] Erasing the citizen-noncitizen distinction, federal law now makes it a deportable offense and a crime to provide "material support" to terrorist organizations, without regard to whether the support provided actually furthered, or was intended to further, any terrorist activity.[10] Virtually every criminal "terrorism" case that the government has filed since September 11 has included a charge that the defendant provided material support to a terrorist organization.[11] And the United States has vigorously pushed other nations to enact similar laws of their own.[12]

Like the PATRIOT Act provision discussed above, the "material support" criminal statute imposes guilt by association. It requires no proof that an individual intended to further terrorist activities, and accordingly punishes moral innocents for constitutionally protected activity. Consider the Humanitarian Law Project (HLP), which I represent in a suit challenging the constitutionality of the "material support" statute.[13] Before the material support statute was passed in 1996, the HLP, a longstanding human rights organization based in Los Angeles, had been training the Kurdistan Workers' Party (PKK) in Turkey in human rights advocacy and peace negotiation skills. The HLP supported the human rights of the Kurds, a much abused minority in Turkey, and sought to encourage the PKK to pursue a peaceful resolution of the conflict there. Its trainings were designed to discourage violence and encourage nonviolence. Yet once the "material support" statute was passed and the secretary of state designated the PKK as a "terrorist organization," the HLP and its members would have faced ten-year prison terms had they continued their training. The government might well exercise its discretion not to prosecute such individuals, but one cannot know that in advance, and as a result the law has a sweeping chilling effect even on activity that seeks to reduce violence.

In shutting down three of the largest Muslim charities in the United States, the government has extended the "material support" ban still further, invoking an obscure administrative regime that allows it to bypass the criminal process altogether.[14] Under the International Emergency Economic Powers Act (IEEPA), the president has unilaterally banned all transactions with the charities, frozen millions of dollars, and effectively closed them down, all without a criminal conviction, a criminal charge, or even an administrative hearing.[15] Here, the executive branch has transformed a law directed at foreign nations into a tool for proscribing U.S. citizens' associations with political groups. IEEPA was designed to authorize economic sanctions against foreign countries in emergency situations. In 1995, however, President Bill Clinton used it to block all transactions with "specially designated terrorists," twelve political organizations in the Middle East—ten Palestinian groups opposed to the peace process and two Jewish organizations.[16] Shortly after the attacks of September 11, President Bush issued a similar executive order naming a different group of "specially designated global terrorists," and authorizing the secretary of the treasury to add to the list anyone who "assist[s] in, sponsor[s], or provide[s] . . . support for," or is "otherwise associated" with, a designated terrorist.[17] Designation results in the immediate blocking of all of an entity's or person's assets, and makes it a crime to engage in any economic transactions with the designated entity or individual.

When IEEPA was used to impose economic embargoes on foreign countries, it was a relatively noncontroversial form of nation-to-nation diplomacy. But when that same authority is applied to blacklist disfavored political groups and individuals, it raises serious constitutional concerns. The transformation of IEEPA essentially resurrects the Cold War practice of generating official lists of proscribed political organizations. As in the Cold War, the IEEPA lists of designated terrorists are created entirely in secret, using undisclosed criteria, and are then used to impute guilt by association. IEEPA does not define "specially designated terrorist," and therefore allows the president to blacklist any group he chooses without substantive standards or meaningful procedural safeguards; President Bush's executive order goes further and allows the secretary of the treasury to extend those sanctions to others based solely on their associations, regardless of the character of those associations.

A little-noticed provision in the PATRIOT Act amended IEEPA to authorize the Treasury Department to freeze assets on the mere assertion that an individual or entity is under investigation for potentially violating IEEPA. It also authorizes the government to defend that freeze order in court with secret evidence, presented behind closed doors, and not disclosed to the party whose assets are frozen.[18] Under these provisions, the Treasury Department after September 11 froze the assets of the Holy Land Foundation, the Global Relief Foundation, Inc., and the Benevolence International Foundation, three of the largest Muslim charities in the United States. In all three cases, it did so without a hearing, based not on allegations of criminal conduct, but on their alleged associations with other groups blacklisted by the president.[19]

The lengths to which IEEPA can be put are illustrated by the internal banishment imposed on Mohammad Salah, a U.S. citizen. In the early 1990s, Salah, a longtime resident of the Chicago area, was arrested, interrogated, and pleaded guilty in Israel—after Israeli troops allegedly extracted his confession through torture—to having distributed money to the families of deported leaders of Hamas. (This was at a time when U.S. State Department officials were arguing in Congress that one could not assume that persons associated with Hamas were terrorists because Hamas was engaged in a wide range of nonviolent social service activities).[20] Salah served a five-year prison sentence in an Israeli jail, was freed, and returned to Chicago, where he now lives. In 1995, without notice, trial, hearing, or appeal, the Clinton administration listed Salah as a "specially designated terrorist."[21] He had no opportunity to present evidence concerning the circumstances of his confession, his activities in Israel, or anything else. Because Salah is now a "specially designated terrorist," it is a crime for anyone in the United States to have any economic transactions whatsoever with him. The designation bars him from buying a loaf of bread from the corner grocer, going to a doctor, hiring a lawyer, or even taking a donation from a friend. If literally enforced, the order would lead to his starvation.[22]

These are extraordinary powers. In effect, the president can target any groups or individuals he chooses, label them "specially designated terrorists" without substantive criteria, notice, or a hearing, and put organizations out of business and individuals into internal economic exile. The statute gives the president a blank check to blacklist political organizations or activists at will. This authority was initially intended to be directed at foreign nations, but has now been extended to U.S. organizations and citizens; the only statutory requirement is some tie to a foreign interest.

These security initiatives have sparked relatively little protest, despite the fact that they potentially affect the freedoms of all Americans. The explanation likely rests on a perception that the tactics have been and will be targeted principally, even if not exclusively, at Arab and Muslim foreign nationals. The same explanation likely applies to Attorney General Ashcroft's relaxation of the guidelines that regulate FBI domestic spying. The guidelines originated in 1976, after a congressional committee revealed that the FBI had engaged in widespread illegal spying on and disruption of domestic political organizations, including many civil rights and antiwar groups.[23] The 1976 guidelines, adopted by then–Attorney General Edward Levi, were designed to focus the FBI on the investigation of crime, and to prohibit political spying by barring investigations where there was no basis for concern about federal crime. These guidelines had already been relaxed twice, by William French Smith in 1983, and by Louis Freeh in 1995.[24] But Smith and Freeh left in place the fundamental requirement that the FBI have some indication of at least the potential for criminal activity before it undertook an investigation. Since September 11, however, one of the most commonly heard complaints is that the FBI was and continues to be too focused on crime. In May 2002, Ashcroft amended the guidelines to authorize the FBI to undertake certain types of investigations—monitoring any gathering open to the public, including religious services; visiting Web sites, electronic bulletin boards, and chat rooms; and obtaining information from commercial data-mining services—without any reason to believe that those being monitored may be engaged in or preparing for criminal activity.[25]

This is a dangerous road, one the FBI has already traveled with disastrous consequences for political freedom in the United States. The conventional wisdom about the FBI being too focused on crime ignores the abuses of the past. Moreover, the pre-Ashcroft guidelines hardly erected a major obstacle to investigations; all that was required to initiate a preliminary inquiry was "an allegation or information indicating the possibility of criminal activity."[26] Since terrorism is a crime, the guidelines did not inhibit legitimate investigations of terrorism. If the FBI is not to be guided by concerns about potential crime in its investigations, what is it to be guided by? History suggests that intelligence gathering not focused on crime tends to sweep far too broadly, and to expend substantial resources tracking the activities of wholly lawful political groups simply because they dissent from the mainstream. This has costs not only for political freedoms but also for security, as resources used to investigate the innocent are resources that cannot be used to investigate the guilty.

Here, too, a double standard operates. It is likely that the new guidelines have not sparked substantial protest because people feel the FBI will focus these new powers on Arab and Muslim foreign nationals; since all of its overt information-gathering techniques have been so focused, one would presume that its covert information gathering will have a similar focus. The Bureau's recent mosque-counting directive only underscores that sense. Thus, most Americans are unlikely to feel that their rights are at risk.

Although the Ashcroft guidelines were announced as an integral part of the war on terrorism, they do not even govern most September 11–related investigations. International terrorism investigations are governed instead by the "foreign counterintelligence" guidelines.[27] These guidelines dispense with probable cause of criminal activity altogether. They authorize investigations of any individual or group with ties to a foreign government, a foreign-based political organization, or a group engaged in international terrorism.[28] Thus, when foreign nationals or citizens with foreign ties are investigated, the notion that the FBI should be focused on crime often does not apply at all.

Finally, the Bush administration has also sought to limit the right to counsel in ways that are applicable to citizens as well as foreign nationals. In October 2001, the Justice Department issued a new regulation authorizing eavesdropping on attorney-client communications in prison whenever the attorney general has "reasonable suspicion . . . to believe that a particular inmate may use communications with attorneys to further or facilitate acts of terrorism."[29] The regulation generally requires the government to provide notice to the inmate and his attorney that their conversations will be overheard, and requires the government to ensure that lawyers involved in the prosecution of the individual not have access to the eavesdropping.

The necessity, wisdom, and constitutionality of this regulation are all questionable. It is unnecessary because the government could always obtain court orders to listen in on attorney-client communications where it had probable cause to believe that the communications would be used to further a crime. Now, however, the government can eavesdrop without going to a court, and without showing probable cause. (Reasonable suspicion, required by the new regulation, is a substantially lower threshold.) It is unwise because if the government seeks to obtain information about terrorist activity, it is much more likely to do so if it does *not* tell the inmate and his attorney that they are being overheard, and under prior law, such confidential taping was permissible in international terrorism investigations. And the regulation may be unconstitutional because it authorizes an intrusion on one of the most sacrosanct of private communications—the counseling of a prisoner by his or her lawyer—without either a warrant or probable cause. While this rule change applies equally to citizens and foreign nationals, as of May 2003, the government had applied it only to Sheikh Omar Abdel Rahman, the Egyptian cleric incarcerated for life for plotting to blow up the bridges and tunnels around Manhattan.

As these measures reveal, citizens have been affected by the war on terrorism. But the sacrifices citizens have been asked to make pale in comparison with those imposed on foreign nationals. And the political process has taken citizens' sacrifices much more seriously, and has even blocked some security measures altogether. As a political matter, the government's war on terrorism has been sustainable in significant part because it is targeted at noncitizens—at "them," not "us." Imagine the public response if the police chief of a major American city responded to a horrific crime by rounding up several thousand "suspects," virtually all from one ethnic group, refused to disclose most of their names, tried them in secret, and ultimately failed to come up with the perpetrators. He would almost certainly be out of a job. Yet John Ashcroft's treatment of foreign nationals has sparked only muted criticism.

Perhaps most significantly, most of the measures that do affect citizens are extensions of authorities initially directed either exclusively or predominantly at foreign nationals, or are justified by pointing to citizens' alleged foreign connections. As Part 2 will show, that pattern is an all-too common one, and suggests that citizens should be skeptical of claims that measures directed at foreign nationals will leave their rights secure.

PART 2
HISTORY LESSONS

6. CROSSING THE CITIZEN-NONCITIZEN DIVIDE: AN OVERVIEW

The pattern of selectively sacrificing noncitizens' fundamental rights reflected in the government's response to the attacks of September 11 has a lengthy pedigree in American history. It turns out that the United States government has responded to virtually every national security crisis by adopting measures that selectively target noncitizens' rights. But the secondary pattern only now beginning to emerge in the wake of September 11—in which antialien measures are extended to U.S. citizens—has an equally impressive historical record. Virtually every significant government security initiative implicating civil liberties—including penalizing speech, ethnic profiling, guilt by association, the use of administrative measures to avoid the safeguards of the criminal process, and preventive detention—has originated in a measure targeted at noncitizens. The government has frequently defended such measures—legally and politically—by arguing that the threat stems from abroad, and that noncitizens do not deserve the same rights and protections as U.S. citizens, as Vice President Cheney did with respect to military tribunals. But almost inevitably, government officials have thereafter extended similar security measures to U.S. citizens. Ultimately, when a sufficient number of citizens are affected, the political and legal processes react, and only then are the measures seen as mistakes.

Part 2 illustrates this phenomenon by focusing on several periods of political crisis and repression. The history presented here is neither new nor comprehensive. What I offer is a new perspective on the history, one that highlights both the important function that antialien sentiment and tactics have played in the development and rationalization of political repression, and the virtually ineluctable tendency of such measures to extend across the citizen-noncitizen divide. In some instances, the use of antialien measures was an intentional opening gambit in a plan to extend political control more broadly; more often, as Acting Secretary of Labor Louis Post put it in describing the Palmer Raids of 1919–20, it was a matter of following "the course of least resistance." It is natural to avoid difficult choices, and targeting noncitizens is a convenient way to avoid having to decide which of one's own liberties to give up in the name of security. Because most security crises have an international element and the nation is generally quick in such periods to demonize foreigners as the "other," foreign nationals have always been an especially easy target. And the targeting of immigrants allows the government to reassure the electorate that its initiatives are contained, and do not directly implicate their own rights. But history shows that the promise that only foreign nationals will feel the effects is illusory.

Part 2 begins, in Chapter 7, by examining perhaps the most shameful episode of American history since slavery—the Japanese internment of World War II. It maintains that the internment, which ultimately led to the incarceration of 70,000 United States citizens as well as 40,000 Japanese nationals, had deep roots in antialien measures dating back to the Enemy Alien Act of 1798. The internment marked the extension to U.S. citizens of practices long imposed on foreign nationals, as the citizen-noncitizen divide was bridged by racial animus. This example illustrates not only the danger to U.S. citizens of denying noncitizens basic human rights, but also the close interconnections between antialien initiatives and racial discrimination. If, as the Jewish philosopher Hermann Cohen argued, "in the alien . . . man discovered the idea of humanity,"[1] it is also in discrimination against the "alien" that mankind may have honed its tendency to target vulnerable minorities.

I then turn, in Chapters 8 through 11, to the McCarthy era and its historical antecedents and consequences. Here, too, the government's tactics of repression reflected an extension to citizens of measures that had been introduced earlier—in the beginning of the twentieth century—against foreign nationals. In this case, the bridge to crossing the citizen-noncitizen divide was politics, as radical citizens were targeted in much the way that radical foreign nationals had been targeted earlier. The political repression that achieved its height in the Cold War ultimately extended far beyond anticommunism to reach civil rights and antiwar groups in the 1960s and 1970s. Only when the government's tactics affected a sufficiently large number of citizens did the country recognize the errors of its ways.

Part 2's final chapter tells a more recent and more personal story. I have devoted a significant part of my legal career to defending foreign nationals targeted for their alleged political associations in cases raising national security claims and allegations of terrorist ties. Long before the attacks of September 11, I saw firsthand what can go wrong when, in the name of preventing terrorism, the government targets the vulnerable, substitutes ideological litmus tests and guilt by association for individual culpability, and employs administrative shortcuts on basic due process guarantees of a fair adversarial process. Here, too, tactics initially targeted at noncitizens have been extended to the citizenry. The last two decades thus replay the patterns of the first 200 years, reminding us that we have not sufficiently learned from our mistakes, and that all of our rights are deeply at stake in the choices our elected representatives make in a war on terrorism that is likely to be with us for the rest of our lives.

7. ENEMY ALIENS AND ENEMY RACES

When the Japanese attacked Pearl Harbor on December 7, 1941, Masuo Yasui, a Japanese immigrant businessman and farmowner in Hood River, Oregon, sent a telegram to his son, Minoru—Min for short—a young lawyer working for the Japanese consulate in Chicago: "NOW THAT THIS COUNTRY IS AT WAR AND NEEDS YOU, AND SINCE YOU ARE TRAINED AS AN OFFICER, I AS YOUR FATHER URGE YOU TO ENLIST IMMEDIATELY." Masuo Yasui was a respected leader in the Hood River Valley, a Rotary Club member, the director of a bank, and a prominent figure in both the largely white apple growers' association and the valley's Japanese-American community. He had raised his seven children as Methodists, and put them all through college. His son, Min, was an officer in the Army Infantry Reserve. In the wake of the Pearl Harbor attack, Masuo, a Japanese national, made the difficult call of urging his son to go to war on behalf of the country the Yasuis had made their home and against the country of the parents' birth.

Min answered his father's call, resigned his job, and reported to Fort Vancouver, near Portland, Oregon. The army initially placed him in charge of a platoon, but the very next day discharged him. A few days later, Min's father was arrested. His name had appeared on a list generated in Washington of potentially dangerous Japanese nationals to be considered for internment as "enemy aliens." The list, which contained over 2,000 names, included Japanese nationals who were influential in their community, Japanese-language teachers, newspaper editors, and Shinto and Buddhist priests. Masuo was taken to an enemy alien internment camp in Missoula, Montana.

Min sought to represent his father in his internment hearing, but under the rules governing the hearings, internees were not allowed lawyers. Min was permitted to attend the hearing, however, and described it as follows:

They produced some very childish maps of the Panama Canal, and they were saying, "Do you know what these are?" Dad looked at them and said, "They look like maps of the Panama Canal." "How did you get them?" he was asked. "Well my kids drew these maps in school." The maps were illustrations of how the locks worked. The questioner said, "This shows how you were really trying to disguise a nefarious plot to blow up the Panama Canal." Dad said, "Of course not, I had no such intention." "Well, prove that you didn't have such an intention," they replied.[1]

Unable to prove a negative, Masuo Yasui was interned from 1942 until 1945.

Weeks after Yasui was first interned, President Franklin Delano Roosevelt signed Executive Order 9066, imposing a curfew not only on Japanese nationals, but on all persons of Japanese ancestry on the West Coast, including United States citizens. Min, a U.S. citizen by birth, and raised very much as an American, was deeply offended by the order. Five hours after the curfew took effect on March 28, 1942, he walked into a police station in Portland and demanded to be arrested for violating the curfew, thus launching the first test case of the military's campaign to restrict the rights and freedoms of Japanese-Americans. Shortly thereafter, Min and his entire family were ordered to leave their homes and report for internment as part of the military's wholesale evacuation of Japanese and Japanese-Americans from the West Coast. The evacuation order read: "All persons of Japanese ancestry, aliens and nonaliens, will be evacuated." Recalling that language years later, Yasui asked, "What's a *nonalien?* I tell you, they played with words."

Min Yasui took his challenge to the curfew to the Supreme Court, where he lost by a unanimous vote. He ultimately spent more than nine months in solitary confinement in a county jail for standing up for a principle of equality that he had learned as a young boy in American public schools.

This treatment of a father and a son, a foreign national and a U.S. citizen, both locked up without any evidence that they posed a danger to anyone, illustrates how easily the line between noncitizen and citizen (or, as the army preferred, alien and nonalien) can be crossed. The restrictions on and ultimate internment of the Japanese during World War II are widely regarded as comprising one of the most shameful episodes in this nation's history. The consensus that these measures were wrong is so widely shared that the federal government issued a formal apology and reparations to those interned—probably the only instance in which it has made such an admission of wrongdoing to a group targeted for repression in a time of fear. In light of the nearly universal condemnation that now attends this aspect of the government's wartime policy, the interesting question is how it could have happened in the first place. As the story of the Yasuis suggests, the way was paved by measures targeted at foreign nationals. The internment of 110,000 persons of Japanese descent—70,000 of them U.S. citizens—treated citizens as we had long treated "enemy aliens."

The United States has always had a deeply ambivalent attitude toward immigrants. We are a nation founded by immigrants fleeing persecution, and have long seen ourselves as a haven for other refugees. We are justly proud of our diversity, and romanticize the figure of the immigrant in American history.[2] At the same time, nativism, defined by historian John Higham as "intense opposition to an internal minority on the ground of its foreign (i.e., 'un-American') connections," has been a persistent theme throughout our history.[3] From the nation's earliest days, citizens have deemed immigrants suspicious based on their racial, religious, and ethnic difference, and their radical associations and ideas. For well over a century, we have incarcerated and deported foreign nationals for their ideas, their beliefs, and the company they keep, while employing summary procedures to do so. And at critical moments, as during World War II, we have relied upon alienage and national origin as bases for mass arrests and detentions.

As I will argue in Chapter 13, these actions are fundamentally inconsistent with our deepest constitutional principles. They are nonetheless politically tempting because, by selectively targeting immigrants, such measures reassure citizens that their own liberties and rights will be left intact. But that promise has often proved illusory. Security measures targeted at immigrants have virtually always laid the groundwork for future deprivations of citizens' rights. The Japanese internment is thus not a unique case, but only the most extreme example of a deeper pattern in American history.

THE ROOTS OF THE JAPANESE INTERNMENT

Historians tend to trace the Japanese internment to anti-Asian prejudice spurred by the influx of Asian immigrants who came to work on the railroads. In fact, the roots extend back at least to 1798, when, inspired by fears that the "alien" radicalism of the French Revolution might infect the polity here, Congress enacted the infamous Alien and Sedition Acts.[4] The Alien Act gave the president the power to deport any noncitizen he deemed dangerous without judicial review.[5] The Sedition Act made it a crime for anyone to criticize government officials.[6] The Alien Act was never enforced, and the Sedition Act was enforced exclusively against Republican critics of the Federalist administration from 1798 to 1800. Both laws sparked substantial protest, and were not reenacted when they expired under sunset provisions two years later. When Thomas Jefferson, a Republican, succeeded Federalist John Adams as president, Jefferson pardoned all those convicted under the Sedition Act. The Alien and Sedition Acts are now widely viewed as an illustration of what can go wrong when we fail to adhere to basic respect for First Amendment freedoms and due process. In *New York Times Co. v. Sullivan,* one of the Supreme Court's most important cases establishing the right to criticize government officials without fear of sanction, the Court pointed to the rise and rapid fall of the Sedition Act as support for the principle that political debate must be free from government control.[7]

The story of the Alien and Sedition Acts has the status of a founding myth—in standard accounts, it reflects an early moment of misguided censorship and repression, from which we have learned the importance of respect for political freedom and due process. Far less well known is the fact that at the same time, Congress enacted the Enemy Alien Act. While the Alien and Sedition Acts were short-lived and ultimately proved more important for the precedent set by their repudiation than by their adoption, the Enemy Alien Act remains on the books to this day.[8] It authorizes the president during a declared war to detain, expel, or otherwise restrict the freedom of any citizen fourteen years or older of the country with which we are at war. It requires no hearing to determine whether the individual is in fact suspicious, disloyal, or dangerous; instead, the Act creates an irrebuttable presumption that enemy aliens are dangerous, based *solely* on their national identity. It authorizes unilateral executive detention without hearings, and precludes judicial review of a president's determination that a given alien is dangerous. In stark contrast to the ignominious and brief history of the Alien and Sedition Acts, the Enemy Alien Act has been enforced repeatedly during declared wars, and was upheld by the Supreme Court in 1948, even when applied to detain and deport foreign nationals *after* hostilities had ceased and peace had been declared.[9]

James Madison, a leading critic of the Alien and Sedition Acts, was also the first president to invoke the Enemy Alien Act, when he used it against the British during the War of 1812.[10] President Woodrow Wilson invoked it in World War I to regulate and detain Germans and Austro-Hungarians. He required all enemy aliens to register, and barred them from possessing guns, coming within half a mile of any military base or munitions factory or within three miles of a shore line, entering the District of Columbia, "ascend[ing] into the air in any airplane, balloon, airship, or flying machine," or publishing any "attack . . . against the Government or Congress of the United States . . . or against the measures or policy of the United States." In addition, all enemy aliens were subject to detention on an administrative determination of "reasonable cause to believe [the alien] may be aiding or about to aid the enemy."[11] In the course of the war, the government arrested approximately 6,300 enemy aliens, placed about 4,000 on parole, and held the remaining 2,300 in internment camps.[12]

President Franklin Delano Roosevelt invoked the Enemy Alien Act against Japanese nationals the day that Pearl Harbor was attacked; the next day he extended those regulations to Italian and German citizens. Of the 5 million foreigners present in the United States in 1940, 900,000 were classified as enemy aliens upon the United States' entry into the war.[13] All enemy aliens were required to register and carry an alien registration certificate at all times. In addition, they were prohibited from traveling more than five miles from their homes without permission; subjected to a dusk-to-dawn curfew; barred from owning cameras, shortwave radios, or guns; and subject to sweeping administrative searches and seizures—without probable cause—for any such "contraband." Thousands of enemy aliens were required to leave their homes on the West Coast under general military "exclusion" orders, based on nothing more than their citizenship or country of origin.[14]

Thousands of others, such as Masuo Yasui, were interned without charges for the course of the war. The initial detentions were based almost entirely on a "custodial detention list" of potentially dangerous persons prepared by the FBI at President Roosevelt's request. The detainees were not informed of the bases for their detentions, and the entire process was conducted largely in secret, but FBI records reveal that placement on the list turned largely on political and ethnic associations. The list was constructed from subscription lists to German, Italian, Japanese, and Communist newspapers, membership in political or ethnic organizations, and reports on meetings and demonstrations.[15] Italians, for example, could end up on the FBI's list if they had been members of the Italian War Veterans (IWV) organization; were associated with Italian language newspapers, magazines, or radio shows; or were Italian language instructors in schools sponsored by Italian consulates.[16] Prospero Cecconi, a pasta maker in San Francisco, was detained because, after fighting for Italy (our ally) during World War I, he had joined the IWV. The IWV was a registered, legal organization that, among other things, raised money for Italian war widows and orphans pursuant to an official State Department license. In May 1941, the State Department rescinded that license, and the IWV immediately stopped fund-raising. The organization disbanded entirely two days after the United States declared war against Italy. Yet past membership in the group was sufficient to warrant detaining Cecconi and many Italians for the course of the war.

The military gave interned enemy aliens individualized hearings, but they were not informed of the charges against them or entitled to be represented by a lawyer. The hearings usually took place far from home, so all the individual could generally offer in his defense was his own testimony. And despite the importance of the FBI's "custodial detention list" to internment and exclusion decisions, the Bureau did not provide any information about the organizations on the list to the enemy alien hearing boards, to the army or its intelligence division, or to the commanding generals who had final authority to make exclusion decisions. In effect, the entire process deferred to the FBI's list.

In July 1943, Attorney General Francis Biddle found that this list was "inherently unreliable," and ordered Hoover to stop using it. As Biddle found, "the evidence used . . . was inadequate; the standards applied to the evidence . . . were defective; and . . . the notion that it is possible to make a valid determination as to how dangerous a person is in the abstract and without reference to time, environment and other relevant circumstances, is impractical, unwise, and dangerous." He ordered Hoover to cease making such classifications, and to stamp the following warning on every document that contained such a classification:

THIS CLASSIFICATION IS UNRELIABLE. IT IS HEREBY CANCELLED, AND SHOULD NOT BE USED AS A DETERMINATION OF DANGER-OUSNESS OR OF ANY OTHER FACT.[17]

Yet Biddle's rebuke came too late for most. And contrary to Biddle's order, the FBI continued to maintain lists of subversive and dangerous individuals, concealing that fact from the Justice Department.[18]

The rationale for the Enemy Alien Act is that during a war the government needs the power to confine and neutralize all persons with ties to the country with which it is fighting, because citizens are presumptively loyal to their own country. It substitutes a group-based presumption of potential threat for individualized determinations of actual culpability, and equates nationality with dangerousness. As Samuel Hopkins Adams put it in 1918, "Reckon each [enemy alien] as a pound of dynamite—surely a modest comparison . . . not all these enemy aliens are hostile. Not all dynamite explodes." [19]

The Enemy Alien Act is by definition predicated on a sharp distinction between citizens and foreign nationals; its very justification is the enemy alien's *foreign* nationality. Given the centrality of "alien-ness" to the concept, one might think that this power would pose little threat to the liberties of U.S. citizens. In World War II, however, the military extended the Act's philosophy to *Japanese-Americans* through the prism of race. The army argued that persons of Japanese descent, even if they were American citizens because they were born here, remained for all practical purposes "enemy aliens," presumptively loyal to Japan. Lieutenant General John L. DeWitt, the driving force behind the internment orders, wrote in his report on the Japanese evacuation that "[t]he Japanese race is an enemy race and while many second and third generation Japanese born on United States soil, possessed of United States citizenship, have become 'Americanized,' the racial strains are undiluted." [20] More colloquially, DeWitt testified in 1943 before the House Naval Affairs Committee that "[a] Jap's a Jap. It makes no difference whether he is an American citizen or not." [21] Secretary of War Henry Stimson concurred, reasoning that "[t]heir racial characteristics are such that we cannot understand or trust even the citizen Japanese." [22] On this reasoning, the military issued a series of orders regulating the conduct of Japanese nationals and U.S. citizens of Japanese descent—"aliens and nonaliens"—alike. They were barred from living in certain areas, subjected to a curfew, and ultimately interned en masse.

It is no accident that the enemy alien concept was extended only to Japanese-Americans. German-Americans and Italian-Americans were spared such treatment, although citizens of these backgrounds often had their loyalty challenged in less categorical ways. [23] The justification for targeting only the Japanese was avowedly racist and had deep roots.

The roots extend at least to the mid-nineteenth century, when anti-Chinese sentiment led to frequent lynchings, stonings, and beatings of Chinese immigrants, as well as to laws barring Chinese nationals from testifying in cases involving whites.[24] California Governor John Bigler argued in 1852 "that the Chinese were a moral evil, that as coolies they were little more than slaves, that they degraded white labor and were inherently incapable of playing the role of citizens."[25] In 1876, the California state legislature published "An Address to the People of the United States on the Evils of Chinese Immigration,"[26] and in 1882, Congress enacted the first Chinese exclusion laws, barring Chinese nationals from entering the United States.[27] Shortly thereafter, Congress enacted a law requiring Chinese immigrants already living here to establish the legality of their presence with the testimony of "one white witness."[28] In cases still routinely cited in immigration jurisprudence, the Supreme Court rejected constitutional challenges to the exclusion of the Chinese based on their national origin, and to the "one white witness" rule.[29]

In 1920, Congress banned virtually all immigration from Asia, and adopted a literacy test for immigrants, designed to keep out those who could not speak English. Four years later, Congress enacted national origin quotas on admissions, designed to discourage nonwhite immigration. One year later, the commissioner of immigration boasted that virtually all immigrants now "looked" like Americans.[30]

Like the Chinese before them, the Japanese were considered unassimilable, a breed apart, and an inferior race.[31] In the period immediately preceding World War II, both the federal and state governments adopted a wide variety of anti-Japanese measures, denying people of Japanese ancestry the right to naturalize, to own property, and to work in several industries.[32] When World War II saw such measures extended to Japanese-Americans, there was little popular objection:

> [T]he position of American citizens of Japanese descent, theoretically more secure [than that of aliens], was almost equally precarious. Regarded generally as "descendants of the Japanese enemy," they found their status as citizens more and more in jeopardy. The confusion of alien ancestry

with alien status was compounded in the public mind as newspapers referred indiscriminately to all Japanese—whether citizens or aliens, enemy
forces or peaceful residents—as "Japs." . . . [T]he cry of "once a Jap, always
a Jap" was heard on all sides.[33]

The *difference* of the Japanese—a difference founded initially on
alienage but ultimately on race—made it easier for the white majority
to accept measures targeted at the Japanese. Their difference simultaneously facilitated deeply rooted stereotypes, diminished empathy,
and offered assurances that the same fate would not befall the majority. The close interrelationship between anti-Asian racism and anti-
immigrant sentiment made the transition from enemy alien to enemy
race disturbingly smooth.

The role that racial stereotypes played in the transition is underscored by the fact that there was never any evidence to support the
concern that the Japanese living among us posed a threat. None of the
interned Japanese was ever charged with, much less convicted of, espionage, sabotage, or treason. But the absence of evidence did not stop
the demands for internment. Instead, in arguments that foreshadow
the "sleeper" theories advanced about Al Qaeda today, government
officials argued that the very fact that Japanese aliens and citizens living among us had *not* taken any subversive action only underscored
how dangerous they really were. Even Earl Warren, then governor of
California and later chief justice of the most liberal Supreme Court
the country has ever seen, argued, "It seems to me that it is quite significant that in this great state of ours we have had no fifth column activities and no sabotage reported. It looks very much to me as though
it is a studied effort not to have any until the zero hour arrives."[34] General DeWitt argued similarly that the lack of any evidence of sabotage
by the Japanese to date "is a disturbing and confirming indication that
such action will be taken."[35]

Reviewing challenges to the government's anti-Japanese measures,
the Supreme Court deferred to the military, accepted the racial prejudice that underlay the wartime restrictions, and upheld both the initial curfews and the ultimate internment.[36] In these cases, the Court

made little reference to the fact that citizens' rights were at issue. The citizen-noncitizen line was crossed virtually without comment. In 1943, for example, the Court upheld Gordon Hirabayashi's conviction for violating the military's curfew. Hirabayashi, a Quaker, had been born and raised in Seattle, had never been to Japan, and had no connection with anyone in Japan. The Court reasoned that the curfew was permissible because the Japanese "have in large measure prevented their assimilation as an integral part of the white population," because some of the Japanese had dual citizenship, and because "we cannot close our eyes to the fact, demonstrated by experience, that in time of war residents having ethnic affiliations with an invading enemy may be a greater source of danger than those of a different ancestry."[37] Adopting the military's equation of ancestry with suspicion, the Court wrote that "[t]he fact alone that the attack on our shores was threatened by Japan rather than another enemy power set these citizens apart from others who have no particular association with Japan."[38] As General DeWitt put it, "a Jap's a Jap."

One year later, in *Korematsu v. United States*,[39] the Court went still further and upheld not just the imposition of a curfew, but lengthy internment, based on racial identity alone. The Court said that laws treating people differently on the basis of race or national origin are generally subject to the most stringent judicial scrutiny, but in fact it deferred blindly to the military's judgment that internment of the entire West Coast Japanese population was required. The Court rejected the argument that the Japanese were the victims of racial prejudice by deferring to the military's assertions that some Japanese were disloyal, and that it was impossible to separate the disloyal from the loyal. In retrospect, history has vindicated dissenting Justice Frank Murphy's view in *Korematsu* that the Japanese internment was "one of the most sweeping and complete deprivations of constitutional rights in the history of this nation in the absence of martial law."[40] In the 1980s, Congress paid reparations to the survivors, and federal courts overturned Gordon Hirabayashi's and Fred Korematsu's convictions on the ground that the military had "knowingly withheld information from the courts when they were considering the critical question of military necessity."[41] While *Korematsu* itself has not been overruled, it is widely viewed with shame. Eight of the nine sitting Justices on today's Supreme Court have stated that *Korematsu* was wrongly decided; Justice Antonin Scalia has placed *Korematsu* on a par with *Dred Scott*.[42]

But despite this collective repudiation of the Japanese internment, the Enemy Alien Act remains on the books. Some, including Chief Justice Rehnquist, have argued that the error of the Japanese internment was only its extension to U.S. citizens; had it been limited to the 40,000 Japanese nationals, Rehnquist implies, the internment would have been constitutionally justified.[43] In my view, it was as wrong to intern the Japanese nationals without individualized determinations as it was to intern the U.S. citizens of Japanese descent. Perhaps that is why, when Congress eventually paid reparations, it recognized that "a grave injustice was done to both citizens and permanent resident aliens of Japanese ancestry," and paid reparations to both citizen and noncitizen survivors.[44]

Yale Law professor Eugene Rostow, writing in 1945, summarized what was wrong with the Japanese internment as follows:

> The Japanese exclusion program thus rests on five propositions of the utmost potential menace: (1) protective custody, extending over three or four years, is a permitted form of imprisonment in the United States; (2) political opinions, not criminal acts, may contain enough clear and present danger to justify such imprisonment; (3) men, women, and children of a given ethnic group, both American and resident aliens, can be presumed to possess the kind of dangerous ideas which require their imprisonment; (4) in time of war or emergency, the military, perhaps without even the concurrence of the legislature, can decide what political opinions require imprisonment, and which ethnic groups are infected with them; and (5) the decision of the military can be carried out without indictment, trial, examination, jury, the confrontation of witnesses, counsel for the defense, the privilege against self-incrimination, or any of the other safeguards of the Bill of Rights.[45]

Each of the five propositions Rostow identified stems from the enemy alien law, which similarly authorizes prolonged protective custody, without any constitutional safeguards, on the basis of military assessments of dangerousness based on political opinion presumed from national origin. These propositions do not become wrong only when applied to U.S. citizens, but are wrong as applied to any human being. Still, even if one is inclined to believe, as Chief Justice Rehnquist apparently does, that the wholesale internment of Japanese nationals may have been justified, the fact that the internment was expanded so smoothly to 70,000 U.S. citizens illustrates how antialien laws, themselves fundamentally flawed, can pave the way for serious inroads on citizens' liberties as well.

More broadly, the treatment of noncitizens has proved a prototype for the treatment of other minority groups whom the majority sees as different, or "other." Double standards predicated on the citizen-noncitizen line are easily extended to racial, religious, and political minorities within the citizenry. In this regard, citizen-noncitizen discrimination is all the more insidious today, precisely because discrimination against noncitizens remains one of the few group-based categories that many people still feel comfortable employing. Overt racism, sexism, and religious intolerance have become taboo, but discrimination against noncitizens has retained a degree of legitimacy, as the current Justice Department's defense of its targeting of Arab and Muslim foreign nationals demonstrates. But as the Justice Department's targeting campaign also shows, discrimination on the basis of nationality can easily be a cover for racial, religious, and political discrimination, and frequently has spillover effects along the pathways of race, religion, and politics.[46]

HOOVER'S LITTLE LIST

While most Americans are familiar with the fact that we interned the Japanese during World War II, few are aware that long after that episode, the federal government continued to make internment plans, this time not limited to the Japanese, but aimed more broadly still at *any* citizen whom the government deemed suspicious or dangerous.

In 1948, the Justice Department secretly adopted a program known as "the Portfolio" for interning "dangerous persons" during emergencies.[47] Under this program, the president would suspend the writ of habeas corpus, and mass arrests would be made under a single "master warrant" issued by the attorney general, bypassing the courts altogether. The master warrant would also authorize widespread searches and seizures without probable cause. Those detained would have no right to seek judicial review, but would be limited to an administrative hearing before specially constituted boards of review not bound by the rules of evidence. The only appeal would be to the president.[48] By July 1950, the FBI had compiled a list of 11,930 persons who would be subject to such detention in the event of a national emergency. The criteria for the list included membership in the Communist Party "or similar ideological groups," and some active role promoting or being trained in the group's "aims and purposes." [49]

The Portfolio program was devised without congressional authorization, and indeed without notice to Congress or the public. In September 1950, however, Congress independently created its own detention plan, enacted as Title II of the Internal Security Act.[50] This authority, which remained on the books until 1971, permitted emergency detention of dangerous persons, albeit under slightly more restrictive terms than "the Portfolio." As historian Richard Longaker described the program:

> [it authorized] detention without arraignment before a judge, the possibility of bail, or a jury trial. . . . Apprehension and incarceration were based on an administrative finding of prospective guilt in which nonjudicial officers utilized a standard of reasonable belief, not probable cause, that a suspect should be held . . . The authority of the Attorney General was uncontrolled. He could issue warrants at will and withhold evidence selectively, including the identity of the detainee's accusers, thus bypassing the right of a defendant to confront and cross-examine his accusers.[51]

In 1952, Congress authorized and funded six detention centers for suspected subversives in Arizona, California, Florida, Oklahoma, and Pennsylvania.[52]

No one was ever actually detained under these programs. But the FBI used their existence to justify widespread political spying for decades in the name of developing and refining its lists of suspicious persons. At its peak, in 1954, the FBI's "Security Index" of people to be detained in an emergency numbered 26,174 persons.[53] In the 1960s, the list included civil rights and antiwar movement activists, including Dr. Martin Luther King Jr. By the late 1960s, the FBI instructed its agents to investigate for potential inclusion on the lists Students for a Democratic Society (SDS), other "pro-Communist New Left–type groups," and persons living in "communes." [54]

In 1971, Congress repudiated the concept of emergency detention. It repealed the Internal Security Act provisions and enacted a new law stating unequivocally that "no citizen shall be imprisoned or otherwise detained by the United States except pursuant to an Act of Congress." [55] Yet the FBI continued to maintain a list of subversive persons until at least 1975, when disclosure of the list by a congressional committee investigating intelligence abuses effectively forced the FBI to abolish the practice.

In the 1980s, the concept of emergency detention of suspicious people made a comeback. In 1986, an antiterrorism task force comprised of high-level Justice Department officials considered an INS "Contingency Plan," which, among other things, called for the use of immigration law to intern "alien terrorists" and "alien activists" in a federal detention center in Oakdale, Louisiana. The plan specifically identified nationals of Algeria, Libya, Tunisia, Iran, Jordan, Syria, Morocco, and Lebanon as potential targets for such emergency detention. When the "Contingency Plan" was leaked, the government quickly backed away from it, insisting that it was merely a "thought experiment." Still, the fact that such a program was even thinkable so soon after the FBI had closed its detention lists demonstrates the persistence of the felt need to lock up "dangerous people" in emergencies.[56]

There things stood until September 11. For twenty-five years no plans for emergency detention were adopted, and as far as we know, the FBI did not create another "Subversive Index." But as recounted in

Chapter 2, the Justice Department's first response to the attacks of September 11 was immediately to resurrect preventive detention under several guises. As in the past, the government's initial targets were foreign nationals. But before long, it had extended its campaign to U.S. citizens, sometimes charging them with pretextual criminal violations, sometimes holding them as material witnesses, and, in the cases of Yasser Hamdi and Jose Padilla, invoking military custody— the ultimate form of executive preventive detention. As in the past, the government is once again detaining people based not on past conduct, but on predictions about their potential for danger in the future. And, as in the past, the government has resorted to extremely broad and wildly inaccurate proxies for potential danger; so much so that by the FBI's own account, virtually all of those it has preventively detained have had no connection to terrorism whatsoever.

As the Japanese internment and the emergency detention schemes of the Cold War reveal, preventive detention measures against foreign nationals make preventive detention of U.S. citizens thinkable. With each successive step the scope of those potentially subject to detention expanded—from nationals of countries with which we were at war, to U.S. citizens of Japanese descent, and ultimately to any U.S. citizen considered dangerous by virtue of association with a suspicious organization or even a "commune." In 1971, the nation seemed finally to have repudiated the concept, but the INS "Contingency Plan" of the 1980s and the preventive detention and enemy combatant approach of today's war on terrorism illustrate how quickly this practice can be revived.

Still, it may be that we have learned something from our mistakes. Congress's renunciation of preventive detention in 1971 and its reparations to the Japanese detainees in 1988 are significant events in our legal culture and history. Perhaps in part because of that history, Arabs and Muslims have not been interned en masse in the wake of September 11 in the way that the Japanese were during World War II. While undoubtedly Arab and Muslim identity played a decisive role in the selection of most of the 4,000 persons incarcerated in Attorney

General Ashcroft's preventive detention campaign, as far as we know the government has not yet locked up Arabs and Muslims *solely* for their national or religious identity.

But is that because we have learned our lesson, or is it simply that the political forces are not sufficient to sustain such a strategy? As terrifying as Al Qaeda undoubtedly is, the threat we face today is less severe than that presented during World War II, when we were fighting a world war against an enemy that had largely prevailed in Europe and was making strong gains in the Pacific, and when millions of our own citizens were risking their lives on the front lines. In addition, unlike the Japanese, who constituted a small and geographically concentrated minority in the United States in the 1940s, there are many millions of Arabs and Muslims interspersed throughout American society, making anything like mass internment highly impractical, to say the least. At the same time, the government has targeted foreign nationals based on their Arab or Muslim identities for questioning, selective enforcement of deportation, differential visa treatment, registration and fingerprinting, and automatic detention of asylum applicants. In doing so, it has indulged the same kind of ethnic stereotyping that defined the Japanese internment. We have resurrected the theory and practice of preventive detention, incarcerating as "suspected terrorists" literally thousands of Arabs and Muslims who have not been charged with any terrorist conduct. And, as in World War II and its aftermath, we have once again extended antialien measures to U.S. citizens through the prisms of race and political association.

8. ALIEN RADICALS AND RADICAL CITIZENS: FROM ANARCHISM TO SEDITION

In 1920, Eugene Victor Debs ran for president on the Socialist Party ticket, and managed to garner nearly 1 million votes. This was quite an accomplishment, considering the handicap placed on his campaign: he was at the time serving a ten-year federal prison sentence for violating the Espionage Act of 1917. Leader of the Socialist Party, which opposed U.S. involvement in World War I from the outset, Debs was prosecuted for making a speech in Canton, Ohio, in which he praised several persons who had been convicted for encouraging others to resist the draft. He did not directly advocate draft resistance, but the Supreme Court in 1919 found that the audience might have inferred such a message, and unanimously concluded that that inference was sufficient to uphold his conviction.

Thirty years later, in 1949, Dorothy Bailey, a civil servant with the United States Employment Service in Washington, D.C., with no responsibility for or access to sensitive information, lost her job. A loyalty review board had found "reasonable grounds" to suspect that she was disloyal to the United States. A friend of Bailey's worked for the prestigious Washington law firm of Arnold, Fortas, and Porter, and the firm agreed to represent her. Thurman Arnold had been assistant attorney general, Abe Fortas went on to become a Supreme Court Justice, and Paul Porter had been the head of the Office of Price Administration in the New Deal. But even with three of the best lawyers in the country on her side, Bailey could not effectively rebut what she could not see. She was told that she was suspected of having been associated with the Communist Party, the American League for Peace and Democracy, and the Washington Committee for Democratic Action, all organizations deemed suspect by the attorney general. Bailey admitted past membership in the American League, but denied all other charges. She asserted her loyalty, offered seventy supporting affidavits and four witnesses to attest to her character, and submitted to all questioning by the hearing examiners. No witness offered evidence against her. As a court later summarized it, "the record consists entirely of evidence in her favor." Yet the hearing board ruled against her, solely on the basis of undisclosed FBI reports relaying accusations by unidentified informants. The hearing board itself had not heard directly from the unknown informants or even from the FBI agents who interviewed them. For all practical purposes, the board simply deferred to a written FBI report, submitted to it in secret, relaying the second-hand accusations of anonymous accusers. Yet the U.S. Court of Appeals for the District of Columbia found nothing illegal or unconstitutional about the process, reasoning that Bailey had no right to a government job, and therefore was entitled to no due process with respect to her termination. The Supreme Court affirmed the decision by an equally divided vote. In the end, the best Arnold, Fortas, and Porter could do for Bailey was to hire her as their office manager.[1]

Debs and Bailey are just two of thousands of U.S. citizens who have been penalized for their political beliefs and associations. During World War I, the federal government prosecuted 2,000 people for merely speaking out against the war. About half were convicted and sentenced to prison terms of up to twenty years. During the Cold War, hundreds of thousands of Americans had their loyalty questioned, and tens of thousands lost their jobs and were blacklisted for their suspected associations with the Communist Party, without regard to whether they actually engaged in or furthered any illegal or violent activity, and usually without any meaningful chance to confront their accusers or defend themselves. In retrospect, these actions, like the Japanese internment, are widely perceived as terrible mistakes. The lessons they taught have resulted in some of the most fundamental principles of modern American constitutional law. They ultimately led the Supreme Court to rule that one may not be punished even for advocating criminal violence unless one's speech is both intended and likely to spark imminent lawless action.[2] They led the Court to prohibit "guilt by association," holding that people cannot be punished for their associations—even with a group that engages in illegal activity—unless the government proves that the individual specifically intended to further the group's illegal activities.[3] And they prompted the Court to insist on fair notice and a meaningful opportunity to respond before the government can take any valuable right from an individual.[4] Yet these rules, now seen as central to a democratic society, were a long time in coming. Before they were adopted, millions of Americans were compelled to take loyalty oaths, subjected to proceedings lacking basic requisites of fairness, or laid off for nothing more than their speech or association.

With the Japanese internment, the McCarthy period stands as one of the most shameful periods of political repression in our nation's history. Less widely recognized is the fact that, as in the Japanese internment cases, the government's Cold War tactics were extensions of practices it had long directed against foreign nationals. Measures initially employed against foreign radicals in the early decades of the twentieth century were direct precursors of the much broader censorship and repression of the Cold War. Where racism was the bridge for crossing the citizen-noncitizen divide in the case of the Japanese internment, here the link was political association, as efforts to suppress radical aliens turned into a war on radical citizens as well.

The story begins, at least at the level of national legislation, with Leon Czolgosz's assassination of President McKinley in 1902. Czolgosz was a U.S. citizen, but he had a foreign-sounding name and called himself an anarchist, and that was enough to spur Congress to enact an immigration law in 1903 that barred entry to "anarchists, or persons who believe in or advocate the overthrow by force or violence of the Government of the United States or of all government or of all forms of law."[5] At the same time, Congress considered but rejected bills that would have imposed similar prohibitions on the political advocacy and beliefs of U.S. citizens. As a result, as of 1903, foreign nationals could be excluded for speech and beliefs that were wholly lawful for U.S. citizens; the double standard with respect to political freedom was born.[6]

This particular double standard had deep roots in American nativists' association of subversive ideas with foreigners. As discussed above, the link between subversion and noncitizens dates back at least to the Alien and Sedition Acts of 1798. Nativist and patriotic organizations carried it forward, and politicians played to it. It affected even Supreme Court Justices; Justice Samuel Miller warned an 1888 graduating class at the University of Iowa: "[Socialists and leftists] come here and form clubs and associations; they meet at night and in secluded places; they get together large quantities of deadly weapons; they drill and prepare themselves for organized warfare; they stimulate riots and invasions of the public peace; they glory in strikes." [7] As Professor William Wiecek has written, "Since the early nineteenth century, Americans have nurtured a consistent fear that alien ideologies, as well as the foreigners who were thought to be their vectors, were invading the pristine American republic." [8]

As an immigration regulation, the 1903 law was by definition limited to foreign nationals, but its focus on subversive speech, and specifically on advocacy of "overthrow by force and violence of the Government of the United States," was to become the template for all future anti-Communist laws. Within two generations, the prohibition on advocacy of violent overthrow was the central feature of an extensive web of federal and state laws, ultimately penalizing not just speech but association, possession of literature advocating forbidden views, and even belief in disfavored doctrines. In World War I and the Cold War, the philosophy underlying the 1903 immigration law— that individuals could be punished for radical speech, beliefs, and associations without any nexus to harmful conduct—reached citizens as well.

Within a year of the 1903 Immigration Act's passage, John Turner, a British trade union leader, provided the Supreme Court's first opportunity to review a law penalizing seditious speech. Turner entered the country surreptitiously, and lectured in New York City on the trade union movement. He was arrested ten days after entering, held in solitary confinement in a six-foot-by-nine-foot cage on Ellis Island without access to any visitors other than his lawyers, and ordered expelled in a secret hearing for espousing anarchist ideas.[9] In the Supreme Court, he was represented by two of the nation's most prominent lawyers, Clarence Darrow and Edgar L. Masters. They contended that his deportation violated his First Amendment speech rights, but the Supreme Court disagreed. It stressed Congress's sovereign prerogatives over immigration, treated Turner as if he had never actually entered the United States, and concluded that "those who are excluded cannot assert the rights in general obtaining in a land to which they do not belong as citizens or otherwise."[10] Thus, the Supreme Court's first review of a First Amendment challenge to a seditious speech law arose in the immigration setting, and its outcome expressly rested on the distinction between citizens and foreign nationals. The Immigration Act passed constitutional muster, the Court reasoned, precisely because it was limited to foreign nationals who could not assert the "rights in general obtaining" to citizens.

Fear of anarchism and "aliens" continued. In 1908, the *Washington Post* called for the death penalty for all anarchists, reasoning that "an avowal of anarchy has been found to be equivalent to an intention to commit murder," and therefore "an anarchist is, in fact, a murderer, even before he has done the deed."[11] The government responded to the public fervor by announcing a campaign to deport *alien* anarchists. But the 1903 law authorized deportation only if a noncitizen had been here less than three years, and the government could not find any anarchists who fit that bill.[12] In 1917, however, as fear of foreign subversion increased with the onset of World War I, Congress expanded the immigration law to bar entry not only to persons who advocated overthrow of the government by force and violence, but also to those who advocated the unlawful destruction of property, "disbelieve[d] in or [were] opposed to organized government," or were members of organizations espousing such ideas.[13] The exclusion law now encompassed not only advocacy of violence, but philosophical anarchism, namely the view that people will coexist more peacefully and fruitfully without an organized government. And the 1917 immigration law's inclusion of mere membership as a ground for exclusion marked the first federal law to adopt the principle of guilt by association. At the same time, Congress also expanded the grounds for deportation of noncitizens already here, authorizing deportation of any foreign national who, within five years of entry, had advocated anarchism, the destruction of property, or the overthrow of the United States government.

Many of the early targets of the immigration law's anarchist provisions were members of the Industrial Workers of the World (IWW). Created in 1905, the IWW organized unskilled workers, had a largely foreign-born membership, and was sharply critical of capitalism. After several prominent IWW strikes in 1916 and 1917, federal law enforcement officials, prompted by business leaders, turned to immigration law as a tactic for attacking the IWW. As William Preston describes, prosecutors saw "deportation as the most flexible and discretionary weapon available for their attack upon radical labor agitators."[14] This was because "[p]roof of individual guilt was the greatest stumbling block in labor disturbances," and the immigration law appeared to support guilt by association.[15] In Seattle, an IWW stronghold and a focal point for many of the deportation cases, government officials "argued that an alien's support of the [IWW] automatically helped to spread its doctrines. An individual could therefore 'advocate' [illegal doctrine] simply by paying his dues or contributing to a defense fund."[16]

These local initiatives were initially overridden in Washington by a progressive Secretary of Labor, William Wilson. Wilson had little formal schooling, and had worked in the mines from the age of nine, but had risen far, first to the executive board of the United Mine Workers, and then to the Cabinet. He was personally opposed to guilt by association, and refused to treat membership in the IWW as sufficient grounds for expulsion.[17] But as historian Paul Murphy describes, "Wilson's strict criteria of individual guilt could not prevail in the face of wartime intolerance and hysteria," and in 1918, with the IWW very much in mind, Congress amended the immigration law to make aliens deportable for membership in groups advocating proscribed views, and extended the reach of deportation charges to all foreigners, no matter how long they had lived here.[18]

Until the United States entered World War I, the federal government's campaign against anarchists and other radicals focused exclusively on foreign nationals.[19] But even before we entered the war, anti-German sentiment increased pressures to extend such measures to U.S. citizens of German descent. President Woodrow Wilson himself gave voice to this sentiment in his annual address to Congress in December 1915:

> There are citizens of the United States, I blush to admit, born under other flags but welcomed under our generous naturalization laws to the full freedom and opportunity of America, who have poured the poison of disloyalty into the very arteries of our national life; who have sought to bring the authority and good name of our Government into contempt, to destroy the industries wherever they thought it effective for their vindictive purposes to strike at them, and to debase our policies to the uses of foreign intrigue.[20]

Exploiting nativist bias, Wilson notably did not target all citizens, but only those "born under other flags," just as during World War II the U.S. Army limited its internship program to citizens of Japanese descent.

With the country's entry into the war in 1917, Congress enacted the Espionage Act, which criminally prohibited speech intended to cause insubordination or disloyalty in the military, but also proscribed any advocacy of resistance to federal law.[21] At the same time, Wilson publicly branded as disloyal all those who dissented from the war effort, and warned, "Woe be to the man or group of men who seeks to stand in our way in this day of high resolution."[22] Attorney General Thomas Gregory echoed that message, stating in November 1917 that: "Our message will be delivered to the [antiwar dissenters] through the criminal courts all over the land . . . [M]ay God have mercy on them for they need expect none from an outraged people and an avenging Government."[23]

Patriotic societies added their voices. Former President Theodore

Roosevelt, then head of the nativist American Defense Society, wrote in 1917 that "either a man is a good American, and therefore is against Germany . . . or he is not an American at all."[24] One year later, William Hornady, a trustee of the American Defense Society, explicitly linked disloyalty to immigration: "we have welcomed the lame and the lazy, the ignorant, the vicious, the veneered criminal and the 'assisted' immigrant with envy in his eye, greed in his heart, and a knife inside his shirt, all coming to exploit America for their own benefit."[25] Even the president of the American Bar Association sounded the nativist alarm, arguing in 1918 that:

> Inasmuch as men have come to this country from foreign lands and, whether they have become citizens or not, are enjoying the privileges and protection afforded by residence here, they should be taught in no uncertain way that they have no right to place America and American institutions second to any other nation or proposed nation on earth, and we should start the fires under our melting pot and keep them burning, until every man, whether born in this country or out of it, has either become thoroughly and wholly American, or, if he is incapable or refuses to become American, is driven back to the country from which he came and upon which he has bestowed his first and best devotion.[26]

In May 1918, Congress passed the Sedition Act, which swept even more broadly than the Espionage Act and made it a crime to utter "any disloyal, profane, scurrilous, or abusive language . . . as regards the form of government of the United States, or the Constitution, or the flag."[27]

With these wartime laws, the punishment of political dissent crossed the line from noncitizen to citizen. During the course of the war more than 1,000 persons, many of them citizens, were convicted under the Espionage and Sedition Acts. As Harvard Law Professor Zechariah Chafee described the effect of these laws:

> It became criminal to advocate heavier taxation instead of bond issues, to state that conscription was unconstitutional though the Supreme Court had not yet held it valid, to say that the sinking of merchant vessels was legal, to urge that a referendum should have preceded declaration of war, to say that war was contrary to the teachings of Christ. Men have been punished for criticism of the Red Cross and the YMCA, while under the

Minnesota Espionage Act it has been held a crime to discourage women from knitting by the remark, "No soldier ever sees these socks." [28]

The Supreme Court reviewed only a handful of the convictions under these laws, and upheld them all, most by a unanimous vote. It upheld the prosecution of Joseph Gilbert for saying, "We are going over to Europe to make the world safe for democracy, but I tell you we had better make America safe for democracy first." [29] It found no fault with Charles Schenck's conviction for distributing a leaflet arguing that the Conscription Act violated the Thirteenth Amendment, and urging its readers merely to petition for its repeal. In an opinion by Oliver Wendell Holmes, Jr., the Court proclaimed that "[w]hen a nation is at war many things that might be said in time of peace are such a hindrance to its effort that their utterance will not be endured so long as men fight and that no Court could regard them as protected by constitutional right." [30] It unanimously affirmed Jacob Frohwerk's conviction and sentence of ten years' imprisonment for publishing an article in a Missouri-based German-language newspaper that depicted "the sufferings of a drafted man." [31] And in the only case that occasioned a dissent (from two Justices, Oliver Wendell Holmes, Jr., and Louis Brandeis), the Court, in *Abrams v. United States,* upheld the conviction of a group of Russian Jews sentenced to prison terms of three to twenty years for throwing leaflets from a New York factory window that criticized the war and called for a general strike. [32]

The punishment of political opinion generated little criticism from organizations and institutions that one might have expected to oppose such censorship. The American Association of Universities recommended dismissal of professors who made antiwar comments, the American Federation of Labor showed no concern, and the *New Republic* applauded the prosecutions of IWW members. [33] In 1917, the American Bar Association unanimously adopted a resolution eerily similar to Attorney General Ashcroft's remarks to Congress almost eighty-five years later, stating:

> We condemn all attempts in Congress and out of it to hinder and embarrass the government of the United States in carrying on the war . . . Under

whatever cover of pacifism or technicality such attempts are made, we deem them to be in spirit pro-German and in effect giving aid and comfort to the enemy.[34]

Law professors at the time generally defended the constitutionality of the wartime sedition laws, arguing that the First Amendment did not protect seditious libel against the government, or that the exigencies of war justified suppression of antiwar sentiment.[35] Professor John Wigmore, defending the result in *Abrams*, called the defendants "alien parasites," and wrote of their cause: "There was . . . nothing American in them. They were engineered by alien agents, who relied primarily on an appeal to the thousands of alien-born and alien-parented of their own races earning a livelihood in this country." [36] Professor Chafee prominently dissented from the chorus of approval, but for doing so in the pages of the *Harvard Law Review,* the university charged him as unfit to teach, and he was acquitted only by the barest of margins, six to five. It was later revealed that the Justice Department had actively helped behind the scenes to prepare the charges against Professor Chafee.[37]

Thus, World War I saw the first wholesale extension of antialien measures to citizens, both "hyphenated" naturalized citizens accused of divided loyalty, and native-born pacifists, socialists, and critics of conscription. Throughout the conflict, even as the line between native and foreign-born was repeatedly crossed, distrust of foreigners fueled the fire. As Professor Thomas Lawrence sums up the period:

The World War I war hysteria . . . was fed by nativist impulses in Americans which resulted from the immigrant's rising political power and a basic distrust of that which was foreign and dissimilar. Immigrants seemed especially susceptible to ideas which powerful and influential groups condemned at every opportunity. . . . The War afforded an opportunity to Americanize these alien elements. . . . An essential part of this process was the suppression of alien propaganda and the destruction of alien ideologies.[38]

At one level, it is ironic that nativist fears prompted the government to breach the line between citizens and foreign nationals; after all, nativism is predicated on the importance of policing that very line. But as the foremost scholar of nativism, John Higham, has shown, nativists fear noncitizens not simply because they are foreign, but because nativists associate foreigners with other religions, different races, and radical ideas.[39] These fears of religious, racial, and political difference, respectively, provide the pathways by which antialien sentiment is directed toward citizens who share the faiths, colors, and ideas viewed as "alien." In World War I, Congress and the executive branch moved swiftly from laws selectively targeting the seditious speech of foreign nationals to laws that penalized anyone who questioned the war effort. Much of the impetus underlying that transition was antialien, but as the war progressed, it became virtually impossible to untangle antialien from antidissident sentiment. To criticize the war was to be "un-American," when what was needed was "100 percent Americanism."[40] The culture and the law thus treated dissident citizens as themselves "alien," providing the rationale for bridging the citizen-noncitizen divide.

9. "THE COURSE OF LEAST RESISTANCE": J. EDGAR HOOVER'S FIRST JOB AND THE PALMER RAIDS OF 1919–20

First jobs can be habit-forming. In July 1917, a young J. Edgar Hoover, fresh out of the night program at George Washington Law School, landed his first legal job in the Justice Department. The nation had just entered World War I, and Hoover's initial assignment was to work with the department's Alien Enemy Bureau, administering the identification, regulation, and internment of "enemy aliens."[1] After the war, he headed up the Justice Department's Alien Radical division, where he maintained lists of subversive foreigners and masterminded the first nationwide roundup of radicals, the "Palmer Raids" of 1919–20. Thus, Hoover, who went on to lead the Federal Bureau of Investigation for nearly fifty years, from 1924 until his death in 1972, began his legendary career employing expansive powers to target, regulate, and imprison "dangerous" foreign nationals without criminal charges, using loose administrative procedures that dispensed with the protections associated with the criminal process.

As Hoover went on to play a central role in the Cold War and the surveillance of civil rights, antiwar, and other progressive political groups in the 1960s and early 1970s, the marks of his first assignment remained with him. He advocated for years for a peacetime sedition law, maintained extensive lists of "subversives" for potential detention during a national emergency, personally prosecuted some of the most high-profile anti-Communist cases, and, when the Supreme Court effectively put an end to criminal prosecutions of Communists, launched COINTELPRO, a secret infiltration, surveillance, and disinformation program that began with the Communist Party and ultimately targeted even Dr. Martin Luther King Jr. In each of these campaigns, Hoover applied what he learned during his first years at the Alien Enemy Bureau and the Alien Radical Division. One might even say that he spent his entire career seeking to exercise over "dangerous" *citizens* the power that he wielded in his first days on the job over enemy aliens. To Hoover, the line between citizen and noncitizen was little more than an inconvenience, and he consistently sought to exploit connections between radical foreigners and radical citizens in order to extend the tentacles of FBI control and intelligence over both. The relative ease with which the nation bridged that divide over the course of Hoover's career—all the while lauding Hoover as a national hero—illustrates the illusory nature of promises that security measures will be restricted to noncitizens. Hoover "succeeded" only because he had widespread institutional and public support, support that only began to dissipate at the very end of his career, when tactics initially limited to a handful of noncitizens had been extended to millions of Americans.

When World War I ended, the Enemy Alien Act, the Sedition Act, and the Espionage Act—all wartime authorities—could no longer be invoked to target the disloyal. But the country's nativist fears did not abate. They were simply redirected from Germany to Communism, which in 1919 appeared to be on the verge of conquering much of Europe. Revolutions had broken out in Hungary, Austria, Bulgaria, and Germany; workers had seized factories in Italy; and radical Communist movements were taking hold in France and Britain. At the same time, a massive wave of domestic labor strikes broke out in the United States; in 1919 alone, the nation saw 3,600 strikes involving 4 million workers.[2] Hoover was moved to claim that "[c]ivilization faces its most terrible menace of danger since the barbarian hordes overran Western Europe and opened the Dark Ages."[3]

In April 1919, the threat became violent. On April 28, an undetonated mail bomb was discovered in the office of Seattle Mayor Ole Hanson, who had played a prominent role in violently suppressing a major strike earlier that year. The next day a similar package arrived at the home of a former senator from Georgia, Thomas Hardwick. His maid opened the package, and lost both of her hands in the explosion. One day later, a vigilant postal employee in New York City discovered sixteen similar packages, and after a national alert was sent out, eighteen more were discovered in other post offices. The packages were addressed to a wide array of public figures, including Supreme Court Justice Oliver Wendell Holmes Jr.; Attorney General A. Mitchell Palmer; Commissioner of Immigration Frederic Howe; Senator Lee Overman, chair of the Senate Bolshevik Investigation Committee; Postmaster General Albert Burleson, who had administered the war censorship of the U.S. mails; and business leaders John D. Rockefeller and J. P. Morgan.[4] Everyone agreed that action had to be taken or, as one newspaper said, "we may as well invite Lenin and Trotsky to come here and set up business at once."[5] As the country was reading about the mail bomb plot on May 1, riots broke out during May Day celebrations in Cleveland, Boston, and New York. One month later, on June 2, bombs exploded in eight different cities within the same hour; two people were killed. Among the targets was Attorney General Palmer's home in Washington, D.C. The bomber of Palmer's home was killed in the explosion, and fragments of the bomber's clothing and body indicated that he was an Italian alien from Philadelphia. In the rubble police discovered a pamphlet from "The Anarchist Fighters" warning that "There will have to be bloodshed . . . there will have to be murder."[6]

Despite a nationwide hunt for the perpetrators, the bombers were never discovered. Instead, the Justice Department, under Hoover's direction, launched a series of dragnet raids directed at deporting radical foreign nationals.[7] The reason for targeting noncitizens was not that they were the prime suspects, but that the law made it easier to round them up. As Hoover's biographer Richard Powers put it, "No law then in effect permitted the Justice Department to attack radical citizens for their beliefs and associations. . . . However, it was possible to attack aliens for their beliefs and associations."[8] Attorney General Palmer himself wrote in his 1920 annual report that federal laws were "inadequate to properly handle the ultra-radical situation by criminal prosecution," and therefore the Justice Department "became centered upon the activities of alien agitators, with the object of securing [their] deportation."[9] Louis Post, acting Secretary of Labor, put the point more poetically, explaining that "the force of the delirium turned in the direction of a deportation crusade with the spontaneity of water flowing along the course of least resistance."[10]

The first of the "Palmer Raids" was conducted in eighteen cities on November 7, 1919, and directed at suspected members of the Union of Russian Workers, a social organization of Russian immigrants. Over 1,100 individuals were arrested, most without warrants.[11] Less than two months later, on December 21, 1919, 249 individuals were deported to Russia on the *Buford*, dubbed the "Soviet ark" by the press. Fifty-one were deported as "anarchists," and 184 as members of the Union of Russian Workers, which the government found had advocated the overthrow of government by force because its founding charter committed it to "a Socialistic revolution by force."[12] But as Assistant Secretary of Labor Louis Post wrote a few years later, "[o]f an enormous proportion . . . it is a reasonable probability that they were totally ignorant of the objectionable clauses in the organic law of the organization."[13]

One of those deported on the *Buford* was Joseph Polulech, a twenty-seven-year-old Russian who had been living in the United States since 1912. Polulech was arrested without a warrant as he was taking a math class at the People's House in New York City, the Union of Russian Workers headquarters. He was held incommunicado for six weeks. At his hearing, he denied membership in any organization other than his church. His pastor testified that he was an ambitious and well-behaved member of his congregation. The only evidence against him was a page from the Union of Russian Workers membership book. But that was sufficient in the eyes of the immigration law.[14]

The public and the press hailed Attorney General Palmer for the deportations. In a typical reaction, the New York *Evening Mail* wrote that "Just as the sailing of the Ark that Noah built was a pledge for the preservation of the human race, so the sailing of the Ark of the Soviet is a pledge for the preservation of America."[15] The Farmers National Congress went still further, recommending, in keeping with their own agrarian practices, that the Justice Department "burn a brand in the hide of those fellows when you deport them so that if they ever dare return the trademark will tell its tale and expose them." [16] On December 3, the *New York Times* endorsed the peacetime sedition law that Hoover and Palmer wanted.[17] Buoyed by this support, Palmer and Hoover began to prepare for the next set of raids, this time directed at the Communist Party and the Communist Labor Party.

The Communist raids were planned for January 2, 1920. But first, Hoover convinced the Secretary of Labor to change the ground rules regarding detained aliens' right to consult lawyers. Progressive union lawyers had produced a pamphlet entitled *Our Constitutional Rights, Notice to Aliens,* advising detainees to remain silent and to consult a lawyer before answering questions. Hoover's response was to amend immigration regulations to delay the right to a lawyer until the case had "proceeded sufficiently in the development of the facts to protect the Government's interests." [18] The amendment took effect on December 31, 1919, one business day before the raids began. Hoover also urged immigration authorities to set high bail amounts in order to make release impossible; if aliens were set free, he argued, the rule change designed to permit interrogations without counsel would be "virtually of no value." [19] A contemporaneous review of a random sample of 200 cases found, not surprisingly given the rule change, that "in no case was the alien informed at the preliminary examination that he was entitled to be represented by counsel at the trial [and] [i]n some cases this information was not given until the hearing was nearly over." [20]

Federal agents obtained arrest warrants for nearly 3,000 noncitizens in preparation for the January raids, but in the end, most people were arrested without warrants in dragnet raids at meeting halls, schools, and other places where foreigners were thought to gather. Two-thirds of the warrants were never executed at all, yet officials arrested between 4,000 and 10,000 persons. As one historian described them, the raids involved

[i]ndiscriminate arrests of the innocent with the guilty, unlawful searches and seizures by federal detectives, intimidating preliminary interrogations of aliens held incommunicado, high-handed levying of excessive bail, and denial of counsel. . . . The Department of Justice concerned itself with the preservation of its informers rather than with the protection of the rights of alien defendants. Sworn and extorted confession became the substitute for due process.[21]

Many of those arrested were members of the Communist Party only by virtue of a 1919 split in the Socialist Party, in which one faction had become the Communist Party, and automatically transferred all its members, with or without their consent, to the new party. Elia Matushko, for example, a twenty-five-year-old Russian who worked in a cafeteria in Chicago, admitted membership in the Communist Party and explained

I joined the Socialist Party. My desire was to get an education and there was a school at this branch of the Socialist Party and I joined it. When I started to attend this school they told me I joined the Socialist Party and then the Socialist Party was transformed into the Communist Party. I didn't know the particulars or the reason this thing was done, but I find out later on we are members of the Communist Party. I didn't hear the principles of this organization up to this morning. It is the first time I heard about the program. Part of it I heard, but not all of it. The important part I did not hear until this morning.

Matushko was ordered deported.[22]

Others were deported on pretextual charges, filed when the government realized that it might not be able to sustain deportation on Communist Party grounds. At the time of his arrest on November 8, 1919, Andrew Chuprina, a thirty-six-year-old Russian who had been in the United States for three years, was living in Detroit with his wife and three children. He worked for the Western Electric Company, had registered for the draft, and had purchased Liberty Bonds to support the war. The only evidence against Chuprina was that his surname appeared in the membership book of the Detroit chapter of the Union of Russian Workers. But he adamantly denied membership, showed that the book simply listed "Chuprina" without a first name or any other identifying information, and proved that there were many Chuprinas living in the Detroit area at the time.

In response, the government simply filed a new charge, claiming that he should be expelled on the ground that "at the time of entry he was liable to become a public charge." He had not in fact become a public charge, but in a remarkable feat of retroactive punishment for potential future conduct that never actually came to pass, he was ordered deported for having been "liable to become" a public charge when he had entered three years earlier. The judge set bond at $10,000, which Chuprina could not meet, and he remained in detention. In September 1920, with his case still pending, Chuprina, presumably fed up with the process, left the country.[23]

The nativist sentiment that fueled the Palmer Raids was evident in Attorney General Palmer's public statements. In testimony drafted by Hoover, Palmer charged that "[o]ut of the sly and crafty eyes of many of them leap cupidity, cruelty, insanity, and crime; from their lopsided faces, sloping brows, and misshapen features may be recognized the unmistakable criminal type."[24] When criticized later for the raids' excesses, Palmer explained that when you are "trying to protect the community against moral rats you sometimes get to thinking more of your trap's effectiveness than of its lawful construction."[25] The press was generally supportive of the raids and at least initially dismissed concerns about civil liberties.[26] Two days after the raids took place, the *Washington Post* proclaimed simply that "[t]here is no time to waste on hairsplitting over infringement of liberty."[27]

In the end, the mass arrests produced hundreds rather than thousands of deportations, largely because of the courageous intervention of one man. Louis Post, as Acting Secretary of Labor, was responsible for reviewing the thousands of deportation orders issued by Immigrant Inspectors during the Palmer Raids. A seventy-one-year-old liberal who had previously edited a liberal weekly, and had entertained anarchist Emma Goldman in his home, Post sharply disagreed with Hoover's expansive view of the deportation laws.[28] Working feverishly with a single assistant, he reviewed as many as one hundred cases a day. In a single month, from April to May 1920, Post personally reviewed 1,600 cases. He reversed the deportation orders in 1,140 of them, while sustaining deportation in 460. All told, from July 1919 to June 1920, 2,200 deportation warrants were cancelled, and 556 foreign nationals were ultimately deported.[29]

Where Hoover had sought to exploit the immigration process to deny detainees basic rights like the assistance of counsel, Post did the opposite, extending the rights of the criminal process to the immigration setting. He reversed deportation orders for those who had been automatically transferred into the Communist Party without knowledge, disregarded all statements obtained in custody without warnings and without the ability to be represented by counsel, and refused to rely on evidence that had been illegally seized.[30] He also refused to deport individuals who joined the party without knowledge of its illegal aims. Even so, Post complained that the laws forced him "to order deportations of many aliens whom not even a lynching mob with the least remnant of righteous spirit would have deported from a frontier town.[31] Of the 556 ultimately deported, he noted, "In no instance was it shown that the offending aliens had been connected in any way with bomb-throwing or bomb-placing or bomb-making. No explosives were found, nor any firearms except four pistols personally owned and some guns in the 'property room' of an amateur theatrical group."[32]

Post's cancellation of most of the deportation warrants incurred the wrath of Palmer, Hoover, and many members of Congress. He was brought up on impeachment charges, and forced to defend himself before the Rules Committee of the House. Criticized for applying principles drawn from the criminal process to administrative immigration hearings, Post replied:

> we should not apply to cases involving human rights the rules exclusively that would apply to property questions under administrative process. Administrative process is a very dangerous institution for a country like ours to adopt with reference to personal liberty, and it is pretty near time that some check was put upon its development so far as it affects rights to personal liberty.[33]

Post described many cases in detail, and defended his decisions so adroitly that by the end of the proceeding, one of his most prominent critics on the committee, Congressman Edward Pou, publicly exonerated Post, and then dramatically walked out of the hearing. For all practical purposes, that was the end of the impeachment inquiry. Post had prevailed over his accusers.[34]

Others also stood up to the antialien tide. One was a federal judge, George Anderson, who presided over a fifteen-day trial reviewing deportation orders against twenty foreigners arrested in the Palmer Raids in New England. In June 1920, Judge Anderson issued a stinging rebuke of the government's tactics. He recounted in detail the abusive searches, raids, and interrogations that accompanied the raids, and cited verbatim Justice Department instructions urging law enforcement officials to search without warrants wherever possible, and to hold individuals incommunicado "until after examination by this office and until permission is given by this office."[35] After describing the manner in which the government carried out the raids, Judge Anderson concluded, "A mob is a mob, whether made up of government officials acting under instructions from the Department of Justice, or of criminals, loafers, and the vicious classes."[36] He ruled that most of the detentions and deportation orders were invalid because the hearings failed to guarantee minimal requisites of fairness, and that those who were tried fairly nonetheless could not be deported because the Communist Party did not in fact advocate the overthrow of the United States by force and violence. On the latter point, he was reversed on appeal two years later.[37] But despite the reversal, the fact that a federal judge had accused the government of acting like "a mob," a determination *not* upset on appeal, proved to be a powerful indictment of the Palmer Raids.

Judge Anderson's decision was issued the same month as a highly critical report on the raids by some of the nation's most prestigious lawyers and law professors. The report was signed by, among others, Roscoe Pound, Harvard Law School's dean; Felix Frankfurter, then a Harvard professor and later a Supreme Court justice; Zechariah

Chafee Jr., also a Harvard professor, as well as the leading First Amendment scholar of his day; Francis Fisher Kane, the former United States Attorney in Philadelphia, who had resigned in protest over the Palmer Raids; and political scientist Ernst Freund of the University of Chicago. They accused the government of conducting unconstitutional arrests, searches and seizures; using *agents provocateurs;* imposing "third-degree" torture to extract confessions; and abusing the office of the Attorney General.[38]

These criticisms incurred the wrath of the Justice Department, which responded by launching investigations of its critics and thereby extending its tactics across the noncitizen-citizen divide. The government investigated all of the prominent critics of the Palmer Raids, including the twelve lawyers who signed the report, Judge Anderson, an organization that had sponsored a study of the raids, its critics in Congress, and of course, Louis Post himself, on whom it developed a 350-page file.[39] Palmer publicly accused Post of having "habitually tender solicitude for social revolutionists and perverted sympathy for the criminal anarchists of the country."[40] When it was revealed, however, that the Justice Department was spying on its critics in Congress and looking for pretextual criminal charges to prosecute against them, Attorney General Harry Daughtery was forced to resign in 1924. He was replaced by Harlan Fiske Stone, a former dean of Columbia Law School with a strong reputation for respecting civil liberties, who promptly forbade political spying.[41]

As the first nationally coordinated campaign against radicals, the Palmer Raids had special significance, not only for the young Hoover in his first job, but for the nation. Although the raids were criticized by a minority at the time and are now widely seen as an unpardonable abuse of federal law enforcement authority, they have nonetheless served as a kind of blueprint for subsequent antiradical campaigns, in four respects.

First, the law enforcement theory underlying the Palmer Raids, like that underlying the Japanese internment and Attorney General Ashcroft's post–September 11 detentions, was "preventive." Rather

than identify those individuals who actually played a role in the terrorist bombings that sparked the raids, the Justice Department took a
broad-brush approach and sought to neutralize all persons who it
thought might pose a potential *future* threat. This preventive approach, unmoored from concepts of individual culpability, would
prove to be a recurring feature of law enforcement in times of crisis.

Second, the Palmer Raids were directed at radical "aliens" not because government officials thought the only (or the most dangerous)
radicals were foreign nationals, but because the laws allowed them to
target foreign nationals in ways that U.S. citizens could not then be
targeted. Hoover and Palmer repeatedly pressed for a peacetime sedition law that would allow them to go after radical citizens in like measure, and President Wilson endorsed such a law in his State of the
Union address in 1919, linking the need for such a law to the "transfu-
sion of radical theories from seething European centers." [42] But while
many such laws were introduced—in the winter of 1919–20 alone,
members of Congress introduced seventy peacetime sedition laws—
none passed. Outside of wartime, Congress remained unwilling to
treat its own citizens the way that it had treated noncitizens. As Albert
Johnson, chairman of the House of Representatives' Immigration
Committee, argued, "Free press is ours, not theirs; free speech is ours,
not theirs, and they have gone just as far as we can let them go toward
running over our most precious rights." [43] The rationale for this explicit double standard was that aliens "are merely guests, with no right
to propagate opinions." [44] Thus, the first nationally coordinated campaign against radicals was possible because, and only because, the targets were foreign nationals. But as Louis Post presciently warned, "a
nation devoted to liberty of opinion and freedom of speech cannot
deny either right to resident aliens without launching a tendency to
deny both rights to citizens also." [45]

Third, by going after immigrants through administrative processes, the government could deny its targets the rights associated
with the criminal process. Citizens could not be detained without a
criminal trial, which required, among other things, a public trial, the

right to be represented by a lawyer, the privilege against compelled self-incrimination, the presumption of innocence until proven guilty beyond a reasonable doubt, and the right to confront any evidence used against one. Administrative immigration proceedings, by contrast, afforded none of these rights, and therefore made it far easier to round up and "convict" large numbers of individuals on little or no evidence of crime. One of the central charges in the impeachment inquiry against Louis Post was precisely that he had dared to extend to noncitizens in the immigration process the rights and protections generally associated with the criminal process.

Finally, the substantive theory underlying the Palmer Raids was guilt by association, and marked the first nationwide employment of this theory of liability. Not one of the 4,000 to 10,000 persons rounded up in the wake of the terrorist bombings of 1919 was charged with complicity in those crimes. Instead, they were arrested for being members (or suspected members) of Communist organizations, which in turn were proscribed not for their conduct, but for the ideas they advocated. To Hoover, Palmer, and arguably to Congress as well, mere membership in a group advocating the propriety of forceful overthrow of government was sufficient to warrant detention and expulsion, without regard to whether a particular individual had ever actually engaged in or supported any criminal or violent activity.

These four features of the Palmer Raids serve as leitmotifs in the history of political repression in modern America. Each tactic was justified initially by pointing to an asserted distinction between noncitizens' and citizens' rights, but each inevitably spread to citizens as well. As Hoover's own history so dramatically reveals, having once employed such expansive authorities, law enforcement officials are reluctant to give them up, and almost invariably seek their expansion.

Perhaps the most unusual feature of the Palmer Raids was that, in an important sense, they backfired. Public opinion, at first supportive of the initiative, ultimately turned on Attorney General Palmer, whose presidential aspirations were for all practical purposes dashed by his perceived responsibility for the excesses of the raids that have taken

10. THE SECOND RED SCARE: TARGETING RADICAL CITIZENS

The Red Scare of 1919–20 was but a brief prologue to the much more extensive Cold War of the 1940s, 1950s, and 1960s. As legal historian Arthur Sabin has written, because the first Red Scare targeted "alien radicals," it "was essentially nothing more personal for almost all Americans than an elongated, dramatic newspaper story."[1] During the Cold War, however, J. Edgar Hoover succeeded in applying similar measures to citizens. As a result, the second Red Scare "touched millions personally through required loyalty oaths," not to mention legislative investigations, FBI surveillance, and federal employee loyalty hearings.[2] During the Cold War, some 300 federal, state, and local laws were enacted against Communist "subversives," and the House Committee on Un-American Activities (HUAC) compiled an index of one million suspects.[3] Guilt by association, previously restricted to foreigners, now reached the citizenry, as criminal statutes, loyalty oaths, blacklists, registration requirements, and congressional inquiries sought to identify and penalize those who were sympathetic to or associated with the Communist Party, irrespective of their personal involvement in any illegal conduct. For their associations and beliefs, suspected Communists and sympathizers were prosecuted, deported, and denied university teaching positions, government jobs, admission to the bar, passports for travel abroad, security clearances for work in defense facilities, and employment in Hollywood and elsewhere in the private sector.

Repeating and extending the tactics of the first Red Scare, the federal government again adopted a sweeping preventive strategy and again relied on administrative mechanisms to bypass the rights associated with the criminal process. As historian Regin Schmidt concluded, "It is remarkable . . . the extent to which the FBI's structural role and methods during the 1940s and 1950s were repetitions, although on a greater scale, of the Bureau's activities during the [first] Red Scare."[4]

The courts and the country initially went along with the government's crossing of the line between foreign nationals and citizens; the threat was thought to emanate from abroad, but to have permeated certain segments of the citizenry. Only later, after many thousands of Americans had been harmed, did the Supreme Court and the country recognize the constitutional infirmities in treating people as culpable for their associations and short-circuiting processes designed to protect the innocent.

THE LAWS

The first Red Scare largely ended with the Palmer Raids. But with the rise of the Communist Party during the Depression, the sharp increase in antialien sentiment associated with World War II, and Stalin's alliance with Hitler in August 1939, anti-Communist fervor again reached fever pitch in the late 1930s. In 1938, HUAC was founded, with a mandate to investigate "un-American propaganda activities," "the diffusion of subversive and un-American propaganda," and "all other questions in relation thereto."[5]

In 1939, Congress barred federal employment to any member of an organization "which advocates the overthrow of our constitutional form of government in the United States."[6] The Civil Service Commission interpreted this provision to encompass any "member of the Communist party, the German Bund, or any other Communist, Nazi, or Fascist organization."[7] Subsequent legislation extended that bar to all government contracts and grants.[8] These laws essentially cut and pasted the language of immigration law and applied it to federal employees and contractors, whether citizen or foreign national.

Fear of foreigners and foreign ideas was the driving force behind the Cold War. By the middle of 1939, Congress had over 100 antiimmigrant proposals under consideration. As one congressman reported, "the mood of this House is such that if you brought in the Ten

Commandments today and asked for their repeal and attached to that request an alien law, you could get it."[9] The most significant bill was H.R. 5138, which eventually became the Alien Registration Act of 1940, more commonly known as the Smith Act, for its sponsor, Representative Howard W. Smith.[10] The Smith Act, in many ways the centerpiece of federal anti-Communist legislation, was given an antialien title, and featured several immigration provisions, among them a requirement that all aliens register and be fingerprinted.[11] But the Alien Registration Act was by no means limited to noncitizens. It made it a federal crime for anyone to advocate the overthrow of the government by force and violence, to organize a group to so advocate, or to belong to such a group with knowledge of its ends. It also authorized seizure of any printed matter advocating forceful overthrow of the government. With this statute, the language of the 1903 immigration law was given the force of criminal law, and extended to all U.S. citizens. For the first time since the short-lived Sedition Act of 1798, Congress had enacted a criminal law explicitly proscribing subversive speech outside the context of a declared war.

In 1947, Congress passed the Taft-Hartley Act, which required union officials to swear that they were not members of any organization advocating the overthrow of the U.S. government by force and violence, by then the legal catch-phrase for the Communist Party. The same year, President Truman launched the Federal Employee Loyalty program, mandating a review of all federal employees' loyalty, or more accurately, disloyalty, principally interpreted to mean membership in, affiliation with, or even "sympathetic association with," the Communist Party.[12]

In the Internal Security Act of 1950 and the McCarran-Walter Act of 1952, Congress adopted the most extensive ideological deportation and exclusion provisions yet, consolidating and expanding the law's prior grounds, and for the first time mentioning the Communist Party by name.[13] In addition, Congress expressly authorized the government to bar entry to foreign nationals on the basis of secret evidence that neither the foreign national nor his lawyer was permitted to see or confront.[14] Other provisions of the Internal Security Act required all "Communist-action organizations" to register with the attorney general and to disclose their membership lists and contributions; imposed penalties on registered organizations and their members, including deportation of aliens and denials of passports and federal employment to U.S. citizens; and authorized emergency preventive detention.[15]

These laws, which formed the legal underpinning for the Cold War, were strikingly similar to those of the first Red Scare in all but one respect: the second time around the government's targets included citizens.

"THE SLATE IS NOT CLEAN": IMMIGRATION CONTROL

Despite the Cold War's crossing of the citizen-noncitizen divide, antialien measures continued to provide the driving wedge in the government's efforts to counter the threat of Communism. No case illustrates the persistence of anti-alien sentiment better than that of Harry Bridges, a colorful Australian labor organizer hounded for more than twenty years for his suspected ties to the Communist Party. Bridges came to the United States as a young man in 1920, found work as a longshoreman in San Francisco, and played a leading role in a general strike there in 1934. His role in the strike prompted an unusual alliance of business leaders, conservative unions, and nativist organizations to call for his deportation. The Immigration Service investigated claims that Bridges was a member of the Communist Party in 1934, but concluded that they were unfounded.[16] The pressure for his deportation did not relent, however, and in 1938, the government charged Bridges with membership in the Communist Party. When the secretary of labor put Bridges's case on hold for the perfectly good reason that the Supreme Court was deciding another case directly on point, J. Parnell Thomas, the ranking Republican on HUAC, introduced a resolution to impeach the secretary and two other officials for "conspiracy to 'defer and defeat' Bridges' deportation."[17]

In April 1939, the Supreme Court ruled that the immigration law required proof of current membership in the Communist Party to authorize deportation,[18] and Bridges's case went forward. Given its controversial nature, the secretary of labor appointed a special judge with impeccable credentials to hear the case: James Landis, former head of the Securities and Exchange Commission and then dean of Harvard Law School. Landis presided over an eleven-week deportation hearing, and in December 1939 ruled for Bridges, finding that the government's witnesses lacked credibility and that there was no evidence of Bridges's membership in the Communist Party.[19]

But Landis's credentials and findings were no match for the forces seeking Bridges's deportation. There is no double jeopardy bar against multiple immigration proceedings on the same ground, so the issue remained open. Congressman A. Leonard Allen accordingly introduced a remarkable bill specifically directing the secretary of labor "to take into custody and deport to Australia . . . the alien, Harry Renton Bridges."[20] The bill passed the House by a vote of 330 to 42.[21] Attorney General Robert Jackson strongly opposed the bill, arguing that

> It would be the first time that an act of Congress has singled out a named individual for deportation. It would be the first deportation in which the alien was not even accused either of unlawful entry or of unlawful conduct while here. It would be the first time that Congress, without changing the general law, simply suspended all laws which protect a named individual and directed the Attorney General to disregard them and forthwith to deport "notwithstanding any other provision of law." And it would be the first time since the Alien and Sedition Laws . . . that any law would provide for a deportation without a hearing or without, indeed, the slightest pretense toward giving the accused what our Nation has long known as "due process of law."[22]

Congress was apparently sufficiently convinced to scuttle this particular Harry Bridges law, but not to leave Bridges alone. Instead, it added a provision to the 1940 Smith Act authorizing retroactive deportation for past (legal) membership in the Communist Party, thereby overruling the Supreme Court's 1939 decision to the contrary.[23] As one of its authors, Congressman Sam Hobbs, proudly proclaimed: "this bill will do, in a perfectly legal and constitutional man-ner, what the bill specifically aimed at the deportation of Harry Bridges seeks to accomplish . . . the Department of Justice should now have little trouble in deporting Harry Bridges and all others of similar ilk." [24] With enactment of the Smith Act, another voice joined the choir urging Bridges's deportation—J. Edgar Hoover. Hoover saw the Bridges case as an opportunity to establish that the Communist Party illegally advocated overthrow of the government, as defined by the Smith Act, and thereby to "lay the basis for the contemplated war on domestic Communism." [25] He lobbied a resistant Attorney General Jackson to reopen Bridges's deportation hearings under the new law. [26] In February 1941 Jackson relented and reinstituted deportation pro-ceedings against Bridges.

This time, Bridges was found deportable. Immigration Judge Charles Sears relied on the statements of two individuals: James O'Neil, who had reportedly told the FBI before the hearing that he had seen Bridges posting dues stamps in a Communist Party mem-bership book, but recanted those statements at trial; and Harry Lundeberg, one of Bridges's bitterest enemies, who testified at trial that Bridges had told him over dinner one night that he was a Com-munist, but had told FBI agents three times before trial that he had no personal knowledge that Bridges was a Communist. Thus, both men told conflicting stories at different times. Judge Sears nonetheless credited their statements identifying Bridges as a Communist and ordered him deported.

In 1945, the Supreme Court reversed the deportation order. By a vote of five to three, the Court ruled that the statutory provision ban-ning "affiliation" required a showing of conduct related to the party's illegal purposes, and that the government had failed to establish that. The Court further ruled that the government's only evidence of direct membership consisted of two affidavits that had been admitted in vi-olation of the immigration service's own rules, effectively denying Bridges an opportunity to confront his accusers. [27] While the decision rested on the interpretation of immigration regulations and statutes, it was plainly driven by constitutional concerns of due process and the First Amendment right of association.[28] Justice Frank Murphy, concurring in the opinion of the Court, made this explicit, stating that neither the First nor the Fifth Amendments "acknowledges any distinction between citizens and resident aliens,"[29] and concluding that "the record in this case will stand forever as a monument to man's intolerance of man."[30]

Even victory in the Supreme Court did not end Bridges's troubles. He immediately applied for and obtained naturalization, but that only prompted a criminal case against him for allegedly lying about his membership in the Communist Party in applying for citizenship. After an eighty-one-day trial, Bridges was convicted, denaturalized, and sentenced to five years in jail. On appeal, the Supreme Court again reversed, this time on the technical ground that Bridges's prosecution was barred by the statute of limitations.[31] Still, the government persisted, filing a civil denaturalization case against him in 1955. When the trial court found the government's evidence not credible, the government finally abandoned its twenty-year effort to deport him. Bridges lived out the rest of his life as a U.S. citizen.

As one commentator wrote at the time, Bridges's case was "a reflection of traditional American antipathy for foreign-born radicals. This is compared to relative tolerance of the native-born variety."[32] Had Bridges been a citizen, he might conceivably have been prosecuted under the Smith Act. But because double jeopardy applies to criminal cases, he could have been tried only once. And in a criminal proceeding, the Ex Post Facto Clause would have barred punishing him retroactively for having been a member of the Communist Party at a time when membership was legal. Bridges's vulnerability was due entirely to his status as a noncitizen. Just as in the Palmer Raids, Hoover hoped that by targeting Bridges, a foreigner, the government could establish beachheads to be used against citizens down the road. Ironically, the tactic failed in Bridges's case largely because the Supreme Court insisted on affording Bridges the same basic constitutional rights enjoyed by citizens, just as the Palmer Raids failed in part because Louis Post insisted on extending the same rights to Palmer's detainees that citizens would have been afforded.

For all the harassment he suffered, Bridges ultimately prevailed. Others were not so fortunate. In two cases in 1952, the Court ruled that Communist foreign nationals could be detained without bail and deported, without any evidence that they had engaged in or furthered any illegal activity.[33] Two years later, in *Galvan v. Press,* the Court ruled that Congress could deport permanent resident aliens for having been members of the Communist Party at a time when membership was legal.[34] Juan Galvan had lived lawfully in the United States since 1918, and had joined the Communist Party in 1944 (while the Soviet Union was our ally during World War II). He quit the party two years later. In 1950, Congress made it a deportable offense to have ever been a member of the Communist Party, imposing the deportation sanction retroactively. Galvan argued that the law imposed punishment after the fact in violation of the Due Process Clause. The Court acknowledged that "much could be said for the view, were we writing on a clean slate, that the Due Process Clause" forbids deportation for conduct legal at the time it was engaged in. "But the slate is not clean," the Court continued, pointing to a "whole volume" of precedent deferring to Congress's decisions about the criteria for admission and expulsion of foreigners.[35]

Probably the most troubling of the Cold War immigration developments, however, was the use of undisclosed secret evidence to exclude, detain, and expel noncitizens. From December 1948 to July 1952 alone, approximately 2,000 foreigners were temporarily excluded from the United States based on secret evidence that they never had a chance to confront or rebut, and roughly 500 were permanently excluded.[36] This was a new development in immigration procedure. From at least 1893 until 1941, all noncitizens were entitled to an exclusion hearing in which they could confront the evidence used against them. On November 14, 1941, however, President Roosevelt issued an emergency war proclamation providing for exclusion of aliens whose entry would be "prejudicial to the United States," and regulations promulgated pursuant to that order provided that the exclusion could take place without a hearing, "on the basis of information of a confidential nature, the disclosure of which would be prejudicial to the public interest." [37] The procedure was invoked only rarely during World War II, but the Cold War saw a dramatic expansion of its use. [38] In 1950, Congress codified the practice in the Internal Security Act, for the first time providing express statutory authority for excluding noncitizens based on undisclosed, confidential information. [39]

The Supreme Court's first opportunity to address the issue arose in the case of Ellen Knauff. A German citizen, Knauff fled to England when Hitler came to power and served in both the British Royal Air Force and the U.S. Army during World War II. While working for the army, she fell in love with and married an enlisted American. When the war ended, Knauff came to the United States to join her husband under the War Brides Act, passed precisely to facilitate such unions.

At Ellis Island, however, Knauff was greeted with the charge that her presence would "be prejudicial to the interests of the United States," and was told that she could not see the evidence supporting that charge. The Supreme Court upheld the government's actions, reasoning that because Knauff was an unadmitted alien who had no "right" to enter the United States, she had no due process rights in connection with her entry. [40] The Court could not have put it more bluntly: "Whatever the process authorized by Congress is, it is due process as far as an alien denied entry is concerned." [41] In dissent, Justice Robert Jackson was equally blunt, writing that "Security is like liberty in that many are the crimes committed in its name. . . . The plea that evidence of guilt must be secret is abhorrent to free men, because it provides a cloak for the malevolent, the misinformed, the meddlesome, and the corrupt to play the role of informer undetected and uncorrected." [42]

Perhaps because Knauff was a war bride, the American people appeared to side with Justice Jackson. The Supreme Court decision was strongly criticized. Congress considered a private bill to block Knauff's deportation, and brought her to Washington to testify at a committee hearing. Shortly thereafter, the House voted unanimously to bar her deportation. The political pressure ultimately forced the INS to grant Knauff a new hearing, even if the Constitution did not. At the hearing, three witnesses testified that they had heard, second- and third-hand, that Knauff was a spy. But they offered no direct evidence whatsoever. Knauff speculated that the rumors had been sparked by a jilted former lover of her husband's.[43] The attorney general ultimately decided that the evidence was not substantial, and Knauff was admitted. She had spent more than two and half years barred from entry, much of it detained on Ellis Island, on the basis of evidence she could not see.

Two years later, the Court applied the same reasoning to uphold the exclusion and long-term detention on secret evidence of Ignatz Mezei. Mezei was alleged to be associated with Communists, to have lied to a consular officer, and to have stolen some bags of flour.[44] Unlike Knauff, Mezei had actually lived in the United States for twenty-five years before his departure and attempted return, although it was unclear whether he was ever lawfully here.[45] The Supreme Court concluded that Mezei should be treated as if he were a first-time entrant because his nineteen-month absence from the country had forfeited any entitlement that his prior residence may have afforded. Accordingly, the Court treated Mezei as standing in the same shoes as Knauff.[46]

Unlike Knauff, however, Mezei pressed a distinct due process challenge to his detention. No country would take Mezei back, and he had been detained on Ellis Island for nearly two years before he obtained his release on a petition for habeas corpus. The Court rejected this claim, too, characterizing Mezei's indefinite detention on Ellis Island as a *benefit* because the government could "keep entrants by sea aboard the vessel pending determination of their admissibility."[47] In effect, the Court treated Mezei, indefinitely detained with no place to go, as a first-time entrant knocking at the gate, whose sole claim concerned the benefit of admission.

It is one thing to say that due process does not apply to the denial of admission; it is another matter entirely to say that due process does not apply when the government has locked up a person. As Justice Jackson stated in dissent in *Mezei*,

> Realistically, this man is incarcerated by a combination of forces which keeps him as effectually as a prison, the dominant and proximate of these forces being the United States immigration authority. It overworks legal fiction to say that one is free in law when by the commonest of common sense he is bound.[48]

As these cases illustrate, the immigration process offered ways to regulate Communism without having to provide the safeguards of the criminal justice system, or even of due process. Still, these measures were limited because by definition they could reach only noncitizens. Hoover and others wanted broader control, and in the Cold War they got it.

CRIMINAL PROSECUTIONS

In July 1948, the government indicted twelve U.S. citizen leaders of the Communist Party under the Smith Act. The criminal charges in *United States v. Dennis* pursued the same theory as Harry Bridges's deportation charges: guilt by association with a group whose sin was to have advocated noxious ideas. The defendants were not charged with overthrowing the government, nor with conspiring to overthrow the government, nor even with teaching its overthrow; rather, the charge was conspiracy to form an organization to teach the doctrine of forcible overthrow. The charges thus combined guilt by association and punishment of speech. As in the Palmer Raids, the government's evidence focused almost entirely on the nature of the Communist Party rather than on any specific conduct of the defendants.[49] Because the Communist Party's "latter-day pronouncements . . . had been so mild . . . the government was forced to develop the theory of 'Aesopian' language—that surface fables had a deeper meaning."[50] The jury nonetheless convicted all of the defendants.

The constitutional standard that then governed the regulation of subversive speech was known as the "clear and present danger" test, first established by the Supreme Court in the wake of World War I.[51] The doctrine provided that the government could prohibit speech advocating illegal conduct only when it posed a clear and present danger under the particular circumstances. On appeal, Judge Learned Hand, perhaps the most venerated federal judge never to serve on the Supreme Court, interpreted that test as a balancing inquiry. He reasoned that if the danger to be feared was great, the immediacy of the danger need not be. As Hand put it, "[i]n each case, [courts] must ask whether the gravity of the 'evil,' discounted by its improbability, justifies such invasion of free speech as is necessary to avoid the danger."[52] Under this approach, because the feared evil was sufficiently grave— here, the overthrow of the national government—it did not matter that the probability that it would actually occur was infinitesimal. In fact, there was absolutely no evidence that the Communist Party had any chance of actually overthrowing the federal government, or even that it had taken any concrete steps to do so. On appeal, the Supreme Court adopted Judge Hand's approach, and affirmed the convictions.[53] As Professor Ralph Brown later assessed, "[u]nder the strain of the cold war and the impact of dominant public sentiment against communism, the clear-and-present-danger test crumpled."[54] Somewhat more dramatically, Professor Zechariah Chafee opined that "the Court reinterpreted the First Amendment to mean 'Congress shall make no law abridging the freedom of speech and of the press unless Congress does make a law abridging the freedom of speech and the press.' "[55]

As Brown's and Chafee's comments suggest, the Court's decision in *Dennis* was out of step with its general approach to the regulation of speech. By 1950, the Court's First Amendment doctrine had come a long way from the World War I decisions in which it had affirmed convictions for merely speaking out against the war. With the advantage of hindsight, the Court had become increasingly sensitive to the danger of allowing the government to punish subversive advocacy. Yet in the *Dennis* case, and in other decisions upholding Cold War initiatives against Communists,[56] the Court took a large step backward. Seeking to explain this anomaly, Professor William Wiecek argues that the Court essentially treated the Communists as "something less than full humans, full citizens, fully rights-endowed."[57] Wiecek elaborates:

> A majority of the Justices regarded Communists and their Party as *sui generis*, different from the other radical groups like the Klan, uniquely threatening to American national security. The Court therefore assigned Communists a special status under the Constitution, with diminished protections for their speech, press, and associational liberties.[58]

The model for such a double standard, of course, was the nation's and the Court's prior treatment of those who were literally "less than . . . full citizens"—foreign nationals. In the Cold War, the link between internal enemy—the Communist Party of the United States—and external foreign threat—the Soviet Union—helped to collapse the distinction between foreign national and citizen. To paraphrase General DeWitt, the architect of the Japanese internment, the government's attitude appeared to be: "once a Communist, always a Communist; it doesn't matter if they are aliens or citizens." In *Dennis*, as in *Korematsu*, the Court permitted the government to extend to citizens treatment previously restricted to foreign nationals.

With the Supreme Court's green light in *Dennis*, the government immediately launched a second wave of anticommunist prosecutions. Between 1951 and 1956, federal prosecutors indicted 126 Communists under the Smith Act. Eventually, 105 stood trial, and the government obtained convictions in 94 cases.[59] Meanwhile, Communist Party membership fell precipitously—from 54,000 near the end of 1949 to under 25,000 in early 1953. The specter of criminal prosecution was by no means the only force behind this development—the loyalty review boards and HUAC, discussed below, probably had an even bigger effect—but it certainly played a significant role. The prosecutions targeted the party leadership and forced the party to focus its attention and resources on defending criminal cases. No one knew how far the government would extend its criminal prosecutions were these test cases to succeed. And the government's prominent use of undercover informants hampered recruitment and led the party to undertake an internal witch hunt for potential informants.[60]

By 1956, the combination of domestic repression and world events had reduced the U.S. Communist Party to an almost wholly symbolic enemy. In February 1956, Krushchev publicly acknowledged Stalin's widespread crimes against political enemies. Shortly thereafter, revelations of anti-Semitism in the Soviet Union were widely circulated. Later that year, the Soviet military brutally suppressed uprisings in Poland and Hungary. By the summer of 1958, the Communist Party of the United States had only 3,000 to 6,000 members. According to historian Michal Belknap, "[a]s a political force American communism had for all practical purposes ceased to exist."[61]

With the demise of the U.S. Communist Party, the second Red Scare was left without its raison d'etre, and Cold War hysteria began to ease. This was best exemplified by the fall of Senator Joseph McCarthy, who personified the nation's struggle to extirpate Communism. McCarthy's popularity peaked in late 1953, but by December 1954 he had been censured by the Senate and his career was in shambles. Meanwhile, Congress and the courts, both of which had participated in and sanctioned anti-Communist fervor in the early years of the Cold War, now began to question the legitimacy of the government's actions.[62]

The Supreme Court effectively reversed its position on the Cold War on June 17, 1957, a day that I. F. Stone proclaimed would "go down in the history books as the day on which the Supreme Court irreparably crippled the witch hunt."[63] On that day, dubbed Red Monday by the Court's critics, the Court decided four cases, all upholding rights claims on behalf of victims of anti-Communism. With the significant exception of immigration, the cases spanned virtually every form of anti-Communist repression: criminal prosecutions, loyalty hearings, congressional inquiries, and faculty purges. In the criminal case, *Yates v. United States,* the Court held that convictions under the Smith Act required advocacy of illegal *action,* and not just advocacy of forcible overthrow as an abstract principle; as the Court stated, "[the] essential distinction is that those to whom the advocacy is addressed must be urged to *do* something, now or in the future, rather than merely to *believe* in something." [64] That distinction effectively put an end to prosecutions under the Smith Act's advocacy provisions. The same day, the Court reversed a decision to fire a career foreign service officer as a loyalty and security risk based on Communist associations; held that the desire to expose Communists was an insufficient basis for compelling testimony in a legislative hearing; and upheld academic freedom against an attempt to purge Communists from a state university faculty. [65]

The federal government did not immediately get the message. After *Yates* effectively blocked prosecutions under the Smith Act's advocacy provisions, prosecutors turned to its membership provisions. But in 1961, the Court in *Scales v. United States* extended its First Amendment–protective approach to those provisions as well. In its first review of a Smith Act conviction for membership, the Supreme Court ruled that the government had to demonstrate not only the fact of membership, but also that the defendant specifically intended to further the Communist Party's illegal ends. In our jurisprudence, the Court said, "guilt is personal," [66] and "[i]f there were a . . . blanket prohibition of association with a group having both legal and illegal aims, there would indeed be a real danger that legitimate political expression or association would be impaired. . . ." [67]

After *Yates* and *Scales*, no one was ever again successfully prosecuted under the Smith Act. The statute remains on the books to this day, but is essentially dead-letter. The Court subsequently held that citizens could not be denied jobs, passports, security clearances, or even the use of public university meeting rooms on the basis of their subversive associations or speech. In the end, the Court was unwilling to allow criminal or civil sanctions to attach to citizens' speech and associations. [68]

The fate of the Smith Act suggests that when Congress seeks to extend to citizens through the criminal process treatment that it has previously restricted to foreign nationals, the courts will eventually rebuff it. But "eventually" can be a long time. During the height of the Cold War, from 1948 to 1953, the Court did little to rein in Congress or the executive branch. Only when the Cold War was winding down, long after Joseph McCarthy had been censured, did the Supreme Court step in and uphold the rights of alleged Communists. By that time, much of the damage had already been done. Moreover, while the Court was willing to recognize the errors of anti-Communist ways when they affected citizens through the criminal process, it continued to permit the political branches broad leeway both in dealing with noncitizens through the immigration laws, and, as shown below, in using administrative measures to penalize citizens for Communist ties.

COMPELLING LOYALTY

The principal mechanisms of control during the Cold War were not criminal but administrative. As in the Palmer Raids, the government, seeking prevention, looked to noncriminal mechanisms. This time, it found them not only in immigration law, but in the administrative loyalty review process and the congressional inquiry. In these settings, federal, state, and local governments found a way to apply to millions of U.S. citizens techniques and arguments for control that the federal government had previously directed only at foreign nationals. Like the Smith Act and the immigration laws, the loyalty and security programs and legislative investigations operated by a principle of associational guilt. But their noncriminal character permitted them to be applied en masse to millions of citizens at a time. And because they threatened "only" loss of a job or reputational harm, not prison time, the government successfully argued that these procedures, like immigration proceedings, did not need to adhere to criminal safeguards, or even to the basic fairness guarantees of due process.

The first employee loyalty requirement in federal law was Section 9-A of the Hatch Act, enacted in 1939. It barred federal employment to members of organizations that advocated the overthrow of the

United States government. By 1941, nineteen states had followed suit, and Congress had extended the Hatch Act ban to personal advocacy of overthrow in addition to membership.[69] In 1941, Congress appropriated $100,000 to the Justice Department for the investigation of federal employees who were members of subversive organizations. These laws authorized the Justice Department, and by extension the FBI, to identify and blacklist "subversive" political groups. By 1942, the attorney general had compiled a list of forty-seven "subversive" groups.[70]

In 1947, President Truman dramatically expanded the reach of employee loyalty review by issuing an executive order mandating affirmative review of the loyalty of every federal employee. The Loyalty Order required dismissal wherever there were "reasonable grounds to believe an employee is disloyal," and set forth several criteria for disloyalty, chief among them membership in, or even "sympathetic association" with, "any organization designated by the attorney general as totalitarian, Fascist, Communist, or subversive, or . . . as seeking to alter the form of government of the United States by unconstitutional means."[71] It directed the attorney general to identify "totalitarian, Fascist, Communist, or subversive" groups, but set forth no substantive definition for such groups, and no procedure for adding groups to the list or taking them off. The attorney general employed a secret administrative process, which denied groups any hearing or opportunity to challenge their designation. Alan Barth called the attorney general's authority to blacklist groups "perhaps the most arbitrary and far-reaching power ever exercised by a single public official in the history of the United States. By virtue of it, the attorney general may stigmatize and, in effect, proscribe any organization of which he disapproves."[72] The list of disapprovals expanded exponentially. By 1950, it encompassed 197 groups.[73]

The attorney general's list served not only as a formal guide for federal loyalty review, but as a kind of semiofficial blacklist triggering sanctions from a wide range of public and private sources. The Treasury Department used it to deny tax exemptions; immigration authorities used it to deny entry to aliens associated with listed groups;

federal prosecutors used it to impeach defense witnesses; states adopted it as a litmus test for teachers, public employees, and elected officers; and the radio and movie industries relied on it to blacklist artists and performers.[74]

The existence of the list, its mysterious provenance, and its ever-expanding nature had a widespread chilling effect on political associations. Just as immigrants could be deported for past membership in proscribed groups, so employees and government contractors could have their loyalty challenged for past membership or "sympathetic association" with any listed group, even if their association predated the group's listing. Because the process for listing groups was secret, no one knew which organizations would be listed next. As a result, anyone who worked for the government, thought they might want to work for government in the future, or might be in a position to obtain a government contract or grant, effectively had to steer clear of all associations not only with the listed groups, but with any groups that might potentially be listed in the future.

The process for reviewing individual loyalty cases was at least as troubling as the process for designating subversive groups, as the tale of Dorothy Bailey recounted in Chapter 8 illustrates. "Loyalty" is such an open-ended term that charges ranged far and wide. Individuals were accused of "advocat[ing] the Communist Party line, such as favoring peace and civil liberties," of possessing or reading Communist literature, and of having "convictions concerning equal rights for all races and classes [that] extend beyond the normal feeling of the average individual."[75] Some were charged with being related by blood to Communists, a charge which came to be known as "guilt by relationship."[76] Abraham Chasanow, a forty-three-year old native of Greenbelt, Maryland, and civilian employee at the Navy Hydrographic Office for twenty-three years, was suspended for disloyalty because, among other things, the wife of one of his friends had "signed Communist nominating petitions during 1939."[77] Loyalty review boards interpreted "sympathetic association" to include "contributions of money, no matter how small, sponsorship of or attendance at meetings, the presence of one's name on the organization's mailing list, and marching in a May Day parade."[78] Loyalty hearing officers inquired into employees' views on HUAC, marriage, and civil rights, their reading habits, and even their musical tastes.[79]

In one hearing, the board grilled a medical scientist at length on his views about whether individuals should have a right to advocate the overthrow of the United States government. He replied that while he personally was "not in favor of advocating or of doing it," he believed that people have "the right to express any opinions, whether they're cockeyed or reasonable," so long as they took no concrete action toward that end and the conditions were not such that their speech might incite such action. The loyalty board chairman's response: "What causes us concern is your basic philosophy, which seems to go so far as to defend the right of advocacy even to overthrow the government of the United States." Later, the chairman made his point even more clearly: "The point that I'm disturbed about is that while you would neither advocate communism nor do anything consciously to implement it, nevertheless you would go the limit in defending the right of other people, or groups of people, to advocate communism, . . . and the only limitation that you placed . . . was that you would limit it . . . if the conditions at the time happened to be such that a political upheaval of some kind might result."[80] In essence, the scientist had articulated the "clear and present danger" test, the then-reigning test for First Amendment protection of subversive advocacy in the Supreme Court. His views were probably closer to the dissenting Justices than to the majority that affirmed the Communist leaders' convictions in Dennis v. United States, but they were still well within the realm of reasonable First Amendment interpretation. Indeed, the scientist's views presaged almost exactly the approach to subversive advocacy that the Supreme Court itself adopted in 1969, and has consistently maintained ever since. Yet for expressing such views, the scientist was deemed disloyal, and his termination sustained on appeal.

The loyalty review standard effectively presumed employees disloyal and required them to rebut that presumption. The initial standard required dismissal where there were "reasonable grounds" to believe that the employee was disloyal, requiring the employee to prove that no such grounds existed.[81] In 1951, President Truman raised the employees' burden still higher, requiring dismissal whenever "there is a reasonable doubt as to the loyalty of the person."[82] Now employees had to resolve all doubts. In 1953, the standard was amended once again, requiring dismissal unless employment was "clearly consistent" with national security.[83] With each successive change of standard, some cases that had been resolved in favor of the employee under the prior standard were reopened. John Service, a State Department employee, was cleared six times and then terminated after the standard was changed to "reasonable doubt."[84]

Extending to U.S. citizens the tactics used against Ellen Knauff, President Truman's Loyalty Order authorized review boards to base their decisions on undisclosed evidence. The boards did no independent investigation, but relied exclusively on FBI reports. The rules expressly authorized the FBI to submit reports without revealing their sources.[85] Thus, much like the "enemy alien" review process of World War II described in Chapter 7, the loyalty review process not only relied on secret evidence, but essentially deferred to the FBI.

As in the Palmer Raids, the government exploited the administrative character of the loyalty review process to deny employees such basic rights as fair notice of the charges against them, the presumption of innocence, and an opportunity to confront their accusers. And just as the government defended its immigration procedures by arguing that deportation is not punishment and that aliens have no right to enter or remain here, so it defended the loyalty procedures on the ground that "[n]o person has an inherent or Constitutional right to public employment. Public employment is a privilege, not a right."[86]

The administrative character of the loyalty review process also meant that the government could reach many more people than it could ever hope to ensnare in criminal trials. From 1947 to 1957, some 11,000 workers were fired as disloyal from federal, state, and local government jobs, while 6,300 private employees lost their jobs for the same reason.[87] And those numbers are barely the tip of the iceberg. In an exhaustive 1958 study, Professor Ralph Brown estimated that approximately 13.5 million workers in private and public employment, or one of every five workers nationwide, had been exposed to the loyalty process, either by taking a loyalty oath, completing a loyalty statement, obtaining security clearance, or undergoing a private employers' scrutiny.[88] The administrative character of the process thus not only allowed the government to avoid the safeguards of the criminal process, but also permitted the tentacles of anti-Communism to reach far more deeply into American life.

TRIAL BY PUBLICITY: THE LEGISLATIVE COMMITTEE

"The rights you have are the rights given you by this Committee. We will determine what rights you have and what rights you have not got before the Committee."[89] So witnesses were greeted upon appearing before the House Un-American Activities Committee (HUAC), with language that echoed the Supreme Court's description of Ellen Knauff's lack of rights as a foreign national seeking admission. HUAC mastered the art of using the congressional investigation to control, deter, and punish political dissent. Like the immigration and loyalty review processes, it did so by relying on guilt by association and refusing to accord its targets the rights and guarantees of the criminal law system. Founded in 1938, HUAC operated until June 1975, and formed a central component of the public war on Communism. Where the loyalty review process sought to regulate dissent by close monitoring and confidential procedures, HUAC did so through broad public exposure. Its purpose was exposure for exposure's sake, knowing full well that private and public employers would react by blacklisting those so identified. As HUAC itself described, "the purpose of this committee is the task of protecting our constitutional democracy by . . . pitiless publicity."[90] HUAC's Chairman, J. Parnell

Thomas, stated in 1947 that "[t]he chief function of the committee, however, has always been the exposure of un-American individuals and their un-American activities."[91]

Like so much else in the arena of government repression, HUAC's genesis was driven by concern about foreigners and foreign influence: its original mandate was to investigate "the diffusion within the United States of subversive and un-American propaganda that is *instigated from foreign countries* or of a domestic origin and attacks the principle of the form of government as guaranteed by the Constitution.[92] It heard from friendly witnesses who would identify others as Communist sympathizers and activists, and it would subpoena unfriendly witnesses to grill them about their alleged Communist ties. The names of those identified as Communists or called as unfriendly witnesses were widely publicized, and merely to be so identified could lead to the loss of one's job.[93] In 1950, for example, Michael Cvetic named more than 300 individuals as Communists and fellow travelers before the committee; over 100 of those named were fired.[94] From 1945 to 1960, HUAC interrogated over 3,000 witnesses in 230 hearings, and issued more subpoenas and cited more witnesses for contempt than all other House committees combined.[95] In effect, it conducted a thirty-seven-year trial by publicity.

HUAC witnesses were afforded even less process than those who appeared before loyalty review boards. Targets of the committee were afforded little or no notice of the accusations against them, which were frequently based on secret informers. Witnesses were also denied the right to counsel. In some circumstances, they were unable even to bring a lawyer into the room. When the lawyer was allowed to be present, he was not permitted to raise objections or to call witnesses, but was "just a bystander, with no chance to conduct the defense."[96] During one of the committee's most famous hearings, investigating Communist influences in Hollywood, a lawyer who represented a number of subpoenaed witnesses asked for permission to cross-examine John Moffit, who was naming Communists. The following exchange ensued:

LAWYER: Mr. Thomas, I represent a number of persons who have been subpoenaed—

THE CHAIRMAN: I am very sorry. You are out of order. We have a witness on the stand, so please go back and sit down.

LAWYER: You have said—

THE CHAIRMAN: I said you are out of order.

LAWYER: You have said you want a fair hearing. Cross-examination is necessary.

THE CHAIRMAN: Will you take this man out of the room, please? Take him out of the room.[97]

Other congressional committees have placed similar restrictions on the rights of witnesses and their counsel during hearings. But most committees do not take as their mandate the exposure and vilification of "guilty" individuals, and accordingly far less is at stake for any particular person. As Professor Robert Carr put it, "because [HUAC] has personalized its hearings to a degree seldom reached by other committees of Congress, the inability of counsel to render to a witness the kind of assistance he could give were his client a defendant in a court trial becomes a serious matter."[98]

Alan Barth aptly summed up the use of congressional committees and administrative tribunals to effect political control during the Cold War:

> By the simple stratagem of charging a man with disloyalty, instead of with treason or espionage or sabotage, it is possible to evade the constitutional requirements that he be indicted by a grand jury, that he enjoy a speedy and public trial by an impartial petit jury, that he be informed of the nature and cause of the accusation and confronted with the witnesses against him, that he be accorded the benefit of compulsory process to obtain witnesses in his favor. He is indicted and tried and sentenced by congressional committee or administrative tribunal, with the same men acting as prosecutors, judges, and jury. The presumption of innocence supposed to surround him is ignored. The mere charge of disloyalty is treated as evidence of guilt.[99]

For similar reasons, Harvard Law Professor Zechariah Chafee dubbed the Cold War the "Period of Subtle Suppression." Chafee, who had himself personally experienced the more heavy-handed tactics of suppression in the early part of his career during World War I, argued that "there is ever so much more suppression today [than during World War I] through proceedings which have no juries, no substantial supervision by judges, and vague definitions of wrongdoing."[100]

Lawyers challenged the constitutionality of HUAC and its procedures on a variety of grounds. They argued that the inquiry violated the First Amendment because it was intended to and had the effect of punishing constitutionally protected speech and associations. They maintained that contempt convictions for refusing to testify before the committee violated the Fifth Amendment Due Process Clause because the committee mandate was so vague and overbroad. And they contended that HUAC effectively inflicted punishment on individuals in contravention of the constitutional prohibition against "bills of attainder," which bars Congress from targeting punitive legislation at specific individuals. But despite strong dissenting views from respected jurists, the courts uniformly rejected such claims.[101] The courts reasoned, just as they had in the immigration settings, that the hearings were not criminal or punitive in nature and therefore need not adhere to the protections that attend the criminal sanction.

In short, the tactics of the Cold War were a reprise of those developed during the first Red Scare: targeting political associations; relying on administrative mechanisms to avoid criminal safeguards; and denying such basic procedural rights as access to lawyers and the right to confront the evidence used against one. As in the first Red Scare, the measures were sparked by fears of an "alien" invasion; but this time, the government's tactics did not stop at the citizen-noncitizen line.

We now recognize that these McCarthy-era tactics were not merely mistaken, but unconstitutional. We now acknowledge that, however real the threat seemed at the time, it did not justify the injuries imposed on so many innocent people without regard to individual culpability. We now recognize the importance of tolerating dissent and insisting on fair government procedures. But what we do not sufficiently recognize is the extent to which measures directed against noncitizens provided the template for all of the wrongs done to citizens during the Cold War. In the Cold War, as in World War II, we began to see the errors of our ways only when our ways began to affect not just "enemy aliens," but us.

11. EXTENDING THE BOUNDARIES: FROM MARTIN LUTHER KING, JR., TO WATERGATE

Even as Congress censured Joseph McCarthy and the Court repudiated guilt by association, the FBI was actively developing new ways to monitor, control, and disrupt radical political activity. When the Supreme Court in 1956 agreed to review the conviction of Oleta O'Connor Yates, Hoover saw the handwriting on the wall even before the Court issued its opinion in *Yates v. United States.* Unwilling to surrender his authority to monitor and control political dissent, but seeing his legal avenues closing off, Hoover sought to open new avenues for control. Where neither criminal nor administrative processes were available, he substituted illegal measures for legal ones. As before, he used foreigners and foreign influence as his justification for inroads on Americans' civil liberties. But this time the government's tactics reached an even wider cross section of the American mainstream, and ultimately provoked a critical reaction, profoundly altering Americans' views of the FBI and its proper role in society.

The most dramatic development of the post-McCarthy period was COINTELPRO (Counter-Intelligence Program), a secret FBI program that bypassed the courts (and the law) altogether. It consisted of a kind of low-level guerrilla warfare directed at disfavored political groups. Under COINTELPRO, the FBI conducted illegal break-ins of targeted groups and installed bugs and wiretaps without obtaining warrants. It placed *agents provocateurs* within target organizations to spread false rumors and foment internal dissent. It dropped "snitch jackets"—falsified documents designed to create the impression that an individual was an FBI informant—on leaders of disfavored groups. Through misinformation, it sought to get meetings cancelled and people fired from their jobs. It worked with the Internal Revenue Service to prompt politically motivated audits, pressured universities and schools to dismiss "radical" teachers, and tipped off local police to carry out drug arrests of political activists. Demonstrating that it could be equally underhanded at both ends of the political spectrum, the FBI sent anonymous letters to wives of Black Panthers and Ku Klax Klan members falsely accusing their husbands of infidelity.[1]

With the development of these largely illegal tactics of repression, the FBI placed new emphasis on the need for secrecy. The Bureau had long relied on asserted confidentiality needs to deprive individuals in loyalty review hearings (and the boards themselves) of access to the identity of their accusers. It had also relied on secrecy within the government itself, as when it secretly continued to maintain a list of subversives even after Attorney General Francis Biddle had ordered the FBI to stop doing so in 1943.[2] But because COINTELPRO was almost entirely illegal, it required a whole new level of secrecy, not so much to protect national security as to protect the Bureau itself from embarrassing disclosures. The FBI accordingly developed a "Do Not File" file for any information that reflected its illegal break-ins.[3]

While the Communist Party was COINTELPRO's initial target, the FBI ultimately applied the program to the Socialist Workers Party, white hate groups, black nationalist groups, and a wide variety of New Left groups, from Antioch College to Students for a Democratic Society.[4] By 1960, the FBI had created files on over 430,000 groups and individuals that it had identified as "subversive," and was devoting more resources to domestic intelligence gathering than to criminal law investigations.[5]

Like so much other political repression in the United States, COINTELPRO had its origins in measures directed at foreigners. It was the capstone of a campaign of monitoring domestic dissent that dates back at least to 1919, when the director of the Justice Department's Bureau of Investigation, the FBI's predecessor, told his agents to investigate "anarchistic and similar classes, Bolshevism, and kindred agitators," and instructed them that "this investigation should be particularly directed to persons not citizens of the United States, with a view of obtaining deportation cases."[6] The campaign's modern phase began in earnest in 1936 as World War II was beginning, when

President Roosevelt issued a secret directive ordering the FBI to investigate "subversive activities" in the United States.[7] Four years later, FDR authorized the FBI to conduct warrantless domestic security wiretaps, restricted "insofar as possible to aliens."[8] By the Cold War and COINTELPRO, however, the government's targets included citizens and noncitizens equally.

Much of the justification for FBI and other federal agency surveillance was founded on age-old concerns about foreign influence. Hoover exploited this fear to the fullest, announcing in 1940 that "foreign 'isms' had succeeded in boring into every phase of American life, masquerading behind front organizations."[9] Many of the FBI's investigations of domestic political organizations were rationalized as attempts to determine whether the Communist Party, a "foreign agent," had infiltrated the group. In 1962, the FBI formally launched a program of surveillance called COMINFIL (Communist Infiltration), designed to identify Communist infiltration of domestic organizations. In 1965, President Johnson asked the FBI to report on Communist influences in the antiwar movement.[10] In order to determine whether infiltration had occurred, the FBI itself had to infiltrate suspected groups. On this justification, the FBI during World War II investigated, among many others, the Independent Voters of Illinois, a New York child-care center, and the League of Fair Play, a group that provided speakers to Kiwanis, Rotary, and other clubs around the nation.[11] On this justification, the FBI, CIA, and the National Security Agency (NSA) monitored mail and international communications of Americans suspected of being sympathetic to hostile foreign countries.[12] The CIA alone illegally opened 215,000 letters from 1956 to 1973, indexed 1.5 million names, and sent much of the information drawn therefrom to the FBI.[13] Using the same rationale, the CIA also launched Operation CHAOS, a program ostensibly designed to study foreign connections to American dissidents, which ultimately gathered information on the wholly domestic, lawful activity of numerous political groups, including Clergy and Laity Concerned About Vietnam.[14] Information sharing was routine: at its peak, CHAOS provided the FBI with more than 1,000 reports per month on political activities of Americans at home and abroad.[15] And on this justification, the FBI spied on and infiltrated the American Friends Service Committee, the NAACP, and even a coalition of legal organizations and lawyers who had merely come together to call for the abolition of HUAC.[16] It was a relatively small step from such free-wheeling surveillance to the affirmatively illegal operations of COINTELPRO.

Martin Luther King, Jr. was the FBI's most famous target during this period. Hoover was obsessed with monitoring King, and did so for years, even obtaining explicit approval from Attorney General Robert Kennedy to bug King's home and office in 1963. A year earlier, Hoover had ordered all field offices to seek out "subversive" information on King that would be "suitable for dissemination." Hoover ultimately obtained taped evidence of King's extramarital affairs (from a bug in King's Washington, D.C. hotel room). He distributed the tapes within the executive branch and threatened to disseminate them to the media on the eve of King's receiving the Nobel Peace Prize. Hoover's ostensible justification? A concern that King's organization, the Southern Christian Leadership Conference, was infiltrated by Communists. Here too, a concern about foreign influence led to an extended campaign of surveillance and harassment directed at a U.S. citizen, in this instance one of the most revered citizens in American history.[17]

The government's concern with foreign influence and infiltration extended during the Vietnam war era to the peace movement and the entire New Left, an unorganized movement loosely committed to participatory democracy, but investigated by the FBI as a "subversive force" because it was allegedly dedicated to destroying "traditional values" and was "anti-war and anti-draft."[18] By the late 1960s and early 1970s, nearly a quarter million Americans were under active surveillance, and intelligence files contained information on hundreds of thousands of individuals and thousands of groups.[19] In 1969, the IRS created a special section to conduct audits on "ideological, militant, subversive, radical, and similar type organizations."[20] When the Watergate break-ins were disclosed, it became clear that the Nixon administration had applied the FBI's tactics—illegal break-ins, political spying, warrantless bugging—to the Democratic Party itself.

By that point, the government had gone too far. No longer content to focus its efforts on small groups of noncitizens, the administration was now targeting popular civil rights and antiwar groups, and even the Democratic Party. Revelations of the government's tactics led to widespread condemnation and criticism, calls for reform of the government's law enforcement and intelligence apparatus, the resignation of President Richard Nixon, reassertion of the judiciary as a check on broad claims of executive privilege and national security, abolition of the attorney general's list and HUAC, repeal of the statute authorizing emergency detention, cessation of the CIA's mail interception program, and imposition of investigation guidelines on the FBI, designed to refocus it on federal crime and bar it from political spying.[21]

But while the need for restraint was now widely recognized, there was little recognition that the methods of repression had virtually all developed out of antialien fears and measures. The 1960s and 1970s saw substantial domestic reform, but those reforms left the immigration law relatively untouched; its ideological provisions, rendering noncitizens deportable for their beliefs, ideas, and associations, remained on the books until 1990. As the next chapter shows, it was precisely through those remnants of the Cold War that the techniques and methods thought to be abandoned in the post-Watergate and post-Vietnam reforms came back to life. After September 11, with renewed calls for prevention, we have resurrected virtually all of these tactics, and have already begun to cross the citizen-noncitizen divide once again.

12. FROM COMMUNISM TO TERRORISM: LESSONS OF A YOUNG LAWYER

It was 1986, but it might as well have been 1956. The place: an immigration courtroom in El Paso, Texas. Fresh out of law school, I was a young lawyer with the Center for Constitutional Rights, and this was my first trial. My client, Margaret Randall, a fifty-year-old poet, author, photographer, and grandmother, faced deportation for having advocated "the doctrines of world communism" in her written work, a deportable offense under the 1952 McCarran-Walter Act, still on the books in the 1980s.[1] Government attorneys had obtained much of Randall's prodigious literary output of oral histories, journals, poetry, and essays, and had reviewed them with the proverbial red pen, underscoring every time that she used the words "Communism" or "revolution."

INS attorney Guadalupe Gonzalez had the job of cross-examining Randall. She confronted her again and again with things she had said in print, challenging her for, among other things, having described her three-year-old son as becoming "communist" because he was learning to share. At one point, Gonzalez asked Randall whether it was true that a poetry magazine she once edited had been described as a "revolutionary weapon," prompting the following exchange:

RANDALL: [Revolutionary weapon] is a metaphor, Ms. Gonzalez. I
    think that . . .
GONZALEZ: What's a metaphor?
RANDALL: The use of the word "revolutionary weapon" when refer-
    ring to a magazine which is made of print and words and pictures.
    It is a metaphor. . . . We gave expression in the magazine to many
    of the feelings which were being raised at that time by people of our
    generation.
GONZALEZ: Leftist feelings?

RANDALL: Feelings.

GONZALEZ: Communist feelings?

RANDALL: All kinds of feelings.

GONZALEZ: I mean, did you ever have an article in any of your last three publications extolling the virtues of the free enterprise system?[2]

The INS offered into evidence thousands of pages of Randall's writings, and cited all of the following as reasons why she should not be allowed to remain in the United States:

•She published political cartoons critical of the United States.

•She dedicated an issue of a literary journal to Huey Newton, a Black Panther.

•She ran an advertisement for a book by Karl Marx in the same journal.

•She published poems and articles in Cuban and Nicaraguan journals and newspapers.

•She wrote a poem called "Che" about Che Guevara.

•Her oral histories of Latin America included interviews with Communists.

•She admitted being an atheist.[3]

INS officials twice denied Randall permanent resident status. The first time, in 1985, INS District Director A.H. Guigni wrote:

> [her] writings go far beyond mere dissent, disagreement with, or criticism of the United States or its policies. Her associations with, and her activities and writings in support of the communist dominated governments of Cuba, North Vietnam, and Nicaragua; and her advocacy and support of revolutionary activity in Mexico, as well as her affiliation with and participation in Communist Party activities, warrant the denial of her application for adjustment of status [to permanent resident] as a matter of discretion.[4]

After the 1986 trial, Immigration Judge Martin Spiegel reached the same conclusion. He claimed to rest his decision on all 2,744 pages of

Randall's work that had been introduced into evidence, but managed to cite not a single offending passage. He did specify, however, that one of Randall's oral history books, *Cuban Women Now,* a book of interviews with Cuban women, was "consistent in its praise for the efforts of the Castro communist revolution in improving women's rights and conditions in Cuba as well as being consistently supportive of the communist revolution in Cuba."[5] In this regard, Randall's sin was to have quoted *other* women who praised Communism.

The only reason that there was any question about Randall's right to live in the United States was that the government considered her an "alien." She was born a U. S. citizen in New York City of American parents, but had moved to Mexico City in the 1960s, where she married a Mexican poet. Finding it difficult as a foreigner to find work in Mexico City, and with a family to support, Randall became a Mexican citizen. The State Department concluded that in so doing she had forfeited her U.S. citizenship. Randall subsequently divorced her first husband, and lived and wrote for many years in Cuba and Nicaragua, not returning to the United States until the 1980s.

Were Randall still a U.S. citizen, of course, she would not have been in deportation proceedings. Indeed, the government could not have taken any action against her based on her advocacy of Communism, her atheism, or the fact that her poetry magazine had been described as a "revolutionary weapon." Randall eventually prevailed on appeal, not on the ground that all persons are free to advocate Communism, but on the ground that she was still a U.S. citizen and therefore could not be deported no matter what immigration officials thought of her writings. The Board of Immigration Appeals ruled that she had never lost her U.S. citizenship because she took Mexican citizenship out of economic duress, and not out of any desire to cut her ties to the United States. In other words, Randall won precisely by insisting upon the line between citizen and noncitizen.

Notorious legal cases of this kind are won or lost not only in the courtroom nor only on the law. Just as critical to our victory was Randall's very public identity throughout the case as an American citizen. By all appearances, she was an American, and not just any American, but a white grandmother with long gray hair, a soft warm smile, and an appealing public presence. She simply did not fit the image of a threat to the United States in the eyes of anyone but a few immigration officials. She was not only born here, but had maintained a virtual presence here through her publications, which were a staple of women's studies and Latin American studies programs in colleges across the country. The government's efforts to deport Randall as a subversive turned her into a small-time celebrity. Margaret Randall defense committees popped up on college campuses nationwide, and she was constantly invited to speak at events held to publicize and raise money for her case. PEN American Center helped organize a First Amendment lawsuit on her behalf joined by such noted authors as Norman Mailer, E. L. Doctorow, William and Rose Styron, and Alice Walker. She appeared on numerous national television shows, and was the subject of favorable news articles in all the mainstream media. As a political matter, Randall was one of us, and try as it might, the government could not transform this friendly white grandmother into an "alien" in the eyes of the nation.

GUILT BY ASSOCIATION: THE LA 8 CASE

In 1987, shortly after Randall prevailed, federal officials in Los Angeles arrested a group of student activists (seven Palestinians and the Kenyan wife of one of the Palestinians) and sought their deportation on similar charges: the government claimed that the students were associated with a group that advocated the "doctrines of world Communism," the Popular Front for the Liberation of Palestine (PFLP). The eight, soon dubbed "the LA 8," were arrested at gunpoint in early dawn raids, placed in detention, and described as national security risks. The government argued that they posed such a grave threat to the security of the nation that they should be incarcerated without bond while their deportation hearings proceeded. When the immigration judge asked the government for evidence to support these allegations, the government responded that the evidence was classified and could be considered only in a closed-door hearing, outside of the presence of the students or their lawyers. To his credit, the immigration judge refused to consider any evidence that was not disclosed to the other side, and ordered their release.

Sixteen years later, the LA 8 remain free. Much has changed in the interim. The "world communism" statute they were initially charged under was declared unconstitutional in 1989, and then was repealed by Congress in 1990. The group with which the eight were allegedly associated, once the second largest faction within the Palestine Liberation Organization (PLO), is now a remnant of its former self. The eight individuals themselves are now middle-aged, employed in routine middle-class jobs, all but one with families to support. Most have abandoned their political activism; the leader of the group, initially charged with supporting "world communism," was for a time earning his living by trading initial public offerings on the Internet, and now competes with Starbucks selling coffee. Yet the government still seeks their deportation for their college-day political activities. At this rate, their case is likely to outlast even Harry Bridges's.

From the outset, the government admitted that none of the eight had engaged in any criminal, much less terrorist, activities. In congressional hearings a few months after their arrest, FBI Director William Webster admitted that a three-year FBI investigation had found no evidence of criminal or terrorist activity, that they "were arrested because they are alleged to be members of a world-wide Communist organization which under the McCarran Act makes them eligible for deportation," and that "if these individuals had been United States citizens, there would not have been a basis for their arrest."[6] The INS district director who authorized the deportation proceedings later confirmed that account, admitting that the eight "were singled out for deportation because of their alleged political affiliations with the [PFLP]."[7] He explained that the INS sought their deportation "at the behest of the FBI, which concluded after investigating [the eight] that it had no basis for prosecuting [them] criminally, and urged the INS to seek their deportation."[8]

I became involved in the case initially to challenge the constitutionality of the McCarthy-era law that the eight were charged with violating. With lawyers from the Center for Constitutional Rights, the ACLU, and the National Lawyers Guild, we filed a federal lawsuit arguing that the First Amendment equally protected the associational rights of citizens and foreign nationals living here, and that the McCarran-Walter Act provision the government was enforcing impermissibly imposed guilt by association. The government's response was telling. It did not dispute that citizens had a right to advocate Communism and to associate with groups so advocating. But it contended that the Bill of Rights was essentially irrelevant when it came to the deportation power, and that therefore the government could deport foreign nationals for speech and associations that their U.S. citizen neighbors had every right to engage in. From the very beginning, in other words, the government invoked the citizen-noncitizen distinction to defend its actions.

Government documents disclosed in the case illustrated that the reforms that followed COINTELPRO and Watergate had not succeeded in ending political spying. FBI memoranda urging the INS to deport the eight amount to over 1,000 pages consisting *entirely* of accounts of lawful political activity, including detailed reports on political demonstrations, meetings, and dinners, and extensive quotations from political speeches and leaflets. Over 300 pages are devoted to tracking the distribution of PFLP newspapers, available in public libraries throughout the United States, as if they were illegal drugs. Agents would intercept boxes of magazines imported from abroad at the Los Angeles airport, weigh them to estimate how many magazines they contained, and then carefully track those who picked up and distributed the magazines.

The FBI memos repeatedly criticize the students' political views as "anti-US, anti-Israel, anti-Jordan,"[9] and even "anti-REAGAN and anti-MABARAK [sic]."[10] The principal FBI report on the group admits that the FBI's aim was to "disrupt" political activity, the very goal of COINTELPRO. The memo states that its purpose is "to identify key PFLP people in Southern California so that law enforcement agencies capable of disrupting the PFLP's activities through legal action can do so," even though the memo identifies no illegal activities by any of the eight.[11] The FBI specifically urged deportation of the alleged leader of the group, Khader Hamide, a lawful permanent resident, not because he engaged in any criminal acts, but because he was "intelligent, aggressive, dedicated, and shows great leadership ability."[12]

On the eve of a federal court hearing on our constitutional challenge to the "world communism" charges, the INS dropped those charges against six of the eight, apparently out of concern that the statutory provisions might be invalidated. These six were all here on temporary visas, and the INS substituted technical visa violation charges—such as taking too few credits on a student visa—for its initial ideological charges. In doing so, however, the INS announced that it was changing the charges solely for tactical reasons, and that it still sought deportation of all eight because of their association with the PFLP. INS official William Odencrantz compared the case to a football game, and said that the government didn't care whether it scored a touchdown or a field goal, as long as it obtained their deportation. The INS retained the "world communism" charges against Khader Hamide and Michel Shehadeh, both lawful permanent residents, because there were no "technical" immigration charges available for them.

In January 1989, federal district court judge Stephen Wilson declared the McCarran-Walter Act provisions unconstitutional.[13] He ruled that the First Amendment protects all people in the United States, citizens and noncitizens alike, and that the McCarran-Walter Act provisions violated the First Amendment because they imposed guilt by association. The government immediately appealed. While the appeal was still pending, however, Congress repealed the McCarran-Walter Act provisions.[14] In their stead, Congress made it a deportable offense to engage in terrorist activity.[15] Given FBI Director Webster's admission that none of the LA 8 had engaged in any terrorist activity, we hoped that this would mark the end of the case.

It did not. The INS continued to seek deportation of the six charged with technical visa violations, and now charged Shehadeh and Hamide, the two permanent residents, with having "engaged in terrorist activity" by providing material support to the PFLP. We returned to the federal district court, where we now argued that all eight had been unconstitutionally singled out for deportation based on First Amendment–protected activities.[16] Such selective prosecution claims are notoriously difficult to prove; the courts require a showing both that the government did not take similar measures against others, and that it targeted the individuals before the court for an improper motive, such as race, religion, speech, or association. But in this case we had outright admissions from the head of the FBI and the INS district director that the eight had been targeted for their political associations. We showed that the PFLP, the group they were accused of supporting, engaged in a wide range of fully lawful activities, including the provision of education, health care, social services, and day care to Palestinians in the West Bank and elsewhere.[17] We demonstrated that the government had not sought to deport many persons with the same technical visa violations as our clients; one immigration official testified that he could not recall anyone ever being deported for taking too few credits on a student visa. And we also showed that the INS had not sought to deport many noncitizen members and supporters of the contras in Nicaragua and the *mujahedin* in Afghanistan, other groups that used violence to further their ends. (On the contrary, the United States in the 1980s was actively supporting the violent activities of both the contras and *mujahedin*.)

The government's lawyers did not seriously dispute these factual showings, but argued again that noncitizens enjoyed at best only diminished First Amendment rights. As a result, it contended, there was nothing illegal about singling out noncitizens for their association with and support of a terrorist group, even without any evidence that they sought to further any terrorist activity of the group.[18] The district court and a unanimous court of appeals flatly rejected the government's argument, holding again that noncitizens living here are entitled to the same First Amendment rights as citizens, and ruling that the government's selective prosecution of the immigration laws was unconstitutional.[19] The government did not seek Supreme Court review, and again we hoped that the case might soon be over.

But again our hopes were dashed. Having lost repeatedly in federal court, the INS in 1996 persuaded Congress to repeal the federal courts' jurisdiction to hear cases challenging selective enforcement of the immigration law. We argued that this new statute did not apply to our case, and that if it did, it would be unconstitutional to deny noncitizens any judicial forum to challenge unconstitutional action taken against them. The district court and the court of appeals again agreed with us. But the Supreme Court agreed to hear the government's appeal.

When the Court issued its decision a year or so later, it not only ruled that the 1996 statute had divested the federal courts of power to hear our case, but also went on to resolve an issue it had explicitly declined to review when it agreed to hear the appeal, and that we therefore were not permitted to brief: whether selective enforcement of immigration law was unconstitutional. In an opinion authored by Justice Antonin Scalia, the Court ruled that, except in unspecified extreme situations, selective enforcement claims should not be entertained at all in the immigration setting.[20] In other words, more than ten years after the government started defending its actions against the LA 8 by invoking a double standard, the Supreme Court embraced one. It is undoubtedly unconstitutional for the government to initiate a criminal prosecution based on an individual's political associations.[21] It is also indisputably unconstitutional to inflict any civil penalty, or even to deny a job, based on an individual's political associations.[22] Yet according to the Supreme Court, it is permissible to seek to deport a noncitizen for the same political associations. And so the case continues.

In the decade and a half that the case has lasted, three of the six originally charged with technical visa violations have become permanent residents, so their cases have ended. But the government still seeks to deport the other five, notwithstanding its admission sixteen years ago that they have engaged in no illegal or terrorist activity. From the government's perspective, that admission is simply not material, because any support to a "terrorist group," even to its wholly lawful activities, warrants deportation.[23]

The cases against the LA 8 and Margaret Randall share certain basic affinities: both were charged under the same statute for their political views and ties, and neither was accused of having engaged in any criminal activity. Yet the LA 8 case has proved far more tenacious than Randall's. This is in part because the LA 8 case, focused on Palestinian activism, was less anachronistic. The LA 8 were targeted not solely for their words but for their asserted affiliations with a group that had allegedly engaged in notorious terrorist acts. But another important factor is that the LA 8 are not white birthright citizens, but indisputably foreigners. They are not part of the American majority, but members of a distinct minority group. They are far more likely to be seen as "alien," and therefore far less likely to garner widespread public support.

The LA 8 case has long caused widespread consternation in the Arab community for precisely this reason. The students had done nothing more than had thousands of displaced Palestinians and other foreign nationals across the country: they had spoken out and organized events in support of the rights of their people, attempted to preserve and celebrate their culture, and provided humanitarian support to those suffering back home. Similar initiatives had taken place among displaced immigrant communities in countless cities across the country. Yet only Palestinians had been threatened with deportation for such conduct. If the LA 8 could be deported, most Palestinians living here could be. Thus, the case took on legendary proportions among Arab Americans, cast a chilling pall over their political advocacy, and raised deep suspicions about the fairness of the government's actions.

The plight of the LA 8 initially attracted significant support from the mainstream media, as the *New York Times,* the *Washington Post,* and the *Los Angeles Times* all ran editorials sharply critical of the government's efforts.[24] But sustaining support beyond the Arab community has been far more difficult. Had the government sought to deport a similarly situated group of white immigrants allegedly associated with the Irish Republican Army (IRA), the popular outcry would have almost certainly been much more substantial. Over the course of the LA 8 case, Irish immigrants and citizens living here actively and notoriously supported the IRA, yet the INS never sought to deport a single person for association with the IRA, or for seeking to raise money for its legal activities. It did seek to deport persons accused of engaging in actual terrorist acts on behalf of the IRA, but not persons alleged merely to be associated with the IRA or its legal arms, Sinn Fein or Irish Northern Aid (NORAID). Because the Palestinians were more easily portrayed as "other," the government could treat them in ways that it certainly could not have treated citizens, and probably could not have treated many white immigrants.

At the same time, as discussed in Chapter 4, the principle of guilt by association for supporting terrorist groups, first advanced in the LA 8 case as limited to foreign nationals, has now been extended to U.S. citizens, crossing the citizen-noncitizen line to serve as the linchpin of the government's criminal law arsenal in the war on terrorism.

SECRET EVIDENCE

When the immigration judge hearing the LA 8 case refused to permit the government to submit secret evidence to justify detention, I was more surprised by the government's request than by the judge's ruling. Few constitutional principles are as basic as the notion that before the government locks up a human being, it must permit him to confront and rebut the evidence against him. But as I was to learn over the course of the next decade and a half, INS officials under administrations from Ronald Reagan to Bill Clinton to George W. Bush have all asserted the authority to rely on undisclosed evidence to detain and deport foreign nationals. Their rationale: noncitizens do not deserve the same due process rights as citizens.

Secrecy undoubtedly serves many salutary functions. In a war, for example, no one would want the other side to have access to one's military plans. Ongoing law enforcement investigations often must remain secret lest suspects evade detection. The deliberative processes of courts, legislatures, and executive officials are often promoted by a guarantee of confidentiality. But when the government seeks to take a person's life, liberty, or property, secret evidence ought to be unacceptable because it frustrates the most basic demands of fairness. In criminal cases, the Sixth Amendment Confrontation Clause guarantees that defendants have a right to confront all evidence used against them, and the Fifth Amendment Due Process Clause further requires the government to disclose any "exculpatory information"—evidence supportive of the defendant's innocence—from its otherwise confidential files. Even in noncriminal settings, the government may not take a person's property or liberty without providing notice and a meaningful opportunity to respond, a right that would seem minimally to require access to the evidence used against one. Yet in immigration cases, the government has relied on the citizen-noncitizen line to defend its refusal to give foreign nationals access to the evidence used against them.

Hany Kiareldeen, a stereo store sales clerk from Newark, New Jersey, spent nineteen months incarcerated in a New Jersey jail on the basis of secret evidence that he never saw. A Palestinian in his thirties, Kiareldeen came to the United States on a student visa in 1990, married a U.S. citizen, divorced, remarried another U.S. citizen, and applied for permanent resident status.[25] In March 1998, without processing his pending application for permanent residence, the INS arrested Kiareldeen, charged him with failing to maintain his student visa status, and detained him without bond as a threat to national security. With the Center for Constitutional Rights and immigration lawyers Houeida Saad and Regis Fernandez, I represented Kiareldeen in a constitutional challenge to his detention.

From the outset, the INS claimed that the information showing Kiareldeen to be a threat was classified and therefore could not be revealed without jeopardizing national security. Accordingly, it submitted the information to the immigration judge in camera (behind closed doors) and ex parte (without the presence of Kiareldeen or his lawyers). The INS did give Kiareldeen an unclassified summary of the evidence, but the summary initially disclosed only that he was allegedly associated with unnamed terrorists and posed an unspecified threat to the attorney general, charges so vague that Kiareldeen could not possibly rebut them.[26]

Subsequently, the INS expanded its disclosure, and ultimately revealed three allegations: (1) that Kiareldeen was associated with an unidentified "terrorist organization," and with other members and suspected members of terrorist organizations, also unidentified; (2) that about a week before the 1993 World Trade Center bombing, Kiareldeen hosted a meeting at his residence in Nutley, New Jersey, where some individuals discussed the planned bombing; and (3) that "Kiareldeen expressed a desire to murder Attorney General Janet Reno."[27] The summary provided no further details. It did not, for example, identify the sources for any of these allegations, nor explain the context or time frame for the alleged relationships and statement.[28]

Kiareldeen nonetheless sought to respond to the government's case as best he could. He denied meeting with the World Trade Center bombers and proved that he did not even live in the apartment where he supposedly hosted the meeting until a year and a half *after* the alleged meeting (and bombing) took place.[29] He showed that his phone records revealed no phone calls to any of the many conspirators in the World Trade Center case, while the conspirators' phone records showed extensive calls among themselves.[30] Guessing (correctly, it turned out) that his ex-wife might be one of the sources of secret evidence against him, he showed that she had made numerous false reports to the police about him in the course of a custody battle over their child, all of which had been dismissed by the local police.[31] Kiareldeen sought to examine his ex-wife in open court, but the INS vigorously opposed his attempts to do so, and she refused to testify about her discussions with the FBI.[32]

In the end, Kiareldeen's defense was sufficient to lead Immigration Judge Daniel Meisner to reverse his initial ruling and to rule that Kiareldeen was not in fact a threat to national security. The government appealed, but in the end, all seven immigration judges who examined the complete record in Kiareldeen's case rejected the government's claim that he posed a threat to national security. Kiareldeen was released in October 1999. He had spent nineteen months in jail.[33]

Although the judges were not allowed to reveal the substance of the confidential information, two judges sharply disparaged the quality of the evidence. Immigration Judge Meisner stated that Kiareldeen had "raised formidable doubts about the veracity of the allegations contained in the [classified information]," and that in the face of repeated requests for more information, the INS had refused "to answer those doubts with any additional evidence, be it at the public portion of the hearing or even in camera."[34] He concluded that the classified evidence was "too meager to provide reasonable grounds to believe that [Kiareldeen] was actually involved in any terrorist activity."[35]

Board of Immigration Appeals (BIA) Judge Anthony Moscato, dissenting from a preliminary decision not to release Kiareldeen, complained that the bare-bones character of the government's in camera evidence made it "impossible" for the BIA to exercise independent judgment in assessing "either the absolute truth or the relative probity of the evidence contained in the classified information."[36] Judge Moscato criticized the INS for having provided no original source material and "little in the way of specifics regarding the source or context of the classified information."[37] He further noted that despite the immigration judge's continuing requests, the INS had provided "no witnesses, neither confidential informant nor federal agent, to explain or document the context of the actions and statements referenced in the classified information or to document the way in which the classified information became known to the source of that information."[38]

Kiareldeen was not alone. Another noncitizen I represented, Nasser Ahmed, an Egyptian man who lived in New York with his wife and three young U.S.–citizen children, spent three and a half years in detention based on secret evidence, most of that time in solitary confinement. When he was first detained, INS officials claimed that the secret evidence used against him could not even be summarized without jeopardizing national security. As a result, he was told nothing about the government's evidence against him, could not refute what he could not see, and was detained as a national security threat. A short while later, the INS informed Ahmed that it could give him a summary, but the summary said only that he had an "association with a known terrorist organization."[39] The INS maintained that even naming the group would jeopardize national security. The immigration judge characterized this summary as "largely useless," but INS regulations did not require anything more.[40] Again, Ahmed was unable to refute such an open-ended charge. The immigration judge ruled that, on the public record, Ahmed would be entitled to political asylum, finding that he would very likely be tortured if sent back to Egypt. But, the judge continued, the secret evidence precluded him from granting Ahmed asylum.[41]

After we filed a constitutional challenge on Ahmed's behalf in federal court, the INS changed its tune. Facing a lawsuit, it declassified approximately fifty pages of previously secret evidence, and gave Ahmed an expanded summary with substantially more specifics about the charges against him. He was now alleged, among other things, to be associated with Sheikh Omar Abdel Rahman, the Muslim cleric tried and convicted for conspiracy to bomb the tunnels and bridges around Manhattan; to be associated with al Gama al Islamiya, the previously unnamed "known terrorist organization"; and to have transmitted a letter from prison for Sheikh Abdel Rahman that was subsequently published and, the government implied, sparked a terrorist incident.[42] Finally apprised of the substance of the charges against him, Ahmed was able to rebut them. He explained that he had met the sheikh when the sheikh came to speak at his mosque, had gone to the sheikh for marital counseling at one point, and had served as the sheikh's court-appointed (and federally approved) paralegal and translator during the sheikh's criminal trial. He denied membership in the Egyptian group, but also offered substantial evidence showing that it was less a group than a widespread movement, and that most of those associated with it had no involvement in violence.

Ahmed also showed that the most specific and potentially serious charge, the allegation about the letter, was false. He denied that he had transmitted the letter, and showed that many others, including journalists, had visited the sheikh in prison around the time the letter appeared. He introduced the letter itself (from the newspaper in which it appeared), which merely complained about the sheikh's prison conditions and did not call for violence. Most importantly, he introduced State Department documents showing that the government itself had concluded that the terrorist incident had actually been prompted by an Israeli attack in Lebanon and not by the sheikh's letter. When the immigration judge later confronted the government's witness about this, the witness admitted that the government never actually had proof that Ahmed had transmitted the letter. After hearing Ahmed's account and hearing again from the government behind closed doors, the same judge who initially ordered Ahmed detained and denied him asylum reversed himself, ordered Ahmed's release, and granted him asylum. The BIA affirmed that decision, the attorney general declined to intervene, and in November 1999, Ahmed was a free man. He remains a permanent resident in New York.

Ahmed's case illustrates the danger of unnecessary reliance on secrecy. The evidence declassified in his case should never have been classified in the first place. Information may be classified only if its disclosure could reasonably be expected to damage the national security or the government's international relations.[43] The fact that "Ahmed worked as one of RAHMAN's paralegals," one of the allegations in the secret evidence, was never a secret to anyone, much less the kind of information whose disclosure would jeopardize national security. Other declassified evidence revealed that the INS's witness in the secret proceedings, an FBI agent, had argued that Ahmed should continue to be detained because his detention by INS had made him a hero in the Muslim community and his release would increase his political stature.[44] While one might understand why the government would want to keep secret the fact that it had made such a patently illegal argument, it hardly merited classification as information whose disclosure would imperil national security.

The case of Dr. Ali Yasin Mohammed Karim may be the most unusual of all the secret evidence cases. He came to the United States in 1997, having been airlifted by the United States after he and a group of other Iraqis participated in an unsuccessful CIA-backed coup attempt against Saddam Hussein. At the border, the INS detained Karim and several others, claiming it had secret evidence that showed them to be double-agents. When former Director of Central Intelligence James Woolsey learned of the Iraqis' plight, he was sufficiently troubled that he offered to represent them pro bono. He argued that surely a former director of the CIA could be trusted to review the classified evidence. When the INS refused to let even Woolsey see the evidence, he went to Congress and the press. The Senate held hearings, and CBS's *60 Minutes* featured the case. Under this pressure, the government discovered that it could declassify over 500 pages of the previously secret evidence.[45] The disclosures revealed a wealth of unreliable information and pure mistakes. For example, the FBI charged one of the Iraqis as being a member of a terrorist group referred to as "KLM." Examination of the Arabic translator who participated in the interrogation revealed that the interpreter had made up the term KLM as shorthand for any of numerous Iraqi Kurdish groups; there was in fact no "KLM."[46] Armed with the government's belated disclosures, Dr. Karim was able to rebut the government's charges, and was released in August 2000, after three and half a years in detention.[47]

As these cases show, the evidence used in secret proceedings is often unreliable. Attorneys who know that their evidence cannot be challenged by their adversaries have less incentive to ensure that it is true. In its closed-door presentations, the INS has relied on double and triple hearsay assertions by FBI agents, and has refused to produce original declarants even when asked to do so by the immigration judge in the closed-door proceedings.[48]

Since 1987, I have represented thirteen noncitizens against whom the government has sought to use secret evidence. In each case, the government initially claimed that the evidence showed the noncitizens to be threats to national security. Yet in each case, the noncitizens were eventually granted relief by court order. In several cases, federal courts concluded that reliance on classified evidence was unconstitutional. In others, judges reversed themselves after the government disclosed the substance of its charges and the individual had an opportunity to present his side of the story. In each case in which the charges were disclosed, they consisted of little more than guilt by association.[49] In no case was the noncitizen ultimately determined to pose any threat to national security.

In my experience, when the government uses the immigration process to target a "terrorist," one can be fairly certain that it does not have evidence that the individual has actually engaged in or supported any terrorist act. In every case in which I have been involved, the government has loosely invoked the label of "terrorism," but has never even *alleged*, much less proven, that any of my clients engaged in or supported any terrorist activity. There is a certain perverse logic to this: if it had evidence of actual terrorist activity, the government would not be satisfied to send the person abroad, where he would be free to plan and carry out further terrorist acts. But that fact only raises further questions about the bona fides of the government's national security claims.

Before September 11, the tide was turning against the use of secret evidence in immigration proceedings. The government had suffered a string of embarrassing public losses. Each time it sought to rely on classified evidence its actions were criticized by editorial pages of major newspapers, including the *Washington Post,* the *New York Times,* the *Los Angeles Times,* and the *Miami Herald.*[50] A bipartisan group of over one hundred members of Congress sponsored a bill in 2001 to require that any use of classified evidence be accompanied by an unclassified summary that preserves the immigrant's ability to defend himself, and a similar bill was favorably reported out by the House Judiciary Committee over only four dissenting votes in the previous Congress.[51] President Bush had even publicly criticized the use of secret evidence against Arab noncitizens in one of the televised presidential campaign debates.[52]

In addition, every federal court that had addressed the practice over more than a decade prior to September 11 had declared the use of secret evidence unconstitutional.[53] The U.S. Court of Appeals for the District of Columbia had compared the position of a noncitizen having to disprove charges based on secret information to that of Joseph K. in Franz Kafka's *The Trial,* and stated that "[i]t is difficult to imagine how even someone innocent of all wrongdoing could meet such a burden."[54] Another court of appeals had ruled that "[o]nly the most extraordinary circumstances could support one-sided process."[55]

In these cases, judges of all political stripes uniformly expressed discomfort with the government's tactics. But that was before September 11. On November 28, 2001, in a decision declaring a secret evidence appeal moot, the U.S. Court of Appeals for the Eleventh Circuit in Miami went out of its way to credit the government's arguments that noncitizens have no right to confront the evidence used to detain them in immigration proceedings.[56] About a week later, the Court of Appeals for the Third Circuit issued an opinion in Hany Kiareldeen's case overturning an award of fees to the legal team that had obtained his release, citing the September 11 attacks and saying, "we are not inclined to impede investigators in their efforts to cast out, root and branch, all vestiges of terrorism in our homeland and in far off lands."[57]

Notwithstanding President Bush's criticism of the practice during his election campaign, Bush administration lawyers vigorously defended the propriety of using secret evidence in both the Third and Eleventh Circuit appeals. Government officials have talked frequently about the need to keep information confidential in the war on terrorism, and in particular about the problems presented by having to produce sources for cross-examination in terrorism cases. The authority to rely on secret evidence remains a part of the immigration law, and if history is any guide, it is likely to be exercised as soon as the INS finds itself unable to effectuate detention or deportation in a "terrorism case" without it.

Meanwhile, the government has extended the tactic of relying on secret evidence beyond immigration law. In the PATRIOT Act, Congress authorized the executive branch to use classified information, presented behind closed doors, to defend the freezing of assets under the International Emergency Economic Powers Act, one of the laws the administration has used to penalize financial support for so-called terrorist organizations. The government has invoked that provision to defend its freezing of three Muslim charities' assets with secret evidence.[58] So far, the courts have found no constitutional problems with these actions. This power, moreover, can be used not only against U.S.–based organizations with U.S. board members, like the Muslim charities, but also against U.S. citizens accused of supporting proscribed groups, like Mohammad Salah. So now the government has invoked the same power to rely on secret evidence against citizens that it has previously defended in the immigration context on the ground that noncitizens do not deserve the same rights as citizens.

The government has gone even further with respect to the designation of U.S. citizens Jose Padilla and Yasser Hamdi as enemy combatants. In these cases, the government has asserted the authority to arrest and incarcerate indefinitely and virtually incommunicado any citizen whom the president labels an enemy combatant, without any hearing whatsoever. It has reluctantly conceded that detained citizens (but not foreign nationals) may seek habeas corpus review, but has argued that the reviewing court cannot question the government's factual assertions, and has submitted secret evidence in camera and ex parte in support of its actions.[59]

These recent experiences recapitulate the historic patterns identified in the previous chapters. Here, as in the Palmer Raids, the world wars, and the early Cold War, the government has taken extreme security measures against noncitizens, and has defended them on the ground that noncitizens deserve only diminished constitutional protections. And as in the world wars, the Cold War, and the Vietnam era, those measures—in particular, the imposition of guilt by association, reliance on administrative process, and the use of secret evidence—have again been extended to citizens. The lesson of history is that what the government does to noncitizens in the name of security will eventually be extended to citizens. The transition may take many years, or it may happen swiftly. But it will happen. In the long run, all of our rights are at stake in how we treat foreign nationals in the war on terrorism.

PART 3
SECURITY

13. LEGITIMACY AND DOUBLE STANDARDS

On November 26, 2002, the front page of the *Washington Post* featured two stories about Saudi Arabia. The first reported that U.S. officials were strongly dissatisfied with Saudi Arabia's failure to cut off financial support for terrorism.[1] Immediately below it, a second story ran, titled, " 'I'll Never Go Back'; Saudis Who Once Embraced America Now Feeling Embittered and Betrayed."[2] That story told of the impact that our government's treatment of Saudi nationals living in or seeking to go to the United States had had on the views of Saudi citizens living in Saudi Arabia, turning them from supporters of the United States to bitter foes. As Charles Kestenbaum, a former U.S. Embassy official in Saudi Arabia explained, "We're treating all Saudis as if they're terrorists. Our inability to distinguish between who is a friend and an enemy turns everyone into an enemy. It's a self-fulfilling prophecy." On May 12, 2003, three synchronized suicide bomb attacks in Riyadh directed at residential compounds heavily populated by Westerners killed thirty-four people, including eight Americans.[3]

While the *Washington Post* did not make the connection explicit, its two November front-page stories were inextricably interrelated. The Saudi government would much more eagerly support our intelligence and enforcement efforts if the Saudi people favored cooperation with the United States. Because its citizens view the United States as disrespecting them and treating them unfairly, the Saudi government may feel substantial pressure *not* to cooperate. The same problem occurs at home—when law enforcement and intelligence officials treat a wide cross-section of the Arab and Muslim community as suspect largely by virtue of their ethnicity or religion, Arabs and Muslims will be less likely to cooperate with authorities and provide needed information. Denying fundamental rights to foreign nationals in a discriminatory fashion leads to substantially less cooperation at home and abroad. And for security reasons, we can ill afford that result.

UNDERMINING SECURITY

All arguments about the effectiveness of given security measures are necessarily speculative. They rest on judgments about what works and does not work that can rarely be tested in a controlled environment, and therefore inevitably leave lots of unanswered questions about cause and effect. The difficulties are compounded many times over by the secrecy that often attends security measures and their implementation. Nonetheless, security policy is predicated on the judgments of experience, and there are good reasons to believe, based on experience, that the double standards we have adopted since September 11 are unlikely to make us more secure, and may well make us less safe.

Consider ethnic and nationality-based profiling, perhaps the paradigmatic double standard in the administration's war on terrorism. In addition to being morally and constitutionally objectionable, ethnic profiling is also ineffective. For this reason—*not* out of a concern about equality norms—senior federal intelligence experts distributed a memo shortly after September 11 warning against ethnic profiling.[4] In the words of Bill Dedman, who reported on the memo for the *Boston Globe*, the experts argued that "profiling adds no security, and in fact can compromise it." As one expert said, "If your goal is preventing attacks . . . you want your eyes and ears looking for pre-attack behaviors, not [ethnic] characteristics." The memo urges police to look at "what a person has done and plans to do, rather than who that person is."

Many law enforcement agencies and experts have recognized that ethnic profiling is bad policing. In October 2002, for example, the Washington, D.C., area was victimized by a three-week shooting spree. Expert profilers predicted that the sniper would be an angry white man, most likely a loner. Yet in the end, the snipers turned out to be a pair of black men working and traveling together. Commenting on the outcome, Oliver Revell, a former FBI deputy director of intelligence, stated, "Profiles have been greatly, greatly overestimated in their value in criminal investigations. [A profile] is not definitive, it is often wrong, and cannot be used as a conclusive road map."[5]

Studies of racial profiling based on presumptions that minorities are more likely to be carrying drugs or other contraband have consistently found no higher "hit rates" among the targeted minority groups. When the Customs Service recently abandoned profiling for a more behavior-oriented approach, it substantially increased its "hit rates," seizing more contraband with fewer searches. In the 1970s, the Secret Service scrapped its profile of assassins, which targeted men, after Sara Jane Moore attempted to assassinate President Ford. And while the FBI's profile of school shooters focused on low-achieving, mentally disturbed boys, school shooters have in fact run the gamut—boys and girls, high and low achievers, of all races, and from all types of backgrounds.[6]

Ethnic, racial, and nationality-based profiling leads agents to miss those who do not fit the profile. Since September 11, law enforcement officials have focused on foreign nationals from Arab and Muslim countries. Yet the defendants in the two cases involving the most serious charges connected to the war on terrorism thus far are a British and a French citizen, respectively—Richard Reid and Zacarias Moussaoui. And as noted above, the majority of those charged criminally with Al Qaeda–related terrorist crimes since September 11 have been U.S. citizens.

The proxies of Arab or Muslim identity or nationality are so inexact and overbroad that virtually all of those questioned, registered, or detained have proven to be innocent of any terrorist activity. Locking up several thousand people with no connection to terrorism is hardly a cost-effective way to improve security. What's more, the predominance of false positives that result when such dragnet tactics are used will inevitably induce investigators to drop their guard and to be less attentive to those few who truly warrant attention.[7] There is simply no reason to think that any of the administration's profiling initiatives would have identified the September 11 hijackers from the hundreds of thousands of other Arab and Muslim residents of the United States.

Guilt by association, a second key tactic in the administration's domestic war on terrorism, also encourages poor policing. Consider a snapshot from the FBI's counterterrorism investigation of the group of students known as the LA 8, discussed in the previous chapter. One of the things the students did was organize annual dinners for the Palestinian community. These events, called *haflis,* were common throughout the Palestinian diaspora. The Los Angeles dinners were widely publicized and open to the public. As many as 1,000 people attended, including many families and children. The events featured Palestinian culture and politics, including traditional food, music, dancing, and political speeches. At the close of the evening there was generally a charitable fund-raising pitch to support the humanitarian needs of those who still lived under occupation or in Palestinian refugee camps. Suspecting that these events might be raising funds for terrorism, FBI agents attended one, and afterward reported as follows:

> The Federal Agents observing the fund raiser did not speak or understand the Arabic language, however, from the posters of Palestinians with AK-47 assaults [sic] rifles and the general mood or tone of the speeches, the agents realized that the PFLP [Popular Front for the Liberation of Palestine] was not attempting to raise money for a humanitarian cause. The music and entire mood of the fund raiser from the entrance ceremony through the speeches sounded militaristic.[8]

The fact that the FBI agent sent to the event could not even speak Arabic illustrates what happens when authorities proceed under a philosophy of guilt by association. If association alone establishes guilt, the difficult work of identifying actual criminal or terrorist activity becomes unnecessary. The FBI never sought to trace the money raised at these events, which was donated to a registered charitable organization in San Francisco for medical and humanitarian aid, to determine whether a single penny actually furthered terrorism or any other illegal purpose. Instead, its agents devoted their time to the easier but less effective tasks of collecting political propaganda, monitoring demonstrations, tracking the distribution of Palestinian magazines, and drawing inferences from the "general mood or tone" of speeches and music they did not understand. In the end, as noted above, the FBI concluded that it had no evidence that any of the individuals had committed any criminal or terrorist activity, but nonetheless urged the INS to deport them for their associations.

Ashcroft's preventive detention campaign raises similar concerns about wasting resources on the innocent and settling for sloppy policing. FBI Special Agent Coleen Rowley, who first made news when she publicly castigated the Bureau for failing to authorize a search of Zacarias Moussaoui's computer, criticized the post–September 11 roundup in a February 2003 letter to FBI Director Robert Mueller:

> The vast majority of the one thousand plus persons "detained" in the wake of 9-11 did not turn out to be terrorists. They were mostly illegal aliens. We have every right, of course, to deport those identified as illegal aliens during the course of any investigation. But after 9-11, Headquarters encouraged more and more detentions for what seem to be essentially PR purposes. Field offices were required to report daily the number of detentions in order to supply grist for statements on our progress in fighting terrorism. The balance between individuals' civil liberties and the need for effective investigation is hard to maintain even during so-called normal times, let alone times of increased terrorist threat or war. It is, admittedly, a difficult balancing act. But from what I have observed, particular vigilance may be required to head off undue pressure (including subtle encouragement) to detain or "round up" suspects particularly those of Arabic origin.[9]

Inspector General Glenn Fine confirmed Rowley's complaints, finding that the Justice Department had detained over 700 foreign nationals on immigration charges, not one of whom was ever charged with terrorism.[10] As Kenneth Elwood, a senior immigration official brought to Washington to oversee the detention campaign, later admitted, "After September 11 there were people arrested who had no business being arrested." Elwood tells of challenging another senior official about the overbreadth of the campaign and insisting to him that the INS "not abandon the Constitution in this crisis." The official's response: "Fuck the Constitution!"[11]

According to eight former high-level FBI officials, including former FBI and CIA director William Webster, the administration may well have compromised security by arresting so many individuals prematurely, before further intelligence could be obtained on their connections, conduct, and associations to determine whether they in fact posed any threat. In counterintelligence and counterterrorism investigations, it is generally preferable to keep suspects under close surveillance rather than to arrest them immediately. Premature arrests may tip off other associates, limit authorities' knowledge of the full scope of the plan, and handicap a criminal trial by foregoing valuable evidence. Surveillance and infiltration, by contrast, may reveal further connections, conspiracies, and evidence that provide a better picture of the threat posed and a better case if criminal charges are ultimately pursued. As William Webster said, effective terrorism investigations are generally long-term and use wiretaps, informants, and undercover operations "so when you roll up the cell, you know you've got the whole group." The risk in arresting early, Webster continued, is that "you may interrupt something, but you may not be able to bring it down. You may not be able to stop what is going on." [12]

The sense of urgency prompted by the attacks of September 11 and the fear that further attacks might follow fast on their heels understandably led officials to err on the side of prevention; the Justice Department presumably felt that it did not have the luxury to adopt a "wait and watch" approach where suspected terrorists were concerned. But as the former FBI officials argue, and the numbers bear out, ethnically based mass sweeps are simply not an effective preventive measure. As of May 2003, only three of the 1,200 "suspected terrorists" arrested in the first seven weeks, and none of the nearly 4,000 more foreign nationals arrested since under related antiterrorism initiatives, turned out to warrant even a *charge* of terrorist-related criminal activity. Attempts to develop better intelligence before detaining could hardly have been less successful.

The utility of other key antiterrorism strategies also seems questionable. Kenneth Walton, former FBI assistant director and leader of the first Joint Anti-Terrorism Task Force in New York City, criticized the Justice Department's program of interviewing thousands of Arab and Muslim immigrant men: "It's the Perry Mason School of Law Enforcement, where you get them in there and they confess. Well, it just doesn't work that way. It is ridiculous. You say, 'Tell me everything you know," and they give you the recipe to Mom's chicken soup."[13] Several months after the interview program, former FBI counterterrorism expert Dale Watson admitted to a Senate Intelligence Committee that the FBI had not discovered any further Al Qaeda cells.[14] A General Accounting Office study in April 2003 found that over half of the law enforcement officers involved "expressed concerns about . . . the value of the responses obtained in the interview project."[15] Similarly, the government's special registration program, which requires male foreign nationals from twenty-five countries to register and be fingerprinted and photographed, is unlikely to develop significant leads. Those who are here illegally are unlikely to turn themselves in voluntarily just because the government has called them in. And if the government is correct that Al Qaeda sleepers lead quiet, unassuming, and law-abiding lives until the call to attack comes, authorities wouldn't know an Al Qaeda cell member if he walked in and shook their hands. Meanwhile, both the interview and registration initiatives have sharply alienated the communities law enforcement authorities should be most eager to work with in the war on terrorism.

LOSING LEGITIMACY

From a security standpoint, the most significant problem with the administration's heavy reliance on double standards is that it undermines the legitimacy of its antiterrorism campaign. As everyone who has ever played a leadership role—from parents to police to presidents—knows, legitimacy is authority's most powerful tool. A leader who is viewed as legitimate will find compliance with his or her wishes much more forthcoming than a leader who has forfeited legitimacy. Lacking legitimacy, authorities must resort to increasingly heavy-handed tactics, which in turn only further undermine their legitimacy. As social scientists (and all parents) have found, legitimacy depends on procedural fairness, especially consistency and equal treatment.[16] The government's decision to impose burdens selectively on the fundamental rights of foreign nationals, and especially on Arab and Muslim foreign nationals, sacrifices the legitimacy of its under-taking, and has costly implications for security at home and abroad.

At home, let us grant the Justice Department's suspicion that there are terrorist threats living among us, and that, given what we know about the makeup of Al Qaeda, they are likely to be Arab and Muslim foreign nationals. The challenge for law enforcement is how to iden-tify the resident enemy. Al Qaeda members don't carry membership cards. The "sleeper cell" phenomenon makes the problem of identifi-cation and prevention all the more daunting. And many Muslim im-migrants lead relatively separate and unassimilated lives, making it more difficult for non-Muslim FBI agents to engage their communi-ties or even to understand social and cultural cues.

Ashcroft's dragnet approach has targeted tens of thousands of Arabs and Muslims for registration, interviews, mass arrests, depor-tation, and automatic detention, effectively treating an entire, overwhelmingly law-abiding community as suspect. Such broad mea-sures deeply alienate the targeted communities, making them far less likely to assist law enforcement efforts to identify the actual perpetra-tors. (This is not to suggest that otherwise law-abiding individuals will knowingly protect and hide terrorists, but that the kind of routine information and connections that are so critical to identifying actual criminals and terrorists will be significantly less forthcoming.) In this regard, one of the leading Arab spokespersons in the United States, James Zogby, director of the Arab-American Institute, found himself in rare agreement with a former FBI counterterrorism chief, both of whom predicted that the Justice Department's plan to interview thou-sands of Arab immigrant men would backfire precisely because of the enmity it would create between law enforcement and the Arab com-munity.[17] Vincent Cannistraro, former head of counterterrorism at the CIA, also criticized the interview plan on similar grounds, stating that it "alienates the very community whose cooperation you need to get good intelligence."[18] These criticisms are borne out in the experi-ences of specific communities. According to an article in *Newsday,* for example, the government's sweeping and heavy-handed treatment of

Muslims in Paterson, New Jersey, transformed that community in a matter of months after September 11 "from willing allies to wary adversaries."[19]

A better way to identify terrorists would be to elicit the relevant communities' affirmative assistance. In criminal law enforcement, police have long recognized the importance of maintaining the public's trust, and have accordingly prioritized "community policing," which seeks to develop positive relationships between the public and the police. In particular, community policing is based on a recognition that those who live within a community are likely to have a better sense of where the problems lie than police officers who are often not themselves part of the community they patrol. Building positive ties promotes trust, which in turn facilitates information sharing between members of the public and the police.

One critical way to break down barriers is to employ members of the targeted community as law enforcement personnel. While by no means a panacea, the presence in the ranks of law enforcement of individuals from targeted communities can open pathways of communication and trust, as well as help law enforcement understand those communities' needs and problems. Such translation and communication is especially important where communities are relatively insular. Without it, the task of differentiating people who pose true threats from others who merely appear different to an outsider is daunting— as the Justice Department's astoundingly low hit rate in locking up "suspected terrorists" has shown.

In choosing dragnet enforcement over forging links with the Arab and Muslim communities, John Ashcroft admittedly confronted a problem not of his own making. The federal government's treatment of Arabs and Muslims *before* September 11 had already created substantial distrust. As illustrated in the preceding chapter, in the 1980s and 1990s, Arab and Muslim political activists found themselves the subject of intrusive investigations by the FBI and of draconian immigration enforcement actions by the INS. The *only* noncitizens expressly targeted for deportation for their political associations were

Arab and Muslim political activists. Virtually all the victims of "secret evidence" were Arab and Muslim. At the same time, there was virtually no representation of Arabs or Muslims in federal law enforcement agencies. As late as 1998, the FBI had only two Arabic translators.[20] On September 11, 2001, the Justice Department's Civil Rights Division employed only two lawyers of Arab descent.[21] So when September 11 happened, the Justice Department was not starting with a clean slate.

Ashcroft's mistake was that he failed to take advantage of a critical opportunity afforded by September 11 to mend relations between these communities and federal law enforcement. He could have used the widely shared shock and revulsion at the attacks to build bridges to Arabs and Muslims, seeking their help in identifying any perpetrators that might reside among them. Such positive outreach, coupled with incentives for assistance, might well have proven far more effective—and could hardly have been *less* effective—than the Ashcroft dragnet, which thus far has yielded not a single person charged with involvement in the September 11 attacks and only a few persons charged with any terrorist-related crimes whatsoever, while generating substantial outrage in the targeted communities.

The Justice Department has undertaken some limited initiatives along these lines. On November 29, 2001, it announced the "Responsible Cooperators Program," through which it would award S-6 class visas, granting a form of legal resident status, to persons who provided information that led to the capture of a terrorist.[22] But this announcement came too late in the day, after the administration had already burned its bridges, and accordingly was met with strong skepticism. In addition, S-visas are likely to appeal most to foreign nationals here in violation of their immigration status, but the Justice Department's simultaneous campaign of aggressively detaining and deporting Arabs and Muslims with any immigration problem chilled cooperation. The fact that the government had detained even people who had come forward voluntarily with information about suspected terrorists only further undermined incentives for cooperation. As the spokesman for the American-Arab Anti-Discrimination Committee,

Hussein Ibish, observed when the S-6 visa program was announced, "This inducement pales in comparison to the disincentive for cooperation that has been offered by the fact that any immigrant found to be even slightly out of status is detained without bond." [23] In the first full year that the program was in existence, not a single S-6 visa for terrorist information was awarded. [24]

In another salutary but belated move, the FBI field offices in Washington, D.C., and Fort Lauderdale, Florida, formed Arab American Advisory Committees in March 2003 aimed at improving relations between the agency and Arab communities. [25] Arab leaders initiated a similar committee in Detroit shortly after September 11 that still meets monthly. These committees are an important step in the right direction, but the Justice Department should have taken the initiative to set them up in Arab and Muslim communities across the country immediately after September 11; to be first doing so in Washington, D.C., a year and a half after the attacks, is inexcusable. And if they are to work, such committees must be treated by the government as more than window-dressing. When I suggested another initiative to a high-level Justice Department official in March 2003 as a way to repair relations with the Arab and Muslim communities, he scoffed at the notion that *anything* could mend the breach at that point.

There is a real danger that Ashcroft's approach will have a downward spiraling effect, as discriminatory treatment breeds greater distrust, requiring more and more broad-brush measures, which will in turn only increase the chasm between law enforcement and the Arab and Muslim communities. As former Deputy Attorney General and Harvard Law Professor Philip Heymann has noted, police in Northern Ireland used internment and custodial interrogation "rather than traditional policing (such as gathering physical evidence or questioning suspects at home or on the street) because communities in Northern Ireland were hostile or intimidating." But the very practice of custodial interrogation, applied discriminatorily to Irish Catholics, only further alienated the population and stimulated IRA recruitment. [26]

Sacrificing legitimacy is also counterproductive in the international arena, where sensitivity to double standards selectively denying foreign nationals' rights is likely to be highest. It is in Osama bin Laden's interest, not ours, to portray the struggle as pitting the United States against Arabs and Muslims. The more we act in ways that support that image, the more likely bin Laden or others will be able to attract adherents to their terrorist cause. Anti-Americanism is at an all-time high.[27] The Bush administration's unilateralism abroad and double standards at home are two sides of the same coin; they both reflect an attitude that the United States need not be governed by the same standards and rules that apply to everyone else. In foreign affairs, we eschew international treaties and international law whenever it is in our interest to do so, even as we maintain that others must be bound by such obligations. So, too, in matters of individual rights, we deny to other nations' citizens the very protections that we insist upon for ourselves. This exceptionalism feeds the view that the United States exploits its status as the world's most powerful nation with arrogance and self-interest, and is virtually certain to spawn new recruits to the causes mobilized against us.

In addition to inspiring recruits for the opposition, double standards impede the international cooperation essential to identifying and capturing those who are already plotting against us. Our military effort may have driven Al Qaeda out of Afghanistan, but the organization apparently survives in a more diffuse form in cells spread across the world. Satellite and aerial surveillance are unlikely to help us find them; human intelligence is our best hope.[28] Because so much critical intelligence will be in foreign hands, we need to foster strong bonds of trust with foreign governments.[29] For these reasons, Paul Pillar, former deputy chief of the CIA's Counterterrorism Center, argues that close cooperation with foreign intelligence services is the most important tool in the war on terrorism.[30] But trust and cooperation are compromised when we impose on foreign nationals, and especially Arab and Muslim foreign nationals, burdens that we do not impose on ourselves. The willingness of members of the international community to cooperate with us by providing intelligence and law enforcement support will turn at least in part on the extent to which we are fighting for a broad principle of justice, rather than for our own parochial self-interest.

Our reliance on double standards has generated widespread foreign criticism. Voices in foreign government and the foreign media alike have sharply criticized the detention of noncitizens, both in Guantánamo Bay and on American soil; the decision to authorize trial of noncitizens in military tribunals; and the sweeping discriminatory treatment of foreign nationals from Arab and Muslim countries. A Pakistani newspaper argued that "the U.S.-led 'war on terrorism' is fast degenerating into a war against Muslims at the collective and individual levels." [31] The Cairo-based *Middle East Times* reported that "Although terrorism is hardly a crime committed only by Muslims, the U.S. war on terrorism is focused solely on Muslims and Muslim countries." [32] In England, *The Guardian* characterized the government's plan to interview male foreign nationals from Arab and Muslim countries as "a new kind of racial profiling which the U.S. government applies but denies." [33] London and Paris newspapers and Iranian radio all criticized the decision to subject only foreign nationals to military tribunals. [34] When the United States announced that it would try U.S. citizen John Walker Lindh in an ordinary civilian court, *The Independent* in London warned that "[a]n effective campaign against terrorism requires the support, not just of Arab and Muslim countries, but of many other countries in the developing world which are quick to sniff out Western hypocrisy. If the alleged terrorists detained in Guantánamo Bay are denied democratic standards of justice or treated inhumanely, the campaign will be seriously damaged." [35]

Foreign governments have also complained. By November 2001 at least seven nations had complained that the Justice Department's domestic preventive detention campaign had held their nationals longer than warranted and had failed to inform the embassies upon taking their foreign nationals into custody, as required by international law. [36] The Deputy Consul General for Turkey, Sedat Onan, expressed concern regarding the detention of forty-three Turkish citizens, complaining that "Turkey is one of the strongest and most loyal allies of the United States. Our citizens are being treated like common criminals."[37] Pakistani Vice Consul Irfan Ahmed warned that the United States' discriminatory actions are "helping to sow the seeds of hatred in the Pakistani community against the U.S. government."[38] Senior officials from our traditional allies—Canada, Great Britain, the Netherlands, France, and Germany—have all objected to the treatment of the Guantánamo Bay detainees.[39] According to one news report, "some foreign governments argue that the conditions in Guantánamo are so improper as to undermine the moral authority of the campaign against al-Qaeda."[40] In May 2003, Secretary of State Colin Powell wrote a letter to Defense Secretary Donald Rumsfeld warning that the Guantánamo detentions were generating constant complaints from some of our most important allies in the war on terrorism.[41]

The Justice Department's special registration program, which selectively imposes registration requirements on male foreign nationals from twenty-five countries, almost all Arab or Muslim, has generated especially strong criticism. When the program was initially proposed, in June 2002, Agence France Press reported that it was "perceived as an attack on Arab communities."[42] The largest-circulation daily in Pakistan editorialized that it "reflects a generally contemptuous and discriminatory attitude toward Muslims," and warned that "pursuing a discriminatory policy . . . will add to the already existing resentment against the US in the whole of the Muslim world . . . [and] creat[e] new enemies for the US."[43] A Saudi newspaper editorial echoed that concern, arguing that "Washington may deny it but American officialdom now apparently thinks that Muslims and Arabs are genetically predisposed to violence," and predicted that the program "will further injure America's image and interests in the Muslim and Arab world."[44] The most widely circulated daily in Jordan wrote that "the recent measures have come to . . . eliminate international support for the war against terrorism, and make the Arabs and Muslims a new target, thereby threatening their interests and rights in the United States and the world."[45] Among others, Pakistani, Saudi, Iranian, Armenian, and Malaysian authorities have all vocally criticized the United States' placement of their nations on the list, and have echoed complaints in the press that these measures undermine the war on terrorism by deepening the divide between the United States and Muslims; Armenians complained sufficiently loudly that the United States actually removed them from the list, but thus far no other country has been so successful.[46]

These criticisms are dismissed at our peril. As Professor Oren Gross and others have argued, the greatest threat that terrorists pose to a democratic state is not to its physical survival, but to what one might call the survival of principle.[47] Gross argues that the terrorists aim to provoke the state into (over)reacting in ways that violate its own principles, and thereby undermine the state's legitimacy and create sympathy for those allied with the terrorists.[48] Many have argued that Great Britain's extreme and discriminatory measures against the Irish Republican Army (IRA)—in particular, internment without charges and coerced confessions—had precisely that effect, inspiring greater support for the IRA.[49]

President Bush's efforts to reach out to Arabs and Muslims in the days immediately following September 11 with public statements that we are not at war with Islam, as well as by including a Muslim cleric in the national memorial service for September 11 victims, seemed to recognize the danger of casting the war on terror as a war of cultures. Yet the government's actions have run contrary to its words. While the president urged that we not treat Arabs and Muslims as suspect based on their ethnic or religious identity, his administration's policies have done exactly that.

WHAT CAN BE DONE

If law enforcement should not target Arab and Muslim foreign nationals in the ways I have criticized, what can be done to make the United States more secure? First, it is important to acknowledge that no combination of measures will ever eliminate the threat of politically motivated violence. This phenomenon has been with us since time immemorial, and cannot wholly be eliminated, even by the toughest security measures imaginable. In this regard, if President Bush is correct that the war on terrorism will not end until "every terrorist group of global reach has been found, stopped, and defeated," it literally will never end.[50] As Tom Ridge, head of Homeland Security, has said, the scope of the undertaking is daunting: "Airports, borders, development of partnerships with the state and local governments, mapping critical infrastructure with the private sector, focusing on cybersecurity, developing plans to enhance our capacity to respond to weapons of mass destruction, enhancement of our public infrastructure—I mean it is an endless list."[51] So endless that *Atlantic Monthly* writer David Carr has argued, only slightly hyperbolically, that "homeland security is the national version of the gas mask in the desk drawer—something that lets people feel safer without actually making them so."[52] Carr quantifies:

> In 2000 more than 350 million non–U.S. citizens entered the country. In 1999 Americans made 5.2 billion phone calls to locations outside the country. Federal Express handles nearly five million packages every business day, UPS accounts for 13.6 million, and until it became a portal for terror, the Postal Service processed 680 million pieces of mail a day. More than two billion tons of cargo ran in and out of U.S. ports in 1999 . . .[53]

Weapons of mass destruction could be smuggled into the country relatively easily in a cargo container, yet before September 11 only 2 percent of all containers coming into the country were actually inspected, and we do not have the means to increase that percentage substantially.[54] In addition, as drug smugglers have shown, a few well-placed bribes can defeat virtually any inspection scheme.[55] One need only walk down any Manhattan street in rush hour to see that if terrorists decide to turn on us the suicide bombing tactics that Palestinians have employed in Israel, there will be little we can do to stop them.

This is not to say that we should throw up our hands. While no measures can guarantee absolute security, we can be made safer. But at the same time, we must accept the reality that we have to live with a certain amount of risk. As former National Security Council (NSC) officials Daniel Benjamin and Steven Simon caution, "Technology and better information sharing within the United States government and between the United States and other countries can improve the probability of finding the needle in the haystack from zero to 'just maybe.' "[56]

A range of steps can be taken to make us more secure without compromising our basic principles. Virtually everyone agrees that better information sharing within the federal government, with other nations, and with state and local authorities, is essential.[57] By most accounts, however, the barriers to information sharing prior to September 11 were more bureaucratic than legal in nature, so amending laws will not solve the problem. The FBI reportedly used legal arguments to rationalize its reluctance to share information with others, but the source of the reluctance was principally Bureau culture, not law.[58] The PATRIOT Act removed legal barriers to sharing information obtained through grand jury investigations, but that does not begin to address the deeper forces of Bureau culture at work. In April 2003, more than a year and a half after the September 11 attacks, both the General Accounting Office and the Police Executive Research Forum issued reports finding that federal agencies were still failing to share critical information about terrorist suspects.[59]

Similarly, the FBI's problem internally was not so much that it was legally hamstrung by restrictions on its investigatory powers as that it was disorganized and decentralized, and did not sufficiently reward intelligence analysis as compared to more traditional law enforcement tasks. As Benjamin and Simon write, "New York doesn't talk to Headquarters. Headquarters doesn't talk to itself. Operations doesn't talk to the analysts as compared to more traditional law enforcement tasks. Field offices don't talk to each other . . . From the inside, the FBI was a disorganized jumble of competing and unruly power centers; from the outside it was a surly colossus."[60] These problems require changes in institutional culture and organization, not an expansion of investigative authority.

There is no question that coordination is essential to effective enforcement. While there are arguably advantages to be gained from multiple agencies and agents competing to solve the same problem, the compartmentalization that characterized our pre–September 11 approach plainly impeded security.[61] Shortly before September 11, for example, the CIA placed two of the September 11 hijackers on a terrorist watch list, and shared that information with the FBI. The FBI, however, did not seek the assistance of the State Department or the INS in locating the two men. Both agencies claim they might well have been able to find the men if asked.[62]

Information sharing is also essential to intelligence analysis. National security intelligence is carried out by multiple federal entities, including the FBI, the CIA, the National Security Agency, the Defense Intelligence Agency, and the State Department's Bureau of Intelligence and Research (INR). Connecting the dots requires that all of these agencies communicate effectively with each other, freely sharing information. Yet there have long been significant barriers to such coordination. Efforts to facilitate that process are far more likely to pay off in security terms than simply authorizing government officials to gather more raw data.

Most important, however, information sharing and analysis is only as good as the information upon which it is based. Improving relations with those communities thought to have access to the most useful information, as well as to individuals with sufficient ties to and familiarity with the communities to be able to understand, interpret, and identify relevant information, cannot be underestimated. This need only underscores the importance of the community relations that Ashcroft's strategy has poisoned rather than fostered.

As virtually all assessments of the government's failure to detect and prevent the September 11 attacks have concluded, the principal problem was not the government's lack of legal authority for gathering information, but its failure to analyze the massive troves of data it had.[63] As so many have said, the government did not "connect the dots." Some of this criticism is unfair; it is always easier to see connections in hindsight than as events are developing. But if the problem is that the government failed to analyze the information it had, sweeping initiatives that will inundate authorities with still more irrelevant information are not likely to provide a solution. The difficulty is that there are already too many extraneous dots. As a Markle Foundation Task Force comprised of national security and technology experts found, "Those who have called for endless mining of vast new government data warehouses are not offering the promise of real security. They instead evoke memories of the walls of clippings collected by the paranoid genius, John Nash, in *A Beautiful Mind.*"[64]

For this reason, freeing the FBI from the requirement that it limit its investigations to individuals and groups presenting some basis for concern about criminal activity—or, for that matter, creating a separate domestic intelligence agency along the lines of Great Britain's MI5—is unlikely to make us safer. The minimal requirement that the FBI's activities have some connection to federal crime serves to focus the agency on those who pose the greatest threat, and to forestall the expenditure of scarce resources on individuals and groups with neither an intention nor a capacity to commit a federal crime. This was hardly an onerous threshold. Pre–September 11 law did not require anything like probable cause to justify investigations. A preliminary inquiry could be instituted where there was any credible indication of concern about criminal activity. Contrary to popular wisdom, the FBI was never prohibited from investigating groups that had not yet engaged in criminal activity, and could always investigate as long as there was some basis for believing that they had the potential to do so.[65]

Another important initiative that can make us safer without infringing on civil liberties would be to limit the threat posed by access to weapons of mass destruction. As Jessica Stern, former NSC official and author of *The Ultimate Terrorist,* has argued, it is essential that we help secure vulnerable stockpiles of nuclear weapons and weapons components, especially those in the former Soviet Union; that we shore up security measures in the states of the former Soviet Union to forestall smuggling, theft, or sale of such weapons; and that we do much more to prepare for attacks with chemical and biological weapons or industrial poisons. With respect to the latter, Stern argues, it is probably impossible to prevent their entry into the United States, but many lives can be saved if emergency responders are better prepared to detect the attacks at an early stage, and to take prompt protective measures to treat victims and to limit the spread of harmful viruses or pathogens.[66]

Other responses to the dangers posed by weapons of mass destruction do present constitutional concerns, but may nonetheless be warranted. Prohibitions on the publication of information about how to build such weapons may be justified, even though they would restrict speech not necessarily intended and likely to incite illegal conduct (the usual standard for prohibiting advocacy of criminal conduct). It is difficult to see what value such publications add to the "marketplace of ideas" that the First Amendment is designed to protect, and the dangers they present grow exponentially with each technological advance. Similarly, efforts to restrict widespread public access to information about the vulnerabilities of critical infrastructure, such as water and energy supplies, Internet and communication networks, and nuclear power plants, make a great deal of sense, even though they also may have the effect of hampering access to that information for legitimate purposes. Because such prohibitions do not target any particularly vulnerable minority, and affect the informational rights of us all, one can be more sanguine that the political process will ensure that the infringements are appropriately circumscribed.

More broadly, we need to think about protecting potential targets of terrorism through limitations on access, metal detectors, concrete barriers, and the like. These measures create inconvenience for many in the name of creating inconvenience for terrorists, but the American public is likely to accept a fair amount of inconvenience if it will make us more safe. Strengthening cockpit doors and placing air marshals on planes are far more likely to deter another terrorist hijacking than ethnic profiling, and do not rely on a double standard or sacrifice constitutional rights. The sheer number of potential targets in the United States, and the wide variety of ways in which attacks might be launched, makes total target protection a fantasy. But the fact that total protection is impossible should not stop us from doing what we can, at least with respect to the most vulnerable targets.

Increased border control and information-gathering about foreign nationals is also not an unreasonable step toward security. There are legitimate questions about how effective the collection of such data will be—it may simply further inundate analysts with still more undigested and largely useless information. Still, constitutional concerns are presented not by registration in general, but only by its selective targeting at foreign nationals only from twenty-five largely Arab and Muslim countries. If registration were implemented across the board, and designed to permit more informed decisions about which foreign nationals are permitted to enter and to remain here, one could not quarrel with it from a civil liberties standpoint.

There is also nothing inherently wrong with pretextual law enforcement as a means for fighting terrorism. No one begrudges the government prosecuting mobster Al Capone for tax evasion, even though it was widely known that the reason the government wanted Capone was his suspected involvement in crimes far worse than failing to pay his fair share. Moreover, prosecuting (or deporting) on a lesser charge may be the most sensible course where proving a more serious charge would require revealing an undercover source that may still be providing useful information. But the discretion that pretextual law enforcement affords the government to go after "bad guys" is also discretion to go after individuals whom the government deems suspicious for their speech, associations, or ethnic or religious identity. And because few people are so confident that they could never be prosecuted for anything, a policy of pretextual law enforcement has a widespread chilling effect on dissent. Where the government is engaged in pretextual law enforcement, for example, a lawyer cannot in good conscience advise any client that he should feel free to speak and associate as he wishes so long as he obeys the law. Many Arabs and

Muslims in the United States today palpably feel chilled from speaking or associating freely, because even fully protected speech or associations might spark a prosecution or deportation on other charges.

Pretextual law enforcement is therefore both potentially useful, when motivated by legitimate concerns, as in the prosecution of Al Capone, and potentially dangerous, when motivated by political, religious, racial, or ethnic bias. Motive is the dividing line between legitimate and illegitimate uses of pretextual law enforcement. In theory, "selective prosecution" doctrine holds that a prosecution motivated by race, gender, ethnicity, religion, speech, or association is unconstitutional. But in practice, selective prosecution has always been a largely illusory defense, defined in doctrinal terms that make it extremely difficult to establish absent an overt admission of discrimination.[67] And in its 1999 decision in the LA 8 case, *Reno v. American-Arab Anti-Discrimination Comm.*, the Supreme Court went out of its way to state in dicta that selective prosecution, except in rare occasions not delimited by the Court, is not a defense to deportation at all.[68] The lower courts had unanimously found that the INS had selectively targeted the LA 8 for their protected political activities and associations, yet the Supreme Court appeared wholly untroubled by such targeting.

Because the lion's share of Ashcroft's pretextual law enforcement campaign has been pursued in the deportation setting, it is not clear that selective enforcement is even an available defense. As a result, Arab and Muslim foreign nationals with any possible immigration problem are well advised to do nothing—such as speaking out, demonstrating, or joining political associations—that might bring them to the attention of the federal government. Courts must provide greater oversight of selective prosecution claims when preventive law enforcement is the order of the day. While pretextual law enforcement is an important tool in the war on terrorism, it needs to be checked by more stringent judicial review for impermissible motives if it is not to have severe negative repercussions on civil liberties.

In developing security responses to the terrorist threat, government should be open to engaging in dialogue with interest groups that advocate on behalf of civil liberties and human rights, from the ACLU to the American-Arab Anti-Discrimination Committee and Human Rights Watch. For reasons discussed earlier, government officials have little incentive to pay attention to civil liberties concerns, especially when measures are concentrated on a vulnerable minority group without a voice in the political process. Involving the groups that make it their job to be concerned about such interests would at least bring that perspective into the room. When the PATRIOT Act was being considered, the House and Senate Judiciary Committees held hearings on civil liberties concerns only after the details of the bill had already been worked out in the respective houses. Government should not be afraid to hear the concerns of those whose rights and liberties it is planning to sacrifice. Hearing such voices does not mean that it must heed their every desire, but it may moderate official policy by identifying legitimate concerns on the other side of the balance.

Finally, it is important not to make the mistake of focusing exclusively on law enforcement and intelligence measures. Security is affected by a wide variety of domestic and foreign policies and actions. As the longstanding, terror-ridden conflicts in Great Britain and Israel painfully illustrate, nations cannot simply police themselves out of politically motivated violence. Israel has cracked down on civil liberties in ways that at least thus far still seem unimaginable in the United States, and yet it continues to be plagued by a seemingly unstoppable stream of terrorist violence. Great Britain only saw a significant decrease in terrorist violence arising out of the conflict over Northern Ireland when it agreed to negotiate a peace settlement with the Irish Republican Army. If we are to reduce the extent of terrorist violence aimed at us, we must consider the root causes of that terror, and seek ways to address it.

We cannot negotiate a peace settlement with Al Qaeda, nor should we appease terrorists. But we must recognize that the seeds of political violence thrive in discontent and despair over real and perceived injustices and inequities, and that our own policies can contribute to or ameliorate those conditions. Thus, for example, two of Osama bin

Laden's biggest recruiting pitches focus on the stationing of United States troops in Saudi Arabia, an Islamic holy land, and the United States's role in supporting Israel's occupation of Palestine. To its credit, the Bush administration has announced that it plans to withdraw most of the troops from Saudi Arabia. President Clinton expended tremendous energy seeking to broker a Middle East peace settlement respecting Israel's security and Palestinians' self-determination, but the Bush administration needs to redouble those efforts. These initiatives are likely to be more critical to ensuring security from terrorism than registering, deporting, and detaining thousands of Arabs and Muslims with no connection to terrorism.

More significantly still, we need to do much more to reduce the massive inequalities in global resources from which we inordinately benefit. As Professor Avishai Margalit has argued, the roots of Islamic fundamentalism lie in the truly desperate situations that face the vast majority of young people in the Islamic world.[69] He argues that there are two ways of dealing with the "explosive gap" between the bleak prospects they face and the "sense of a glittering life elsewhere" communicated by television, movies, and the Internet: "enhance the economic prospects of people in the Islamic world and work for a better life for them," or "change people's expectations of life by changing their notion of what constitutes the good life" through religious ideology. By failing to do much toward the former, we create a vacuum for Islamic fundamentalism to do the latter. We are the richest nation in the world, yet we are dead last in terms of the amount of foreign aid we dole out to other nations as a percentage of gross national income.[70]

Finally, and directly related to our exploitation of double standards at home, our security is likely to be furthered in the long run by a commitment to the rule of law at home and abroad. The rule of law generally furthers stability and peace. "American exceptionalism" at home and abroad poses a direct and serious threat to the rule of law. If the most powerful nation in the world refuses to be bound by the rules, it frees up other nations to adopt similar attitudes. And that development will almost certainly increase the grounds for discontent and desperation among those who lack the power to play by their own rules. There are no silver bullets. But if we are to respond effectively to terrorism, we must not limit ourselves to increasing our police and military capabilities, but must also address the underlying inequalities that sow the seeds for politically motivated violence directed our way.

The events of September 11 have for good reason prompted wide-spread concern about the United States' ability to predict and prevent future terrorist attacks. That concern may well justify recalibrating the balance between liberty and security. But when we seek to strike that balance by selectively denying the fundamental rights of foreign nationals, and especially foreign nationals of Arab and Muslim identity, we undermine security by simultaneously creating more enemies and losing the assistance and cooperation of potential friends.

As I acknowledged at the outset, determinations about the effectiveness of various programs are necessarily speculative. Neither security officials nor their critics can say with certainty that a particular measure has made us safer or has exacerbated the dangers that we face. Rough judgments are the best we can do. The argument of this book does not turn on a claim that every double standard will necessarily make us less safe. Some of the measures that I have criticized may well make us safer. Laws aimed at denying financial support to organizations that engage in terrorism, for example, are likely to hinder those organizations' ability to do evil, even as they also hinder many people's rights to do good. Locking people up in secret might deny Al Qaeda useful information, and interrogating individuals without lawyers is almost certain to result in more confessions than would be obtained with lawyers present. And relaxing the threshold requirements for searches and surveillance may lead to the discovery of evidence that would have otherwise eluded detection.

I do not deny, in other words, that some of the measures adopted since September 11 may well have made us safer. My point is that when the government relies so heavily on double standards to strike the balance between liberty and security, its loss of legitimacy among persons, communities, and nations potentially our partners in the

PART 4
THE RIGHT THING TO DO

14. THE BILL OF RIGHTS AS HUMAN RIGHTS

And if a stranger sojourn with thee in your land, ye shall not vex him. But the stranger that dwelleth with you shall be unto you as one born among you, and thou shalt love him as thyself.

LEVITICUS 19:33–34 KING JAMES

Anyone who lives inside the United States can never be considered an outsider anywhere in this country.

DR. MARTIN LUTHER KING, JR.,
LETTER FROM THE BIRMINGHAM JAIL

One of the most common responses to criticism of the way foreign nationals have been treated in the war on terrorism is to assert, as Vice President Cheney did about the military tribunal order, that foreign nationals do not deserve the same rights as American citizens. That response strikes a chord with the widely shared assumption that citizenship makes a difference, and that the difference warrants the distinct treatment that foreign nationals receive. But are foreign nationals entitled only to reduced rights and freedoms? The difficulty of the question is reflected in the deeply ambivalent approach of the Supreme Court, an ambivalence matched only by the alternately xenophobic and xenophilic attitude of the American public toward immigrants. On the one hand, the Court has insisted for more than a century that foreign nationals living among us are "persons" within the meaning of the Constitution, and are protected by all those rights that the Constitution does not expressly reserve to citizens. Because the Constitution expressly limits to citizens only the rights to vote and to run for federal elective office, equality between non-nationals and citizens appears to be the constitutional rule.

On the other hand, the Court has stated that with respect to immigration, "Congress regularly makes rules that would be unacceptable if applied to citizens," and the Court has just as regularly found those rules acceptable for noncitizens.[1] The Supreme Court has permitted foreign nationals to be excluded and expelled because of their race.[2] It has allowed them to be deported for political associations that were entirely lawful at the time they were engaged in.[3] It has upheld laws barring foreign nationals from owning land, even where the laws were a transparent cover for anti-Japanese racism.[4] It has permitted the indefinite detention of "arriving aliens" stopped at the border on the basis of secret evidence that they could not confront.[5] And it has allowed states to bar otherwise qualified foreign nationals from employment as public school teachers and police officers, based solely on their status as foreigners.[6]

Given this record, it is not surprising that many members of the general public presume that noncitizens do not deserve the same rights as citizens.[7] But the presumption is wrong in many more respects than it is right. While some distinctions between foreign nationals and citizens are normatively justified and consistent with constitutional and international law, most are not. The significance of the citizen-noncitizen distinction is more often presumed than carefully examined. Upon examination, there is far less to the distinction than commonly thought. In particular, foreign nationals are generally entitled to the equal protection of the laws, to political freedoms of speech and association, and to due process requirements of fair procedure where their lives, liberty, or property are at stake.

CITIZENS AND PERSONS

The Constitution does distinguish in some respects between the rights of citizens and noncitizens: the right not to have one's vote discriminatorily denied and the right to run for federal elective office are expressly restricted to citizens.[8] All other rights, however, are written without such a limitation. The Fifth and Fourteenth Amendment due process and equal protection guarantees extend to all "persons." The rights attached to criminal trials—including the right to a public trial, a trial by jury, the assistance of a lawyer, and the right to confront adverse witnesses—all apply to "the accused." And both the First Amendment's protections of political and religious freedoms and the Fourth Amendment's protection of privacy and liberty apply to "the people."

The fact that the Framers chose to limit to citizens only the rights to vote and to run for federal office is one indication that they did not intend other constitutional rights to be limited to citizens. Accordingly, the Supreme Court has squarely stated that neither the First Amendment nor the Fifth Amendment "acknowledges any distinction between citizens and resident aliens."[9] For more than a century, the Court has recognized that the Equal Protection Clause is "universal in [its] application to all persons within the territorial jurisdiction, without regard to differences of . . . nationality."[10] The Court has repeatedly stated that "the Due Process Clause applies to all 'persons' within the United States, including aliens, whether their presence here is lawful, unlawful, temporary, or permanent."[11] When noncitizens, no matter what their status, are tried for crimes, they are entitled to all of the rights that attach to the criminal process, without any distinction based on their nationality.[12]

There are strong normative reasons for the uniform extension of these fundamental rights. As James Madison himself argued, those subject to the obligations of our legal system ought to be entitled to its protections:

> it does not follow, because aliens are not parties to the Constitution, as citizens are parties to it, that whilst they actually conform to it, they have no right to its protection. Aliens are not more parties to the laws, than they are parties to the Constitution; yet it will not be disputed, that as they owe, on one hand, a temporary obedience, they are entitled, in return, to their protection and advantage.[13]

Madison's view was not without its critics, but it prevailed in the long run.[14] On this view, the Constitution presumptively extends not just to citizens, but to all who are subject to American legal obligations, and certainly to all persons within the United States. Madison's view is buttressed by the fact that when adopted, the rights enumerated in the Bill of Rights were viewed not as a set of optional contractual provisions enforceable because they were agreed upon by a group of states and extending only to the contracting parties, but as inalienable natural rights that found their provenance in God.[15]

Natural law theories no longer hold much influence, but the human rights movement of the last fifty years reflects a remarkably parallel secular understanding, namely that there are certain basic human rights to which all persons are entitled, simply by virtue of their humanity. Human rights treaties, including those that the United States has signed and ratified, uniformly provide that the rights of due process, political freedoms, and equal protection are owed to all persons, regardless of nationality. The Universal Declaration of Human Rights, for example, aptly described by Professor Richard Lillich as the "Magna Carta of contemporary international human rights law," is expressly premised on "the inherent dignity and ... the equal and inalienable rights of all members of the human family."[16] Every international law scholar to consider the question has concluded that the Universal Declaration extends its rights to nonnationals and nationals alike.[17] The Universal Declaration explicitly guarantees the rights of due process, political expression and association, and equal protection.[18]

The International Covenant on Civil and Political Rights similarly extends its protections generally to noncitizens; the Human Rights Committee's authoritative commentary provides that "in general, the rights set forth in the Covenant apply to everyone ... irrespective of his or her nationality or statelessness."[19] These principles are also reflected in the Declaration on the Human Rights of Individuals Who are Not Nationals of the Country in which They Live, adopted by the United Nations General Assembly in 1985. It expressly guarantees to non-nationals, among other rights, the right to life, the right not to be subjected to arbitrary arrest or torture, due process, equality before the courts, and the freedoms of thought, opinion, conscience, religion, and expression.[20] The only civil and political rights that international law does not generally guarantee on equal terms to citizens and noncitizens are the right to vote, the right to run for elective office, and the rights of entry and abode.[21]

While state practices diverge in some respects, other nations also generally recognize that foreign nationals are entitled to the same basic human rights as their own citizens. Some constitutions, such as Sweden's, expressly guarantee equal rights and freedoms to non-nationals.[22] Other constitutions, such as Canada's, guarantee basic human rights to "everyone," much as ours does to "persons," and have therefore been read to protect non-nationals living in the country.[23] Italy's Constitution extends fundamental rights, including due process and the freedoms of speech and association, to all persons in Italy, even those who have entered illegally.[24] Germany's Basic Law establishes "human rights" and "everyone's rights" that apply equally to all persons without regard to citizenship. The Basic Law does guarantee certain other freedoms, including the freedoms of assembly and of association, to Germans only, but these rights have been extended by statute to foreigners in the same manner as they apply to citizens.[25] While Great Britain does not have a Constitution, it has recently incorporated the European Convention on Human Rights (ECHR) into its domestic law by statute, and the ECHR generally extends fundamental rights protection to all persons without regard to nationality.[26]

The normative idea underlying this broad consensus is that fundamental rights are owed to persons as a matter of human dignity and should be honored no matter what form of government a particular community chooses to adopt. As David Feldman has written, "there are certain kinds of treatment which are simply incompatible with the idea that one is dealing with a human being who, as such, is entitled to respect for his or her humanity and dignity."[27] The rights of political freedom, due process, and equal protection are among the minimal rights that the world has come to demand of any society. In the words of the Supreme Court, these rights are "implicit in the concept of ordered liberty."[28]

Our own historical experience with restricting fundamental rights on the basis of citizenship should also give us pause about departing from uniformity.[29] Chief Justice Taney's decision in *Dred Scott v. Sandford*[30] sought to define away the rights of even free African Americans by concluding that "persons who are descendants of Africans who were imported into this country, and sold as slaves," were not *citizens* and therefore could not invoke federal court jurisdiction.[31] Chief Justice Taney reasoned that when the Constitution was adopted, blacks were not protected by its provisions because they were "considered as a subordinate and inferior class of beings, who had been subjugated by the dominant race, and, whether emancipated or not, yet remained subject to their authority, and had no rights or privileges but such as those who held the power and the Government might choose to grant them."[32]

With the express intent of overruling that reasoning, Congress provided in the Civil Rights Act of 1866 that "all persons born in the United States and not subject to any foreign power, excluding Indians not taxed, are hereby declared to be citizens of the United States. . . ."[33] The same Congress enacted the Fourteenth Amendment, which provided that all persons born or naturalized in the United States are citizens, and further guaranteed to all persons in the United States—whether citizens or not—due process of law and equal protection. As Yale Law Professor Alexander Bickel wrote, *Dred Scott* teaches that "[a] relationship between government and the governed that turns on citizenship can always be dissolved or denied [because] [c]itizenship is a legal construct, an abstraction, a theory."[34] It is far more difficult to deny that a human being is a "person."

The fact that noncitizens residing among us, even lawful permanent residents, lack the right to vote provides another reason for extending to foreign nationals the rights reflected in the Bill of Rights. Foreign nationals residing here must obey our laws and pay taxes; they are even subject to the draft.[35] Yet because they lack the franchise, they are without a meaningful voice in the political bargains that govern their everyday lives. Members of Congress have little reason to concern themselves with the rights and interests of people who cannot vote. As Professor John Hart Ely has argued, non-nationals' interests will almost by definition be undercounted in the political process; as such, they are a "relatively easy case" of a "discrete and insular minority" deserving of heightened protection.[36] Foreign nationals do enjoy some indirect representation, as co-ethnic groups and business interests may sometimes assert their rights, and foreign governments may use diplomatic measures to protect their nationals in the United States. But such indirect representation is no substitute for the vote. When one adds to this the ignoble history of anti-immigrant sentiment among the voting citizenry, often laced with racial animus, foreigners are a group particularly warranting judicial protection.[37] The Supreme Court itself has acknowledged this, writing that "[a]liens as a class are a prime example of a 'discrete and insular' minority for whom . . . heightened judicial solicitude is appropriate."[38]

FREE SPEECH, DUE PROCESS, AND EQUAL PROTECTION

The specific characters of the constitutional guarantees of political freedom, due process, and equal protection also support their extension to foreign nationals living in the United States. The First Amendment, for example, protects even the speech of inanimate corporations, on the instrumentalist ground that corporate speech contributes to the marketplace of ideas.[39] If protecting corporate speech is essential to preserving a robust public debate, so too is protecting noncitizens' speech. In classrooms, courts, workplaces, private associations, and town hall meetings, noncitizens and citizens routinely find themselves side by side. If noncitizens did not have the same First Amendment rights to express themselves as citizens, the conversations in each of these settings would be considerably less free. If my foreign law students were not as free as their U.S. citizen classmates to speak their minds, our classroom dialogue would be impoverished. And if, for example, Peter Jennings, a Canadian citizen, were unable to speak as freely as Dan Rather, a U.S. citizen, we would all suffer.

Nor does it make sense to maintain, as the United States government has, that foreign nationals enjoy full First Amendment freedoms *except* when facing the immigration power. Just as one cannot be a little bit pregnant, a foreign national cannot be a little bit restricted in his or her right to speak. If a foreign national has no First Amendment rights in the deportation setting, he has no First Amendment rights anywhere; the fear of deportation will always and everywhere restrict what he says.[40]

Those who view the First Amendment as serving the ends of self-government might argue that because noncitizens do not have a right to participate directly in self-government, their expressive rights are less important to protect than those of citizens. But the First Amendment protects speech for a range of reasons not limited to informing the right to vote. Free speech furthers autonomy, critical thinking, self-expression, the search for truth, and the checking of government abuse, all interests that noncitizens share equally with citizens. Corporations, minors, and many ex-convicts cannot vote, yet their speech rights are nonetheless fully protected. Moreover, the very fact that noncitizens cannot vote but nonetheless are bound by the political decisions of the community in which they reside only underscores the importance of protecting their speech and associational rights. At a minimum, those who can vote need to hear from those who cannot if the democratic process is to have any hope of taking their interests into account.

The Fifth and Fourteenth Amendment Due Process Clauses should also apply equally to citizens and noncitizens. If the state cannot take a citizen's life, liberty, or property without due process of law, why should it be able to take a noncitizen's life, liberty, or property without due process? It is generally just as much an imposition on a foreign national's physical freedom to be locked up as it is an imposition on a citizen's freedom. The government sometimes argues that noncitizens are entitled to diminished due process, but it is not clear why that should be so.[41] Determining what process is constitutionally due in any given case requires balancing the individual's interest against the government's interest while considering whether the procedure under challenge is likely to produce erroneous results.[42] Individual interests in life, liberty, and property do not usually vary depending on nationality. There may be particular situations in which a foreign national's interests will be less substantial than a citizen's, but the presumption certainly ought to be that liberty is liberty, life is life, and property is property. Similarly, the significance of the government's interest should not generally turn on the citizen-noncitizen distinction. The interest in national security, for example, would be equally threatened by exposure of confidential information in a criminal case involving a citizen, a criminal case involving a foreign national, or an immigration proceeding. The national security interests implicated by the prosecution of Zacarias Moussaoui, indicted as the so-called twentieth hijacker, would not be different were he a citizen, nor were he in immigration proceedings. Finally, the risk of error from truncated procedures will be precisely the same whether the individual affected is a citizen or noncitizen. Thus, the factors that guide due process analysis generally should not vary depending on the nationality of the individual.

The government often argues that noncitizens detained while in immigration proceedings have a reduced liberty interest because they have the right to leave the country, and therefore hold the "keys to the cell" in their pockets.[43] In some limited settings, this argument may have some traction, as when a foreign national is detained while seeking to enter the country from abroad and is perfectly free to turn around and go home. But it is more often than not illusory. Foreign nationals who have lived here for any significant stretch of time will likely have developed educational, occupational, personal, and community ties that make it less than a simple matter to leave. Immigration law affords every foreign national apprehended in the country the right to contest his removal, and to apply for various forms of relief from removal, but also provides that if a person chooses to leave the country while in removal proceedings he automatically abandons his claim to remain. Similarly, individuals who have applied for political asylum cannot be said to have the "keys to the cell" in their pockets, as their very contention is that returning home will likely result in their persecution. Finally, as illustrated by its policy toward the post–September 11 "special interest" detainees, the government maintains the authority to deny departure and maintain in custody even those foreign nationals who agree to leave, indicating that in fact the government ultimately holds the keys. Thus, the ability to leave the country does not generally warrant denying due process to noncitizens. Citizens and foreign nationals ought to enjoy the same due process protections.

Equal protection is more complicated. There is no dispute that noncitizens are entitled to equal protection of the laws; the Court held as much in 1886.[44] Indeed, the Court has held that even undocumented persons illegally here are encompassed by the Equal Protection Clause, ruling that Texas could not deny public education to the children of "illegal aliens."[45] But what equal protection actually means with respect to distinctions based on nationality, alienage, or national origin is less clear. Equal protection, after all, does not require identical treatment, but only forbids different treatment of similarly situated persons without an adequate justification. Citizens and noncitizens are not similarly situated in all respects, and in some instances their differences will justify differential treatment. A citizen cannot be expelled from the country no matter how egregious his conduct, while a noncitizen may be expelled even for trivial infractions. But in most respects, citizens and noncitizens are similarly situated.

The general rule, then, is that where foreign nationals and citizens are similarly situated, they must be treated equally. Indeed, the Court treats alienage as a "suspect" classification, and *state* laws discriminating on the basis of alienage, nationality, or national origin are generally as presumptively invalid as laws discriminating along racial lines.[46] There are very good reasons for this, given noncitizens' lack of political voice, and the history of alienage and nationality discrimination as a cover for racial animus and political repression. This rule, however, is subject to two significant exceptions. First, because the federal immigration power by definition treats foreign nationals differently from citizens, federal discrimination on the basis of alienage in regulating immigration is generally permissible. As noted above, the Supreme Court has acknowledged that "[i]n the exercise of its broad power over naturalization and immigration, Congress regularly makes rules that would be unacceptable if applied to citizens."[47] But this statement should not be read too broadly. In context, it referred only to Congress's power to exclude and remove foreign nationals, a power that by definition differentiates between citizens and foreign nationals.[48] Second, the Court permits states to bar foreign nationals from public employment connected to the administration of public policy, including such positions as police officers, schoolteachers, and even deputy probation officers.[49] It reasons that a state may limit those who formulate and carry out public policy to citizens of the polity. In adopting these two exceptions, the Court has not declared that equal protection is inapplicable, but only that noncitizens are differently situated from citizens in these areas: with respect to the immigration power, because they are uniquely subject to that power; and with respect to self-government, because they are not necessarily part of the polity.[50]

In short, contrary to widely held assumptions, the Constitution extends fundamental protections of due process, political freedoms, and equal protection to all persons subject to our laws, without regard to citizenship. These rights inhere in the dignity of the human being, and are especially necessary for people, like non-nationals, who have no voice in the political process. The rights to political participation, entry, and abode, by contrast, are rights that may be limited to the citizenry; they are inextricable from a polity's ability to define itself, and they are virtually universally recognized as legitimately limited to the citizenry. By contrast, there are no good reasons specific to the rights of speech, association, or due process that warrant diminished protection for non-nationals. While relevant differences between nonciti-zens and citizens do justify some classifications based on alienage, be-yond those limited differences, noncitizens are presumptively entitled to equal protection of the laws.[51]

To assert that noncitizens are entitled to substantially the same constitutional rights protections as citizens is not to assert that these rights are absolutes, or that the Constitution is a suicide pact. With the exception of the bans on slavery and torture, most constitutional rights are not absolutes, but presumptive protections that may be overridden by compelling showings of governmental need and nar-row tailoring. Thus, for example, the First Amendment creates a strong presumption of protection for speech, but that presumption is overridden where the speech is intended and likely to incite imminent lawless action.[52] My claim is not that such categorical balancing is in-appropriate, but that we should not cheat on the balance by drawing the line differently for non-nationals and citizens. While the defini-tion of most constitutional rights contains an implicit consequential-ist balance, the balance should be struck equally for all—even if it might appear convenient or politically tempting to strike it differently for some.

LOYALTY, PLENARY POWER, THE RIGHT/PRIVILEGE DISTINCTION, AND THE VALUE OF CITIZENSHIP

Defenders of exceptional government power over noncitizens none-theless offer several arguments for not extending the same rights to foreigners that we extend to citizens. Foreign nationals have taken no oath of loyalty to this country and presumably maintain their princi-pal fidelity elsewhere. While citizens have a right to permanent resi-dence in the United States, foreign nationals have no constitutional right to reside here. The political branches' broad authority over im-migration justifies diminished rights in the immigration setting. For-eign nationals come and live among us only as our guests, on whatever conditions we set. And if we were to extend to foreign nationals the same rights that citizens enjoy, we would devalue citizenship itself.[53] For these reasons, it is said, treating foreign nationals differently does not violate basic norms of equality and dignity, but simply reflects that they are in fact different.

None of these arguments warrants affording diminished constitutional protection to non-nationals residing among us. Loyalty is a red herring. Most citizens became citizens by the accident of birth, not by passing any test of commitment. Non-nationals choose to come here, while most citizens were simply born here and did not leave.[54] Presumptive loyalties to other nations are especially irrelevant in the war on terrorism, where our adversary is not a nation, but a criminal organization, and is indeed a common adversary of many of the Arab and Muslim nations whose citizens the government has targeted. Saudi Arabia, Pakistan, and Egypt, for example, are among our most important allies in the war on terrorism, yet their citizens have been discriminatorily subjected to registration, interviews, detentions, and deportations.

Perhaps the most common argument for reduced constitutional protection for noncitizens invokes what the Supreme Court has called the political branches' "plenary power" over immigration.[55] The doctrine, founded on notions of the sovereign's inherent power to control its borders, counsels considerable judicial deference in reviewing the substantive terms Congress sets for admission. But the plenary power doctrine is frequently overstated and has been narrowed by more recent Supreme Court decisions. In 2001, for example, the Court summarily rejected the government's assertion of plenary power in a case involving indefinite detention of criminal non-nationals, insisting that the plenary power "is subject to important constitutional limitations."[56]

In particular, the plenary immigration power does not justify differential treatment of foreign nationals' First Amendment speech and associational rights or Fifth Amendment due process rights. Indeed, the Supreme Court has insisted that the First and Fifth Amendments acknowledge no distinctions between citizens and noncitizens residing here.[57] When the United States government argued in the Cold War that Congress had plenary power to deport foreign nationals for their speech and associations, the Court declined to adopt that contention, but instead upheld the challenged immigration law under the then-prevailing First Amendment standard for citizens.[58] Similarly, with one exception, the Court has generally applied the same due process analysis to preventive detention of foreigners in immigration proceedings and of citizens in criminal and civil commitment settings, treating the cases interchangeably.[59]

The one exception is the Court's 2003 decision in *Demore v. Kim,* which upheld a statute mandating preventive detention during deportation proceedings of foreign nationals charged with certain criminal offenses.[60] Under the statute, even persons who pose no risk of flight and no danger to the community must be detained. In a five-to-four decision, the Court pointed to statistics showing that significant percentages of "criminal aliens" committed more crime upon release and/or failed to appear for their deportation hearings, and reasoned that Congress could therefore make a categorical judgment that no such persons should be released on bond while in deportation proceedings. The decision marks the first time outside of a war setting that the Court has upheld preventive detention of *anyone* without an individualized assessment of the necessity of such detention. And the majority expressly rested its decision on a double standard, noting that Congress can make rules in the immigration setting that would be unacceptable for citizens. But the Court fails to explain the double standard's extension to preventive detention. As noted above, both the liberty interests of the detainee and the government's interests in preventing flight or danger to the community are no different for noncitizens in immigration proceedings than for citizens in criminal proceedings. *Demore* thus asserts but does not justify differential treatment of foreign nationals' due process rights.

A third argument commonly heard as a rationale for affording noncitizens less robust rights protection maintains that because noncitizens are only "guests"[61] who have "come at the Nation's invitation,"[62] their admission and continuing presence may be conditioned on whatever constraints the government chooses to impose. As the Supreme Court put it, "deportation is simply a refusal by the Government to harbor persons whom it does not want."[63] If you don't like it, the argument goes, either don't come, or get out. This argument seeks to transform what we generally think of as inalienable rights into discretionary privileges that can be granted or denied at will. It uses the fact that a foreign national's entry is a privilege to recast restrictions on his or her rights here as conditions on the privilege of entry.

This argument proves too much. It would negate virtually all constitutional rights of noncitizens, and relegate an entire class of the populace to a wholly unprotected status. A law mandating detention of all noncitizens who marry noncitizens of other races, for example, would be immune from due process, privacy, and equal protection challenges because it could be defended as a mere condition on noncitizens' entry. The Supreme Court has rejected such reasoning, in the immigration area and elsewhere, precisely because it would allow the government to achieve indirectly, by attaching conditions to benefits, what it cannot achieve directly. As the Court stated in 1971 in a case involving noncitizens' rights "this Court has now rejected the concept that constitutional rights turn upon whether a governmental benefit is characterized as a 'right' or as a 'privilege.' "[64] Under contemporary constitutional law, equal protection prohibits invidious discrimination in the allocation of benefits as well as of rights, and the Court's "unconstitutional conditions" doctrine provides that the government acts unconstitutionally when even wholly discretionary benefits are denied because of the recipient's exercise of constitutional rights.[65] Thus, the right-privilege distinction does not justify a denial of immigrants' rights.

Finally, some warn that extending substantially equal rights to foreign nationals will dilute the value of United States citizenship, and thereby create fewer incentives for immigrants to become naturalized citizens.[66] Citizenship would undoubtedly be more attractive if basic protections against government intrusions on privacy, equality, liberty, and life were available exclusively or in more generous measure to citizens. But devaluing human beings' basic rights is an illegitimate means toward that end. As long as citizens alone are afforded the rights to vote, to take part in the political process of self-government, and to permanent abode, rights traditionally limited to citizens the world over, there seems little danger that citizenship will be devalued in any deeply troubling way.

Thus, there is little reasoned support for the widely held notion that noncitizens are entitled to substantially less constitutional protection than citizens. While not identically situated in all respects, foreign nationals should generally enjoy the same constitutional protections for fundamental rights and liberties as U.S. citizens. The areas of permissible differentiation—admission, expulsion, voting, and running for federal elective office—are much narrower than the areas of presumptive equality—due process, freedom of expression, association, and religion, privacy, and the rights of the criminally accused.

DOING THE RIGHT THING

In the preceding chapters, I have argued that it is in our interest not to trade immigrants' rights for citizens' purported security because the rights we deny to immigrants will almost inevitably be denied to citizens later and because double standards undermine security by impairing the legitimacy of the war on terrorism. This chapter makes a different and more fundamental argument; it contends that trading non-nationals' basic human rights not only disserves our long-term interest, but is wrong as a constitutional and normative matter. The constitutional argument is a trump card; even if one were to disagree with the first two points, and to conclude that it serves the citizenry's interests to deny foreign citizens basic human rights, it is not a choice we should allow ourselves to make as a constitutional democracy.

When we balance liberty and security, in other words, we should respect the equal dignity and basic human rights of all persons because it is the right thing to do. In the wake of September 11, we have failed to follow that mandate. When we spy on foreign nationals but not citizens, selectively target foreign nationals for registration, detention, and deportation based on their ethnic and religious identities, and lock up foreign nationals in secret or without any hearings at all, we have chosen the easy way out: sacrificing their rights for our purported security. In the end, the true test of justice in a democratic society is not how it treats those with political power, but how it treats those who have no voice in the democratic process. How we treat foreign nationals, the paradigmatic other in this time of crisis, ultimately tests our own humanity.

CONCLUSION: BREAKING THE CYCLE

The standard assessment of emergency power is that in times of crisis, governments overreact, and only later recognize their errors. As Franklin Delano Roosevelt's Attorney General Francis Biddle candidly stated, "The Constitution has not greatly bothered any wartime President." [1] There is an inescapable realpolitik to this: Attorney General Ashcroft and President Bush know full well that they will take a far bigger "hit" politically if there is another terrorist attack than if they lock up innocent Arabs or intrude on foreign nationals' rights. In the midst of security crises, government officials often see rights protections as little more than obstacles to getting the job done. Their message: give us broad powers, and trust us not to abuse them. In such periods, Congress tends to want to be seen as having done something, and readily passes laws giving government more power, whether or not those powers are appropriate or necessary to greater security. And the public, caught up in the panic of the day and generally shut out from critical information by the government's increased reliance on secrecy, typically defers to executive officials, especially where the government's actions seem to be targeted at foreign nationals, not U.S. citizens.

But just as inevitably, at some point after—and often long after—the emergency has passed, the government's conduct is widely acknowledged to have been an overreaction. Thus, we now recognize that it was wrong to incarcerate people for mere speech during World War I; to arrest thousands and deport hundreds for their political associations during the Palmer Raids; to intern 110,000 Japanese-Americans during World War II; to prosecute, publicly shame, and fire Communists during the Cold War; and to infiltrate and deliberately disrupt the lawful political activities of the civil rights and anti-war movements in the 1960s and 1970s. With respect to each of these crises, the judgment of history is not that tragically difficult sacrifices were necessary and appropriate given the threat presented, but that government overreacted, sacrificing far more than the emergency warranted. But that judgment has generally come too late to help the thousands of human beings injured in the name of national security.

In theory, the Constitution is supposed to forestall this. To those officials all too ready to intone "the Constitution is not a suicide pact" as they bypass its protections, one might answer, in the words of Senator John Potter Stockton in 1871: "Constitutions are chains with which men bind themselves in their sane moments that they may not die by a suicidal hand in the day of their frenzy."[2] But the Constitution has all too rarely worked to bind us in our days of frenzy. As Supreme Court Justice William Brennan stated in 1987:

> There is considerably less to be proud about, and a good deal to be embarrassed about, when one reflects on the shabby treatment civil liberties have received in the United States during times of war and perceived threats to national security. . . . After each perceived security crisis ended, the United States has remorsefully realized that the abrogation of civil liberties was unnecessary. But it has proven unable to prevent itself from repeating the error when the next crisis came along.[3]

I have sought to demonstrate that the phenomenon of overreaction is inextricably linked to the double standards that the nation has so frequently exploited in times of crisis. A political process that weighs everyone's security on one side of the balance, but weighs the rights and liberties of only a voiceless and often demonized "alien" minority on the other, is a recipe for overreaction. Inroads on fundamental liberties in the name of security have virtually always been sold as limited to foreign nationals, but once established, have then been extended ineluctably to citizens. It is generally only when their effects touch a sufficiently large number of citizens that the governments' initiatives are recognized as overreactions and curbed.

Given that virtually everyone acknowledges and bemoans the phenomenon of overreaction, the question is whether there is anything we can do to avoid it in the first place. Just as it is better to prevent a terrorist act from occurring than to catch and punish the perpetrators after the bomb goes off, so too it would be better to check the government so that it does not overreact in times of crisis.

Some efforts have been made toward that end, but they are generally retrospective, and often prove vulnerable once the next crisis emerges. In some instances, for example, the lessons drawn from overreactions have been crystallized in Supreme Court doctrine regarding specific practices, and that doctrine may impose some constraint on the government's options in the next emergency. As we have seen, the lessons of World War I and the Cold War led the Court to preclude punishment for speech and association absent extremely strong showings of a close nexus to criminal conduct. The importance of such decisions over the long term should not be underestimated. Penalizing antiwar speech or association per se is now plainly off-limits in the war on terrorism, largely because of Supreme Court doctrine. But as the Bush administration's resurrection of guilt by association under the rubric of penalizing "material support" for terrorist organizations illustrates, these restrictions may simply require the government to put a new spin on old tactics.

In other instances, the lessons of history have become deeply rooted in the broader legal and popular culture. Thus, even though *Korematsu,* the decision upholding the World War II Japanese internment, has never been formally overruled, the internment is widely viewed as a black mark on the Court's and the nation's history, and as a result the government is unlikely to repeat it. But here, too, while the government has not interned people solely for their national origin or race in the war on terrorism, it has engaged in widespread ethnic and nationality based profiling, relying on stereotypes linking suspicion to ethnicity that recall the suspicion of the Japanese during World War II.

Sometimes Congress and the executive branch have been moved (or embarrassed) by revelations of excesses and abuses to adopt reforms themselves. Thus, in 1971, Congress not only repealed the emergency detention provisions of the 1950 Internal Security Act, but affirmatively prohibited preventive detention without express congressional approval.[4] Congress has also attempted to set limits on foreign intelligence gathering through the Foreign Intelligence Surveillance Act, to bring sunshine to government "national security" actions through the Freedom of Information Act, and to prohibit political spying through the Privacy Act.[5] And in 1976, the Church Committee's revelations of FBI abuses prompted Attorney General Edward Levi to adopt guidelines for domestic security investigations designed to forestall such abuses in the future.

In general, however, legislative and administrative reforms alone are less effective than the constitutional and cultural constraints discussed above, because they are susceptible to swift revision by the same entities that put them in place in the first instance. Thus, in the PATRIOT Act, Congress rolled back many of the privacy protections that it had adopted in part as a reaction to the spying abuses of the Cold War and Vietnam eras. Similarly, Attorney Generals William French Smith, Richard Thornburgh, and now John Ashcroft have all relaxed the restrictions on FBI spying instituted by the Levi guidelines. Protections put in place through the normal political process are easily overridden when the next emergency arises, and therefore fail to provide much meaningful restraint in times of emergency.

A different approach with substantially more hope for taming the time-tested proclivity to overreact would be to insist that, as much as possible, all persons share equally the costs and burdens that we have so often selectively imposed on foreign nationals. Rather than seeking to fashion specific limits on particular tactics—a game of catch-up that inevitably fails to respond adequately to innovations—this approach seeks to create a better process by requiring that the balance between security and liberty be struck uniformly across the board. Were we to deny ourselves the easy way out of sacrificing the rights of a vulnerable minority for the purported security of the majority, we would be forced to be more candid and forthright in balancing liberty and security in the first place. The responses to Operation TIPS, the

Total Information Awareness program, and the assertion of un-checked enemy combatant authority against U.S. citizens illustrate that when government measures are seen as potentially applying to all, the nation takes notice, and the political process is far more atten-tive to the rights and liberties at stake in the liberty-security balance. By requiring that we all be willing to forgo the rights and liberties that we are so quick to deny to the vulnerable, we would be less likely to overreact, and more likely to strike an appropriate and just balance. As Justice Robert Jackson noted in describing one of the chief virtues of the right of equal protection, "there is no more effective practical guaranty against arbitrary and unreasonable government than to re-quire that the principles of law which officials would impose upon a minority must be imposed generally." [6]

The targeting of foreign nationals is certainly not the only form of government overreaction in times of crisis, and therefore treating for-eign nationals as we would treat ourselves on matters of basic human rights is not a panacea. As Professor Oren Gross has shown, many other factors contribute to the phenomenon of overreaction, includ-ing the government's political need to be seen as doing something, whether or not it actually makes us safer; the deference to executive authority that stems from fear of attack; the misguided notion that emergency measures will be temporary in duration; and the psycho-logical tendency to exaggerate the likelihood of dramatic risks.[7] But as the history recounted above illustrates, one of the most persistent features of repression of civil liberties in times of crisis has been its genesis in measures directed at foreign nationals. To quote Justice Jackson again: "nothing opens the door to arbitrary action so effec-tively as to allow those officials to pick and choose only a few to whom they will apply legislation and thus to escape the political retribution that might be visited upon them if larger numbers were affected." [8] At no time is this more likely to be true than in periods of national inse-curity, when the tendency to divide "us" from "them" is at its zenith.

Emergency periods and new vulnerabilities may well warrant sac-rifices of rights and liberties. Few rights are absolute; most require balancing, meaning that demands for increased security may properly lead to decreased liberty, as long as the loss in liberty is made up for by sufficient gains in security. But in striking that balance, we should all share the costs of the trade-offs.

This is not to say that citizens and foreign nationals must be treated identically in every respect. As discussed in this book's penultimate chapter, there are relevant differences between citizens and foreign nationals that may justify differential treatment in some settings. But those differences are more limited than is generally assumed, and in particular do not extend to those fundamental human rights extended by the Constitution to all persons on whom the United States imposes legal obligations, and extended by international human rights treaties to all persons as a matter of human dignity without regard to their citizenship status. With respect to these rights and liberties—the rights of speech, association, religion, due process, and equal protection—we should resist the temptation to shortchange foreign nationals. Resisting that illegitimate trade-off by putting ourselves in the shoes of the foreign "other" is not only the right thing to do, but the only hope for breaking the seemingly endless cycle of overreaction and apology. In extending rights to the "alien," Hermann Cohen maintained, "man discovered the idea of humanity."[9] The challenge we now face is whether we can reclaim that idea in the wake of September 11.

NOTES

Introduction

1. Katharine Q. Seelye, "Walker Is Returned to U.S. and Will Be in Court Today," *New York Times,* January 24, 2002, A15.

2. Katharine Q. Seelye and Steven Erlanger, "U.S. Suspends the Transport of Terror Suspects to Cuba," *New York Times,* January 24, 2002, A1; Katharine Q. Seelye, "For America's Captives, Home Is a Camp in Cuba, with Goggles and a Koran," *New York Times,* January 20, 2002, §1, 14; Katharine Q. Seelye, "A Nation Challenged: The Captives; On Defensive, General Says Prisoners Get Mats, Even Bagels," *New York Times,* January 17, 2002, A16.

3. Seelye and Erlanger, *supra.*

4. John Mintz, "Debate Continues on Legal Status of Detainees," *Washington Post,* January 28, 2002, A15; "Secretary of Defense Donald H. Rumsfeld Roundtable Briefing with Radio Media" (As Released by the Pentagon), *Federal News Service,* January 15, 2002 (quoting Rumsfeld).

5. Detention, Treatment, and Trial of Certain Non-Citizens in the War Against Terrorism, 66 Fed. Reg. 57833 (November 13, 2001).

6. Elisabeth Bumiller and Steven Lee Myers, "Senior Administration Officials Defend Military Tribunals for Terrorist Suspects," *New York Times,* November 15, 2001, B6.

7. "News Conference Re: Criminal Charges Filed Against John Walker Lindh," *Federal News Service,* January 15, 2002.

8. In *Ex parte Quirin,* 317 U.S. 1 (1942), the Court upheld against a constitutional challenge to the use of a military tribunal to try a group of "German saboteurs" who had secretly entered the United States posing as civilians with intent to attack U.S. installations. One of those charged claimed that, having been born in the United States, he was a U.S. citizen. The Court held that military tribunals can be used against U.S. citizens and foreign nationals alike; the crucial predicate is not the individual's citizenship, but whether he is an "unlawful combatant" fighting for the enemy in a declared war. *Id.* at 35–36.

9. Stephen J. Hedges, "U.S. Flouts Legal Rights, Lawyer Says; Suspect in Bomb Plot Is a Citizen," *Chicago Tribune,* June 12, 2002, 1.

10. Jess Bravin, "More Terror Suspects May Sit in Limbo: White House Seeks to Expand Indefinite Detentions in Military Brigs, Even for U.S. Citizens," *Wall Street Journal*, August 8, 2002, A4.

11. Pub. L. No. 108-7, §111 (2003); Adam Clymer, "Congress Agrees to Bar Pentagon from Terror Watch of Americans," *New York Times*, February 12, 2003, A1. "United States persons," a term borrowed from the Foreign Intelligence Surveillance Act, includes citizens and lawful permanent resident aliens, but does not include foreigners here in any status other than as permanent residents.

12. Letter from James Madison to Thomas Jefferson, May 13, 1798, quoted in Harold Lasswell, *National Security and Individual Freedom* (New York: McGraw-Hill, 1950), 23.

13. Bonnie Honig, "A Legacy of Xenophobia," *Boston Review*, December 2002/January 2003, 11.

14. See, e.g., Raymond Bonner, "Southeast Asia Remains Fertile for Al Qaeda," *New York Times*, October 28, 2002, A1; Frank Bruni, "Europe Pauses and Grieves, But Takes Issue With U.S.," *New York Times*, September 12, 2002, B1; Zbigniew Brzezinski, "Confronting Anti-American Grievances," *New York Times*, September 1, 2002, §4, 9; Thomas Friedman, "Tone It Down a Notch," *New York Times*, October 2, 2002, A27.

15. See generally, Institute for Energy and Environmental Research and Lawyers' Committee for Nuclear Policy, *The Rule of Power or the Rule of Law?: An Assessment of U.S. Policies and Actions Regarding Security-Related Treaties* (2002), available at http://www.ieer.org/reports/treaties/fullrpt.pdf (criticizing U.S. pattern of rejecting or disregarding international treaties); Anthony Lewis, "Captives and the Law," *New York Times*, January 26, 2002, A15 (maintaining that "the prisoner issue touches a profound resentment abroad at what many see as an American tendency to lecture others about international standards while refusing to comply with those it urges"); "The Guantánamo Story," editorial, *Washington Post*, January 25, 2002, A24 (arguing that administration response to criticism of treatment of detainees at Guantánamo "suggested that the Bush administration would respect international law only so far as it chose to"); Stewart Patrick, "Don't Fence Me In: The Perils of Going it Alone," *World Policy Journal*, September 22, 2001, 18.

16. See Michael Hirsh, "Bush and the World," *Foreign Affairs*, September/October 2002, 18 (arguing that the Bush administration's disdain for international commitments undermines the war on terrorism); David E. Sanger, "A Nation Challenged: The Treatment; Prisoners Straddle an Ideological Chasm," *New York Times*, January 27, 2002, A16; Katharine Q. Seelye and David E. Sanger, "Bush Reconsiders Stand on Treating Captives of War," *New York Times*, January 29,

2002, A1; Katharine Q. Seelye, "Criticized, U.S. Brings Visitors to Prison Camp," *New York Times,* January 26, 2002, A8.

17. See *Abrams v. United States,* 250 U.S. 616 (1919); *Debs v. United States,* 249 U.S. 211 (1919); *Frohwerk v. United States,* 249 U.S. 204 (1919); *Schenck v. United States,* 249 U.S. 47 (1919).

18. See, e.g., *Korematsu v. United States,* 323 U.S. 214, 236 (1944).

19. See, e.g., *Dennis v. United States,* 341 U.S. 494 (1951); Michal R. Belknap, *Cold War Political Justice: The Smith Act, the Communist Party, and American Civil Liberties* (Westport, CT: Greenwood Press, 1977); Victor S. Navasky, *Naming Names* (New York: Viking, 1983); Arthur J. Sabin, *In Calmer Times: The Supreme Court and Red Monday* (Philadelphia: University of Pennsylvania Press, 1999).

20. *Railway Express Agency, Inc. v. New York,* 336 U.S. 106, 112 (1949) (Jackson, J., concurring).

21. *Id.*

22. Jude McCulloch, "Either You Are With Us, or You Are With the Terrorists": The War's Home Front, in *Beyond September 11: An Anthology of Dissent,* ed. Phil Scraton (London: Pluto Press, 2002), 54, 57.

23. *Ludecke v. Watkins,* 335 U.S. 160 (1948), see also 50 U.S.C. §§ 21–24 (2002).

24. *Johnson v. Eisentrager,* 339 U.S. 763 (1950).

25. *Id.* at 785.

26. *Id.* at 774 n.6.

27. *Id.* at 773.

28. *Id.* at 772.

29. *Id.* (quoting *Techt v. Hughes,* 229 N.Y. 222, 237 (1920) (Cardozo, J.)).

30. *Department of Justice Oversight: Preserving Our Freedoms While Defending Against Terrorism: Hearings Before the Senate Judiciary Committee,* 107th Cong. 313 (2001) (testimony of Attorney Gen. John Ashcroft). David Blunkett, the United Kingdom's Home Secretary, similarly told the *Guardian* on November 12, 2001: "We could live in a world which is airy-fairy, libertarian, where everyone does precisely what they like and we believe the best of everybody and then they destroy us." See Paddy Hillyard, "In Defense of Civil Liberties," in Scraton, *Beyond September 11, supra,* 107 (quoting Blunkett).

31. *Kennedy v. Mendoza-Martinez,* 372 U.S. 144, 160 (1963).

32. Letter from Justice William O. Douglas to Washington State Bar Association, Young Lawyer's Section (1976), in Melvin I. Urofsky, ed., *The Douglas Letters: Se-*

lections from the Private Papers of Justice William O. Douglas (Bethesda, MD: Adler & Adler, 1987), 162.

1. Their Liberty, Our Security: An Overview

1. *ABC News Special Report: America Under Attack* (ABC television broadcast, September 11, 2001), http://www.lexis.com; Donald Lambro, "Bush Polls Soar in Attack Aftermath," *Washington Times*, September 14, 2001, A3; Richard Morin, "Poll: Half of All Americans Still Feel Unsafe; Majority Would Give Up Some Civil Liberties to Improve Security After Sept. 11," *Washington Post*, May 3, 2002, A7; National Public Radio et al., *Poll: Security Trumps Civil Liberties* (November 30, 2001), http://www.npr.org/news/specials/civillibertiespoll/011130.poll.html.

2. *Civil Liberties Update*, NPR/Kaiser/Kennedy School Poll, conducted August 7–11, 2002. Results available at http://www.npr.org/news/specials/civilliberties poll2/combinedtoplines.pdf.

3. *O'Rourke v. Warden*, 539 F. Supp. 1131, 1135 (S.D.N.Y. 1982) ("The BIA . . . has construed [8 U.S.C. §1252(a)] to provide that the determination to release an alien pending deportation proceedings is 'not a discretionary form of relief' but rather 'an alien should be detained or required to post a bond, only if he is a threat to national security or is a poor bail risk.' ") (quoting *In re O'Rourke*, A22 607 396, Decision and Order of the BIA, August 13, 1980, 3); see also *In re Drysdale*, 20 I. & N. Dec. 815, 817 (BIA 1994) ("Once it is determined that an alien does not present a danger to the community or any bail risk, then no bond should be required."); *In re De La Cruz*, 20 I. & N. Dec. 346, 349 (BIA 1991) (same); *Matter of Patel*, 15 I. & N. Dec. 666 (BIA 1976) (same).

4. Declaration of Michael E. Rolince at p. 5, submitted in *Matter of Al-Maqtari*, reproduced as Appendix B to Human Rights Watch, *Presumption of Guilt: Human Rights Abuses of Post-September 11 Detainees* (August 2002).

5. *Id.* at 5–6.

6. U.S. Department of Justice, Office of the Inspector General, *The September 11 Detainees: A Review of the Treatment of Aliens Held on Immigration Charges in Connection with the Investigation of the September 11 Attacks* (April 2003) (released June 2, 2003), 79, 89.

7. See "Ali Al-Maqtari's Story," available at http://immigrantcenter.com/almaqtari.htm; *Department of Justice Oversight: Preserving Our Freedoms While Defending Against Terrorism: Hearings Before the Senate Judiciary Committee*, 107th Cong. 212 (2001) (statement of Ali Al-Maqtari); David Firestone, "A Nation Challenged: The Detainees; Ali Al-Maqtari," *New York Times*, November 25, 2001, B5; Hanna Rosin, "Some Cry Foul as Authorities Cast a Wide Net," *Washington Post*, September 28, 2001, A1.

2. The Disappeared

1. Attorney General John Ashcroft, "Prepared Remarks for the U.S. Mayors Conference," October 25, 2001, available at http://www.usdoj.gov/ag/speeches/2001/agcrisisremarks10_25.htm.

2. *Id.*

3. Department of Justice, "Attorney General Ashcroft Outlines Foreign Terrorist Tracking Task Force," October 31, 2001, available at http://www.usdoj.gov/ag/speeches/2001/agcrisisremarks10_31.htm (emphasis added).

4. Department of Justice, "Remarks of Attorney General John Ashcroft, U.S. Attorneys Conference, New York City," October 1, 2002, available at http://www.usdoj.gov/ag/speeches/2002/100102agremarkstousattorneysconference.htm.

5. *United States v. Rahman,* 189 F.3d 88 (2d Cir. 1999), *cert. denied,* 528 U.S. 1094 (2000).

6. See, e.g. *Kansas v. Crane,* 534 U.S. 407 (2002); *Kansas v. Hendricks,* 521 U.S. 346 (1997); *Foucha v. Louisiana,* 504 U.S. 71 (1992).

7. The U.S. citizens are John Walker Lindh, James Ujaama, Enaam M. Arnaout, Ilyas Ali, seven residents of Lackawanna, New York, accused of attending an Al Qaeda training camp, and six defendants in Portland, Oregon, accused of seeking to support Al Qaeda. The foreign nationals are Zacarias Moussaoui (French), Richard Reid (British), one of the Portland defendants, two Pakistanis accused along with Ilyas Ali of conspiring to sell drugs and use the proceeds to send Stinger missiles to Taliban–Al Qaeda forces, and four Yemeni nationals—Sheikh Muhammad Ali Hassan al-Mouyad and Muhammad Mushen Yahya Zayed, charged in Brooklyn with raising money for Al Qaeda, and Jamal Ahmed Muhammad Ali al-Badawi and Fahd al-Qusa, charged in Manhattan with plotting the attack on the USS *Cole* in Yemen in October 2000.

8. Dan Eggen and Susan Schmidt, "Count of Released Detainees Is Hard to Pin Down," *Washington Post,* November 6, 2001, A10 (reporting 1,182 detained); Todd S. Purdum, "A Nation Challenged: The Attorney General; Ashcroft's About-Face on the Detainees," *New York Times,* November 28, 2001, B7 (reporting over 1,100 detained); Amy Goldstein and Dan Eggen, "U.S. to Stop Issuing Detention Tallies," *Washington Post,* November 9, 2001, A16 (reporting 1,182 detained).

9. Goldstein and Eggen, *supra.*

10. "The War on Terrorism: Immigration Enforcement Since September 11," Prepared Statement of Michael T. Dougherty, Director of Operations, Before the House Committee on the Judiciary Subcommittee on Immigration, Border Security and Claims, *Federal News Service,* May 8, 2003 (reporting that 1,139 "absconders" had been apprehended).

11. Michael Powell, "An Exodus Grows in Brooklyn," *Washington Post*, May 29, 2003, A1 (reporting that 2,747 persons had been detained in connection with the Special Registration program).

12. James Ujaama was detained as a material witness in July 2002, and charged on August 28, 2002, with planning to develop a terrorist training camp here to support Al Qaeda. *United States v. Ujaama* (W.D. Wash. August 28, 2002), available at http://news.findlaw.com/hdocs/docs/terrorism/usujaama82802ind.pdf. In April 2003, the United States dropped all but one charge against Ujaama, in exchange for his pleading guilty to providing humanitarian aid to the Taliban in violation of an economic embargo. Robert L. Jamieson Jr., "Ujaama Smoking Gun Goes Up in Smoke," *Seattle Post Intelligencer*, April 16, 2003, B1. Three noncitizens from Detroit initially detained in September 2001 were charged in August 2002 with supporting terrorist activity. *United States v. Koubriti*, No. 01-80778 (E.D. Mich. August 28, 2002), available at http://news.findlaw.com/hdocs/docs/ terrorism/uskoubriti82802ind.pdf. Of those three, two were acquitted of terrorist charges, and one was convicted. Another man not swept up in the preventive detention campaign was also convicted on terrorism charges. Danny Hakim, "2 Arabs Convicted and 2 Cleared of Terrorist Plots Against the U.S.," *New York Times*, June 4, 2003, A1. In April 2003, Maher Hawash, an American citizen who had been detained as a material witness for a month, was charged with conspiring to provide material support to Al Qaeda and the Taliban. Rachel L. Swarns, "Aftereffects: Detainees; Suspect Charged with Plotting to Fight U.S. in Afghanistan," *New York Times*, April 29, 2003, A21.

13. David Firestone and Christopher Drew, "A Nation Challenged: The Cases; Al Qaeda Link Seen in Only a Handful of 1,200 Detainees," *New York Times*, November 29, 2001, A1.

14. Evan Thomas and Michael Isikoff, "Justice Kept in the Dark," *Newsweek*, December 10, 2001, 37.

15. The government's policy has been not to release or deport September 11 immigration detainees until the FBI has affirmatively cleared them. Christopher Drew and Judith Miller, "A Nation Challenged: The Detainees; Though Not Linked to Terrorism, Many Detainees Cannot Go Home," *New York Times*, February 18, 2002, A1. Yet as of late 2002, the government announced that only six immigration detainees from the initial sweep remained in custody, with the rest having been released or deported. Dan Eggen, "U.S. Holds 6 of 765 Detained in 9/11 Sweep," *Washington Post*, December 12, 2002, A20. By the government's own account, all of these individuals had been cleared of any connection to terrorism.

16. Dianne Solis, "Muslims Register with U.S. Immigration as Bombs Pound Iraq," *Dallas Morning News*, March 22, 2003.

17. Whenever the government has given breakdowns of the categories of detainees, those held on immigration charges have been the largest group. In January 2002, for example, the government released a limited amount of information in connection with a Freedom of Information Act (FOIA) lawsuit brought by civil liberties and human rights groups. At that time, the government accounted for 835 individuals detained since September 11 on immigration and criminal charges. (This was several months *after* it had announced that 1,182 persons had been detained). The vast majority—718—were arrested on immigration charges. Another 108 were arrested on criminal charges, mostly minor crimes, such as credit card fraud, fraudulently obtaining a driver's license, or lying to government investigators. (Nine criminal cases were described only as sealed.) The government did not disclose how many were being held as material witnesses, or on state or local charges. See Human Rights Watch, *Presumption of Guilt: Human Rights Abuses of Post–September 11 Detainees* (August 2002), 18 n. 39; *Center for National Security Studies v. Ashcroft,* 215 F. Supp. 2d 94, 99 (D.D.C. 2002).

18. Memorandum from Chief Immigration Judge Michael Creppy to All Immigration Judges Re: Cases requiring special procedures (September 21, 2001) (relaying details of order from Attorney General Ashcroft). See also *Detroit Free Press v. Ashcroft,* 195 F. Supp. 2d 937 (E.D. Mich. 2002) (declaring this closure order unconstitutional as applied to a particular immigration proceeding); William Glaberson, "A Nation Challenged: Secret Trials; Closed Immigration Hearings Criticized as Prejudicial," *New York Times,* December 7, 2001, B7.

19. Letter from Daniel J. Bryant, Assistant Attorney General, to Senator Carl Levin, chair of the Senate's Permanent Subcommittee on Investigations, July 3, 2002, available at http://www.immigration.com/newsletter1/752detained.pdf.

20. William Glaberson, "U.S. Asks to Use Secret Evidence in Many Cases of Deportation," *New York Times,* December 9, 2001, 1B.

21. David Shepardson, "Feds Mum on Fate of Detainee; Ann Arbor Man Arrested after Raid on Suspected Charity," *Detroit News,* December 19, 2001, 1B; "U.S. Holds Suspect with Ties to Group Linked to Terror Aid," *New York Times,* December 18, 2001, B6.

22. *Detroit Free Press v. Ashcroft,* 195 F. Supp. 2d 937 (E.D. Mich. 2002); *Haddad v. Ashcroft,* 221 F. Supp. 2d 799 (E.D. Mich. 2002).

23. *Detroit Free Press v. Ashcroft,* 303 F. 3d 681, 683 (6th Cir. 2002). The government's appeal of Judge Edmonds's due process ruling is pending as of this writing.

24. *North Jersey Media Group, Inc. v. Ashcroft,* 205 F. Supp. 2d 288 (D.N.J. 2002). I am also co-counsel in this case, with the ACLU, the Center for Constitutional Rights, and the law firm of Gibbons, Del Deo, Dolan, Giffinger, and Vecchione.

25. *North Jersey Media Group, Inc. v. Ashcroft,* 308 F.3d 198 (3d Cir. 2002).

26. *Center for National Security Studies v. U.S. Dept. of Justice,* 215 F. Supp. 2d 94 (D.D.C. 2002).

27. *Id.* at 96.

28. *Center for National Security Studies v. U.S. Dept. of Justice,* 217 F. Supp. 2d 58 (D.D.C. 2002) (granting stay pending appeal).

29. U.S. Department of Justice, Office of the Inspector General, *The September 11 Detainees: A Review of the Treatment of Aliens Held on Immigration Charges in Connection with the Investigation of the September 11 Attacks* (April 2003) (released June 2, 2003) (hereinafter "Inspector General's Report").

30. See 8 C.F.R. §287.3(d) (2000) (pre–September 11 regulation); 66 Fed. Reg. 48,334 (Sept. 20, 2001) (amending 8 C.F.R. §287.3(d)).

31. Amnesty International, *United States of America: Amnesty International's Concerns Regarding Post September 11 Detentions in the USA* (2002), 10–11; Human Rights Watch, *Presumption of Guilt, supra,* 50.

32. Inspector General's Report, *supra,* 37–71.

33. Mark Bixler, "Minor Immigration Slip Becomes Costly; Palestinian Faces Ouster on Little-Used Law," *Atlanta Journal and Constitution,* July 10, 2002, 12A; Suzanne Gamboa, "INS Deluged with Change of Address Forms," Associated Press, September 10, 2002.

34. Gamboa, *supra;* see 67 Fed Reg. 48,818 (July 26, 2002).

35. This information stems from communications with Mr. Qayyum's attorneys at NYU Law School's Immigration Rights Clinic. See also Sameer M. Ashar, "Immigration Enforcement and Subordination: The Consequences of Racial Profiling After September 11," 34 *Connecticut Law Review* 1185, 1186–91 (2002).

36. Review of Custody Determinations, Interim Rule, 66 Fed. Reg. 54,909 (October 31, 2001) (codified at 8 C.F.R. §1003.19).

37. *Bezmen v. Ashcroft,* 2003 U.S. Dist. LEXIS 2397 (D. Conn. February 18, 2003); *Almonte-Vargas v. Elwood,* 2002 U.S. Dist. LEXIS 12387, at *19 (E.D. Pa. June 28, 2002).

38. 8 U.S.C. §1229(c).

39. Inspector General's Report, *supra,* 46–66.

40. See *Turkmen v. Ashcroft,* CV-02-30007 (E.D.N.Y. April 17, 2002), available at http://news.findlaw.com/hdocs/docs/terrorism/turkmenash41702cmp.pdf; Susan Sachs, "A Nation Challenged: Detainees; Civil Rights Group to Sue over U.S. Handling of Muslim Men," *New York Times,* April 17, 2002, A11. I am co-counsel in the *Turkmen* case with the Center for Constitutional Rights.

41. Drew and Miller, *supra.*

42. *Carlson v. Landon,* 342 U.S. 524 (1952).

43. *Wong Wing v. United States,* 163 U.S. 228 (1896).

44. In *Zadvydas v. Davis,* 533 U.S. 678 (2001), for example, the Supreme Court held that even aliens who had received a final order of deportation and who were found to be dangerous could not be detained indefinitely if they were not likely to be deported in the foreseeable future.

45. Drew and Miller, *supra.*

46. *County of Riverside v. McLaughlin,* 500 U.S. 44 (1991) (holding that the Fourth Amendment presumptively requires probable cause hearing within forty-eight hours of arrest).

47. Human Rights Watch, *Presumption of Guilt, supra,* 43.

48. *United States v. Salerno,* 481 U.S. 739 (1987) (upholding pretrial preventive detention under the Bail Reform Act of criminal defendants who pose a danger or a flight risk).

49. 18 U.S.C.S. §3161(b) (2002) (requiring that charges be filed within thirty days of an arrest); 18 U.S.C.S. §3161(c)(1) (2002) (requiring that trial must commence within seventy days of filing charges).

50. Human Rights Watch, *Presumption of Guilt, supra,* 13–14 (describing case of Abdi Hassan and Ahmed Shueib Yusuf).

51. *Id.* at 13 (describing case of Ahmad Abdou El-Khier).

52. *Id.* at 59; Tom Brune, " 'Of Special Interest': Immigration System Being Used to Detain Some Suspects," *Newsday,* September 16, 2002, A8 (describing Baloch case); Chisun Lee, "INS Detainee Hits, U.S. Strikes Back," *Village Voice,* January 30–February 5, 2003, 47; *Turkmen v. Ashcroft, supra.*

53. 18 U.S.C. §3144.

54. See Josh Gerstein, "Under Charge: The Real 9/11 Liberties Problem," *The New Republic,* April 22, 2002, 22; Naftali Bendavid, "Material Witness Arrests Under Fire; Dozens Detained in War on Terror," *Chicago Tribune,* December 24, 2001, 1.

55. Department of Justice, "Attorney General Ashcroft Outlines Foreign Terrorist Tracking Task Force," October 31, 2001, available at http://www.usdoj.gov/ag/speeches/2001/agcrisisremarks10_31.htm. Similarly, Assistant Attorney General Viet Dinh, centrally involved in the development and public defense of the Justice Department's post–September 11 strategy, explained in a law review article that:

Each of the detainees has been charged with a violation of either immigration law or criminal law, or is the subject of a material witness warrant issued by a court. The aim of the strategy is to reduce the risk of terrorist attacks on American soil. . . . These detentions may have incapacitated an Al Qaeda sleeper cell that was planning to strike a target in Washington, D.C.

Viet Dinh, "Freedom and Security after September 11," 25 *Harvard Journal of Law & Public Policy* 399, 402 (2001).

56. John Riley, "Held Without Charge: Material Witness Law Puts Detainees in Legal Limbo," *Newsday,* September 18, 2002, A6; Human Rights Watch, *Presumption of Guilt, supra,* 60–67.

57. Steve Fainaru and Margot Williams, "Material Witness Law Has Many in Limbo; Nearly Half Held in War on Terror Haven't Testified," *Washington Post,* November 24, 2002, A1.

58. *United States v. Awadallah,* 202 F. Supp. 2d 55 (S.D.N.Y. 2002); *United States v. Awadallah,* 202 F. Supp. 2d 82 (S.D.N.Y. 2002); Human Rights Watch, *Presumption of Guilt, supra,* 36, 65–67.

59. For example, federal agents used the material witness law to arrest Ahmed "Ed" Badawi, a travel agent and naturalized citizen in Orlando, Florida, who had done nothing more than sell an airline ticket to a person investigators considered suspicious. Like Awadallah, Badawi was established in the community and had fully cooperated with law enforcement. There was no reason to believe that he would not testify voluntarily. Yet he was held for three days in solitary confinement as a material witness. Riley, *Held Without Charge, supra.* Eyad Alrababah, a Palestinian living in Connecticut, was held for six weeks as a material witness after he voluntarily approached the FBI to tell them that he had had casual contacts with several of the hijackers. Riley, *Held Without Charge, supra.*

60. See Amy Goldstein, "A Sept. 11 Detainee's Long Path to Release; After Final Glitch, Ivory Coast Native Is Home," *Washington Post,* November 12, 2002, A3; Amy Goldstein, "No Longer a Suspect, But Still a Detainee; U.S. Won't Release or Deport Prisoner," *Washington Post,* May 27, 2002, A1; Amy Goldstein, " 'I Want to Go Home'; Detainee Tony Oulai Awaits End of 4-Month Legal Limbo," *Washington Post,* January 26, 2002, A1.

61. See Detention, Treatment, and Trial of Certain Non-Citizens in the War Against Terrorism, 66 Fed. Reg. 57, 833 (November 13, 2001).

62. *Abbasi v. Secretary of State for Foreign and Commonwealth Affairs* [2002] EWCA Civ 1598 (November 6, 2002), para. 64; see also *id,* at para. 107 ("We have made clear our deep concern that, in apparent contravention of fundamental principles of law, Mr. Abbasi may be subject to indefinite detention in territory over which the United States has exclusive control with no opportunity to challenge the legitimacy of his detention before any court or tribunal.").

63. "Why Mr. Hamdi Matters," Editorial, *Washington Post,* August 12, 2002, B6; "Detaining 'Enemy Combatants,' " Editorial, *New York Times,* January 10, 2003, A22; "A Question of Freedom," Editorial, *The Economist,* March 8, 2003; "Citizens Beware," Editorial, *Boston Globe,* January 10, 2003, A14; Anthony Lewis, "Marbury v. Madison v. Ashcroft," *New York Times,* February 24, 2003, A17.

64. Geneva Convention Relative to the Treatment of Prisoners of War, August 12, 1949, art. 102, 6 U.S.T. 3316, 75 U.N.T.S. 135.

65. *Id.* at art. 5.

66. *Id.*

67. President Bush, speaking to Congress on September 20, 2001, stated that the war on terrorism "begins with Al Qaeda, but it does not end there. It will not end until every terrorist group of global reach has been found, stopped, and defeated." "A Nation Challenged: President Bush's Address on Terrorism Before a Joint Meeting of Congress," *New York Times,* September 21, 2001, B4.

68. Associated Press, "Guantánamo Becomes an All-Purpose Prison; Suspected Terrorists from Many Countries Detained," *Newsday,* January 20, 2002, A23.

69. Only 310 of 1,196 individuals were determined to be enemy combatants, and all of those were determined to be "privileged combatants." The rest were found to be displaced civilians or refugees. Department of Defense, *Report on the Conduct of the Persian Gulf War, Final Report to Congress* (April 1992).

70. The detainees have been granted access only to the International Red Cross and in a few instances to visiting foreign embassy officials.

71. See Katharine Q. Seelye, "A Nation Challenged: Captives; Detainees are Not P.O.W.'s, Cheney and Rumsfeld Declare," *New York Times,* January 28, 2002, A6 (quoting Vice President Cheney describing the Guantánamo detainees as "the worst of a very bad lot," "very dangerous," and "devoted to killing millions of Americans"); Joseph Lelyveld, "In Guantánamo," *New York Review of Books,* November 7, 2002, 62 (quoting President Bush describing Guantánamo detainees as "killers," and Defense Secretary Donald Rumsfeld calling them "hard-core, well-trained terrorists").

72. "More to be Freed from Cuban Base; Official: Teenagers Are Likely to Leave Guantánamo Bay," *Chicago Tribune,* May 6, 2003, 16.

73. Greg Miller, "Many Held at Guantánamo Not Likely Terrorists," *Los Angeles Times,* December 22, 2002, 1.

74. Frank Griffiths, "Guantánamo Suicide Attempts Continue," Associated Press, February 19, 2003, available at http://washingtonpost.com.

75. *Coalition of Clergy, Lawyers, and Professors v. Bush,* 310 F.3d 1153 (9th Cir. 2002) (finding that lawyers and others challenging legality of Guantánamo Bay

detentions lacked standing to do so); *Al Odah v. United States*, 321 F.3d 1134 (D.C. Cir. 2003) (holding that foreign nationals held outside the United States have no constitutional rights, and therefore no right to seek habeas corpus to challenge the legality of their detentions).

76. *Hamdi v. Rumsfeld*, 296 F.3d 278, 283 (4th Cir. 2002).

77. *Id.*

78. *Hamdi v. Rumsfeld*, 316 F.3d 450 (4th Cir. 2003).

79. *Id.* at 459. ("Because it is undisputed that Hamdi was captured in a zone of active combat in a foreign theater of conflict, we hold that the submitted declaration is a sufficient basis upon which to conclude that the Commander in Chief has constitutionally detained Hamdi pursuant to the war powers entrusted to him by the United States Constitution. No further factual inquiry is necessary or proper, and we remand the case with directions to dismiss the petition.")

80. *Padilla v. Rumsfeld*, 233 F. Supp. 2d 564, 608, 569–70 (S.D.N.Y. 2002).

81. Respondents' Motion for Reconsideration in Part in *Padilla v. Rumsfeld*, 4, 6 (filed January 9, 2003).

82. *Id.* at Exh. A (Declaration of Vice Admiral Lowell Jacoby). Jacoby states that "only after such time as Padilla has perceived that help is not on the way can the United States reasonably expect to obtain all possible intelligence information from Padilla," and that affording him access to a lawyer "would create expectations by Padilla that his ultimate release may be obtained through an adversarial civil litigation process."

83. *Ashcraft v. Tennessee*, 322 U.S. 143 (1944).

84. *Padilla v. Rumsfeld*, 243 F. Supp. 2d 42 (S.D.N.Y. 2003). In a case not arising out of the war on terrorism, the federal government has argued to the United States Supreme Court that as long as it does not use the information in a criminal trial, the due process clause does not bar the government from coercing information from individuals against their will unless its interrogation methods actually "shock the conscience." Brief for the United States as Amicus Curiae Supporting Petitioner in *Chavez v. Marinez*, No. 01-1444 (U.S. 2002), 2001 U.S. Briefs 1444. In May 2003, the Supreme Court remanded the case, leaving unresolved the question whether the coercive interrogation tactics used violated substantive due process. *Chavez v. Martinez*, 2003 U. S. LEXIS 4274 (U.S. May 27, 2003).

85. *United States v. Salerno*, 481 U.S. 739, 755 (1987).

3. Ethnic Profiling

1. Testimony of Nihad Awad, Executive Director, Council on American-Islamic Relations, before the House Judiciary Committee, *The Effect of Racial Profiling in the American Muslim Community Since September 11, 2001*, January 24, 2002; see also Human Rights Watch, *"We Are Not the Enemy": Hate Crimes Against Arabs, Muslims, and Those Perceived to be Arab or Muslim after September 11* (November 2002), 14 (noting that the federal government reported a seventeen-fold increase in anti-Muslim hate crimes from 2000 to 2001); "Bias Incidents Against Muslims Are Soaring, Islamic Council Says," *New York Times*, May 1, 2002, A3; Susan Sachs, "For Many American Muslims, Complaints of Quiet but Persistent Bias," *New York Times*, April 25, 2002, A16.

2. Roper Center for Public Opinion Research, *Do You Approve or Disapprove of the Use of "Racial Profiling" by Police?*, Gallup Poll, December 9, 1999, available at WESTLAW, USGALLUP 120999 R6 009.

3. David Harris, *Profiles in Injustice: Why Racial Profiling Cannot Work* (New York: The New Press, 2002).

4. Gen. Accounting Office, *U.S. Customs Service: Observations on Selected Operations and Program Issues* (GAO/T-GGD/AIMD-00-150) (April 20, 2000); Jerome Skolnick and Abigail Baplovitz, "Guns, Drugs, and Profiling: Ways to Target Guns and Minimize Racial Profiling," 43 *Arizona Law Review* 413, 432–35 (2001) (detailing Customs Service reforms).

5. *Confirmation Hearing on the Nomination of John Ashcroft to Be Attorney General of the United States: Hearing Before the Senate Comm. on the Judiciary*, 107th Cong. 492 (January 22, 2001).

6. In June 2001, Representative John Conyers and Senator Russell Feingold introduced in both houses of Congress a bill prohibiting racial profiling and requiring data collection on the racial demographics of law enforcement. S. 989, 107th Cong. (2001); H.R. 207, 107th Cong. (2001).

7. Sam Howe Verhovek, "A Nation Challenged: Civil Liberties; Americans Give in to Race Profiling," *New York Times*, September 23, 2001, A1. A *Detroit News* poll of Michigan residents found that while "70 percent generally opposed racial profiling, 70 percent also agreed that 'authorities should take extra precautions in screening people of Arab descent when flying.' " Gregg Krupa, "Most in State Support Screening of Arabs," *Detroit News*, February 28, 2002, A1.

8. Stuart Taylor, "The Case for Using Racial Profiling at Airports," 33 *National Journal* 38 (September 22, 2001). Before September 11, Taylor wrote that:

> [R]acial profiling by police should be held to be unconstitutional . . .
> even where there is a statistically valid basis for believing that it will help

catch more drug dealers or illegal immigrants. . . . The negative impact of such profiling is far reaching . . . it subjects thousands of innocent people to the kind of inconvenience and humiliation most of us associate with police states; and it makes law enforcement more difficult by fomenting fear and distrust among potential witnesses and jurors. These costs far outweigh any law enforcement benefits.

Stuart Taylor, Jr., "Cabbies, Cops, Pizza Deliveries, and Racial Profiling," 32 *National Journal* 1891, (June 17, 2000). Others have also endorsed ethnic profiling of Arabs and Muslims in the war on terrorism. See Stanley Crouch, "Drawing the Line on Racial Profiling," *New York Daily News,* October 4, 2001, 41; Michael Kinsley, "When Is Racial Profiling Okay?", *Washington Post,* September 3, 2001, B7; Dorothy Rabinowitz, "Hijacking History," *Wall Street Journal,* December 7, 2001, A18; see generally Henry Weinstein, Michael Finnegan, and Teresa Watanabe, "Racial Profiling Gains Support as Search Tactic," *Los Angeles Times,* September 24, 2001, A1; William Glaberson, "Racial Profiling May Get Wider Approval by Courts," *New York Times,* September 21, 2001, A16.

9. Fox Butterfield, "A Nation Challenged: The Interviews; Police are Split on Questioning of Mideast Men," *New York Times,* November 22, 2001, A1; Laurie Goodstein, "A Nation Challenged: Civil Rights; American Sikhs Contend They Have Become a Focus of Profiling at Airports," *New York Times,* November 10, 2001, B6; Neil A. Lewis, "A Nation Challenged: Immigration Control; I.N.S. to Focus on Muslims Who Evade Deportation," *New York Times,* January 9, 2002, A12; Edward Walsh, "Abusive Behavior, Or Racial Profiling?; Airline, Attorneys Dispute Incident," *Washington Post,* January 4, 2002, A25.

10. Thomas B. Edsall, "Anti-Muslim Violence Assailed; Justice Dept. Probing Incidents Across the Nation," *Washington Post,* September 15, 2001, A9 (quoting Ashcroft).

11. Dana Milbank and Emily Wax, "Bush Visits Mosque to Forestall Hate Crimes; President Condemns an Increase in Violence Aimed at Arab Americans," *Washington Post,* September 18, 2001, A1.

12. Michael Chertoff, "Testimony Before the Senate Judiciary Committee Hearing on Preserving Freedoms While Defending Against Terrorism," *Federal News Service,* November 28, 2001, available at LEXIS, News Library, News Group File, All.

13. Naftali Bendavid, "Bush OK's Terror Tribunals; U.S. Seeks 5,000 Foreign Nationals for Questioning in Investigation," *Chicago Tribune,* November 14, 2001, 1.

14. Fox Butterfield, *supra;* Steven Elbow, "Madison Cops Won't Screen Muslims," *The Capital Times,* December 12, 2001 (quoting Madison police chief stating that Madison police "will not engage in random interviews of any per-

son solely based on their country of origin, race, religion, or any other characteristics unless there is specific evidence linked to that person for a criminal act.").

15. "New Round of Interviews Planned with Foreigners," *Wall Street Journal*, March 21, 2002, A8.

16. Jeanne A. Butterfield, *Executive Branch Actions Since September 11*, available at http://www.ailf.org/lac/2002/adminactions.htm.

17. Dan Eggen and Cheryl W. Thompson, "U.S. Seeks Thousands of Fugitive Deportees; Middle Eastern Men Are Focus of Search," *Washington Post*, January 8, 2002, A1; Department of Justice, Guidelines for Absconder Apprehension Initiative, January 25, 2002, available at http://news.findlaw.com/hdocs/docs/doj/abscndr012502mem.pdf; Susan Sachs, "U.S. Begins Crackdown on Muslims Who Defy Orders to Leave Country," *New York Times*, April 2, 2002, 13.

18. Jill Serjeant, "Hundreds of Muslim Immigrants Rounded Up in California," Reuters, December 18, 2002.

19. Michael Powell, "An Exodus Grows in Brooklyn," *Washington Post*, May 29, 2003, A1; Alex Gourevitch, "Detention Disorder: Ashcroft's Clumsy Round-up of Foreigners Lurches Forward," *American Prospect*, Web Exclusive, January 31, 2003, available at http://www.prospect.org/webfeatures/2003/01/gourevitch-a-01-31.html.

20. Michael Isikoff, "The FBI Says, Count the Mosques," *Newsweek*, February 3, 2003, 6.

21. Eric Lichtblau, "FBI Tells Officers to Count Local Muslims and Mosques," *New York Times*, January 28, 2003, A13.

22. The Lawyers Committee for Human Rights said that the countries are: Afghanistan, Algeria, Bahrain, Bangladesh, Djibouti, Egypt, Eritrea, Indonesia, Iran, Iraq, Jordan, Kazakhstan, Kuwait, Lebanon, Libya, Malaysia, Morocco, Oman, Pakistan, Philippines, Qatar, Saudi Arabia, Somalia, Sudan, Syria, Thailand, Tajikistan, Tunisia, Turkey, Turkmenistan, United Arab Emirates, Uzbekistan, Yemen, and the Occupied Territories. Christopher Drew and Adam Liptak, "Immigration Groups Fault Rule on Automatic Detention of Some Asylum Seekers," *New York Times*, March 31, 2003, B15.

23. "National Press Club Luncheon Address by Homeland Security Department Secretary Tom Ridge," *Federal News Service*, April 29, 2003.

24. See Chertoff, Testimony Before the Senate Judiciary Committee, *supra*.

25. Gerald Neuman, "Terrorism, Selective Deportation and the First Amendment after *Reno v. AADC*," 14 *Georgetown Immigration Law Journal* 313, 339 (2000).

26. *Saint Francis College v. Al-Khazraji,* 481 U.S. 604, 614 (1987) (Brennan, J., concurring).

27. See generally Natsu Saito, "Alien and Non-Alien Alike: Citizenship, 'Foreign-ness,' and Racial Hierarchy in American Law," 76 *Oregon Law Review* 261 (1997); Keith Aoki, " 'Foreign-ness' and Asian American Identities: Yellowface, World War II Propaganda, and Bifurcated Racial Stereotypes," 4 *UCLA Asian Pacific American Law Journal* 1 (1996); Neil Gotanda, " 'Other Non-Whites' in American Legal History: A Review of 'Justice at War,' " 85 *Columbia Law Review* 1186 (1985).

28. Gerald L. Neuman, "Aliens as Outlaws: Government Services, Proposition 187, and the Structure of Equal Protection Doctrine," 42 *UCLA Law Review* 1425, 1452 (1995); see also *id.* at 1428–29.

29. See David Cole, *No Equal Justice: Race and Class in the American Criminal Justice System* (New York: The New Press, 1999), 41–43; Samuel R. Gross and Debra Livingston, "Racial Profiling Under Attack," 102 *Columbia Law Review* 1413, 1415 (2002). But see Richard Banks, "Race-Based Suspect Selection and Colorblind Equal Protection Doctrine and Discourse," 48 *UCLA Law Review* 1075 (2001) (questioning distinction between use of race as a generalization and use of race as an identifying criterion from eyewitness report).

30. Gross and Livingston, *supra,* 1421.

31. Natsu Taylor Saito, "Symbolism Under Siege: Japanese American Redress and the 'Racing' of Arab Americans as 'Terrorists,' " 8 *Asian Law Journal* 1, 12 (2001).

32. Twila Decker, "Muslims Fight Unfairness, the American Way," *St. Petersburg Times,* October 17, 1999, available at 1999 WL 27322848.

33. *Miller v. Johnson,* 515 U.S. 900, 904 (1995).

34. "Muslims Move Into Political Arena in U.S.," *Florida Times-Union,* October 22, 1999, available at 1999 WL 29069360 (reporting on numbers of Muslims and Arabs in the United States); U. S. Census Bureau, Supplementary Survey, Fact Finder, Selected Social Science data, available at http://factfinder.census. gov (estimating 1.2 million Arab-Americans as of 2000 census); United Nations Development Programme, *Arab Human Development Report 2002* (New York: United Nations, 2002) (estimating 280 million Arabs worldwide).

35. See International Policy Institute for Counter Terrorism, "Al Qa'ida—The Base," (reporting that Al Qaeda has 2,830 members), at http://www.ict.org.il/ inter_/orgdet.cfm?orgid=74. The Council on Foreign Relations says the num-ber of Al Qaeda members could range from "several hundred to several thou-sand." See http://www.terrorismanswers.com/groups/alqaeda.html#Q3. The

FBI estimated that by September 2002, "hard-core" Al Qaeda membership had dwindled to around 200. Mark Hosenball, "A War Yet to Be Won," *Newsweek,* September 9, 2002, available at http://www.msnbc.com/news/801470.asp?0sl=-12&cpl=1. The Council of Foreign Relations estimates that about 10,000 persons may have attended Al Qaeda training camps at one time. See http://www.terrorismanswers.com/groups/alqaeda.html#Q3. But as the camps were used to train Taliban military personnel, the fact of attendance does not necessarily entail commitment to Al Qaeda. See Jane Mayer, "Lost in Jihad," *The New Yorker,* March 10, 2003, 50, 52–54.

36. *Craig v. Boren,* 429 U.S. 190, 201–04 (1976).

37. Warran Hoge, "A Nation Challenged: The Convert; Shoe-Bomb Suspect Fell in with Extremists," *New York Times,* December 27, 2001, B6.

38. Bill Dedman, "Memo Warns Against Use of Profiling as Defense," *Boston Globe,* October 12, 2001, A27.

39. Cf. Malcolm Gladwell, "Safety in the Skies: How Far Can Airline Security Go?," *New Yorker,* October 1, 2001, 50 (arguing that it is cognitively impossible to remain alert in reviewing metal detectors at airports because the fact that the vast majority of luggage will pose no threat inevitably causes security personnel to let their guard down).

4. Patriots and Enemies: Redefining Terrorism

1. Pub. L. No. 107–56, 115 Stat. 272 (2001) [hereinafter USA PATRIOT Act or PATRIOT Act].

2. Compare USA PATRIOT Act, §802, amending 18 U.S.C. §2331(5) (defining "domestic terrorism") with USA PATRIOT Act, §411(a), amending 8 U.S.C. §1182(a)(3)(B)(iii)(V)(b) (defending "terrorist activity" for immigration purposes).

3. USA PATRIOT Act, §411.

4. See Immigration and Nationality Act of 1990, Pub. L. No. 101–649, 8 U.S.C.S. §1182(a)(3)(C) (repealing INA §212(a)(27) and (28) (1952), which excluded anarchists; members of the Communist Party; noncitizens who advocated Communism or violent overthrow of the U.S. government; and noncitizens who wrote or published, or even knowingly had in their possession, material advocating such activities).

5. *NAACP v. Claiborne Hardware,* 458 U.S. 886, 932 (1982).

6. *Scales v. United States,* 367 U.S. 203, 224–25 (1961).

7. *Id.* at 224–25, 229–30.

8. See David Cole, "Hanging with the Wrong Crowd: Of Gangs, Terrorists, and the Right of Association," 1999 *Supreme Court Review* 203, 246–50.

9. 18 U.S.C. §2339B.

10. USA PATRIOT Act, §411. The Act defines as a deportable offense the solicitation of members or funds for, or the provision of material support to, any group designated as terrorist. There is no defense available for support to designated groups, not even for those who can show that their support was not intended to and did not further terrorism. The government is free to designate as terrorist any organization that uses or threatens to use violence. In addition, the law makes noncitizens who support even nondesignated groups deportable if the group has engaged in or threatened violence, unless the noncitizen can prove that he neither knew nor reasonably should have known that his support would further the group's terrorist activities.

11. See, e.g., U.S. Department of State, *Patterns of Global Terrorism: 1988*, (1989) 82; U.S. Department of State, *Patterns of Global Terrorism: 1987*, (1988) 65.

12. See *Humanitarian Law Project v. Reno*, 205 F.3d 1130 (9th Cir. 2000) (accepting government's argument that penalizing material support is distinct from penalizing membership), *cert. denied*, 532 U.S. 904 (2001); see also Gerald Neuman "Terrorism, Selective Deportation and the First Amendment After *Reno v. AADC*," 14 *Georgetown Immigration Law Journal* 313, 333–35 (2000) (making similar argument).

13. See, e.g., *United States v. Robel*, 389 U.S. 258, 262 (1967); *Keyishian v. Board of Regents of Univ. of State of N.Y.*, 385 U.S. 589, 606 (1967); *Scales v. United States*, 367 U.S. 203, 221–22 (1961).

14. See *Robel*, 389 U.S. at 262 (invalidating ban on Communist Party members working in defense facilities absent showing of "specific intent" to further the party's illegal aims); *Keyishian*, 385 U.S. at 606 (holding that "[m]ere knowing membership without a specific intent to further the unlawful aims of an organization is not a constitutionally adequate basis" for barring Communist Party members from employment in state university system); *Elfbrandt v. Russell*, 384 U.S. 11, 19 (1966) (invalidating oath requiring state employees not to join Communist Party because "[a] law which applies to membership without the 'specific intent' to further the illegal aims of the organization infringes unnecessarily on protected freedoms"); *Noto v. United States*, 367 U.S. 290, 299–300 (1961) (finding that the First Amendment bars punishment of "one in sympathy with the legitimate aims of [the Communist Party], but not specifically intending to accomplish them by resort to violence"); *Scales*, 367 U.S. at 221–22 (construing the Smith Act, which barred membership in an organization advocating violent overthrow of government, to require showing of "specific intent").

15. See *Meyer v. Grant,* 486 U.S. 414 (1988) (holding that statutory prohibition against paid solicitors violates First Amendment); *Citizens Against Rent Control v. City of Berkeley,* 454 U.S. 290, 295–96 (1981) (holding that monetary contributions to a group are a form of "collective expression" protected by the right of association); *Village of Schaumburg v. Citizens for a Better Environment,* 444 U.S. 620, 632–38 (1980) (ruling that the First Amendment protects a nonprofit group's right to solicit funds).

16. *Buckley v. Valeo,* 424 U.S. 1, 65–66 (1976) (quoting *NAACP v. Alabama,* 357 U.S. 449, 460 (1958)). Monetary contributions to political organizations are a protected form of association and expression. *Id.* at 16–17, 24–25.

17. See Racketeer Influenced and Corrupt Organizations Act (RICO), 18 U.S.C. §§1961–68 (2001); Money Laundering Control Act of 1986, 18 U.S.C. §§1956–57 (2002). Forfeiture of property is authorized by 18 U.S.C. §§981–82 (2002).

18. See Philip Monrad, "Ideological Exclusion, Plenary Power, and the PLO," 77 *California Law Review* 831 (1989).

19. See *supra* note 4.

20. USA PATRIOT Act, §411.

21. *Brandenburg v. Ohio,* 395 U.S. 444, 447(1969).

22. See, e.g., *Kleindienst v. Mandel,* 408 U.S. 753 (1972) (assuming without deciding that a noncitizen outside the United States does not have First Amendment right to object to his exclusion); *United States ex rel. Knauff v. Shaughnessy,* 338 U.S. 537 (1950) (holding that noncitizens outside the United States do not have a right to enter protected by the Constitution).

23. See, e.g., *Kleindienst v. Mandel,* 408 U.S. 775 (Marshall, J., dissenting) (recognizing that exclusion of a noncitizen for his political associations and views infringes on the rights of U.S. citizens to exchange ideas with him); *Abourezk v. Reagan,* 785 F.2d 1043 (D.C. Cir. 1986) (same), *aff'd per curiam,* 484 U.S. 1 (1987); Steven R. Shapiro, "Ideological Exclusions: Closing the Border to Political Dissidents," 100 *Harvard Law Review* 930 (1987).

24. USA PATRIOT Act, §412(a)(3) (amending 8 U.S.C. §1226A(a) (2001)).

25. *Zadvydas v. Davis,* 533 U.S. 678, 690 (2001) (explaining constitutional limits on preventive detention, and interpreting immigration statute not to permit indefinite detention of deportable noncitizens); *Foucha v. Louisiana,* 504 U.S. 71, 80–81 (1992) (holding civil commitment to be constitutional only where individual is mentally ill and poses a danger to the community and adequate procedural protections are provided); *United States v. Salerno,* 481 U.S. 739, 751–55 (1987) (upholding preventive detention only where there is a showing of threat to others or risk of flight, the detention is limited in time, and adequate procedural safeguards are provided).

26. USA PATRIOT Act, §412 (amending 8 U.S.C. §1226A(a)(2) (2001)).

27. *Zadvydas,* 533. U.S. at 702 (holding that INS could not detain indefinitely even noncitizens finally determined to be deportable where there was no reasonable likelihood that they could be deported because no country would take them). The Court in *Zadvydas* reserved for another day the legality of indefinite detention of a deportable noncitizen where applied "narrowly to 'a small segment of particularly dangerous individuals,' say suspected terrorists." *Id.* at 691 (citation omitted). But the PATRIOT Act's definition of "terrorist activity" is not limited to a narrow, "small segment of particularly dangerous individuals," as the Court in *Zadvydas* contemplated, but applies to garden-variety criminals, barroom brawlers, and those who have supported no violent activity whatsoever, but have merely provided humanitarian support to a disfavored group.

28. USA PATRIOT Act, §218 (amending 50 U.S.C. §§1804(a)(7)(B) and 1823(a)(7)(B) (2001)).

29. 50 U.S.C. §§1801–1863 (2001).

30. 50 U.S.C. §1801(a)(5) (2002) (defining "foreign power" to include "a foreign-based political organization, not substantially composed of United States persons"); 50 U.S.C. 1801(b)(1)(A) (2002) (defining an "agent of a foreign power" to include "any person other than a United States person, who . . . acts in the United States as an officer or employee of a foreign power").

31. 50 U.S.C. §1805(a)(3)(A) (2002).

32. 50 U.S.C. §1825 (g) (2002).

33. USA PATRIOT Act, §218 (amending 50 U.S.C. §§1804(a)(7)(B) and 1823(a)(7)(B) (2001)).

34. See Dan Eggen and Susan Schmidt, "Secret Court Rebuffs Ashcroft: Justice Department Chided on Misinformation," *Washington Post,* August 23, 2002, A1.

35. *In re All Matters Submitted to the Foreign Intelligence Surveillance Court,* 218 F. Supp. 2d 611 (Foreign Intel. Surv. Ct. 2002).

36. *In re Sealed Case,* 310 F.3d 717 (Foreign Int. Surv. Ct. Rev. 2002).

37. The draft legislation is available at http://www.publicintegrity.org/dtaweb/downloads/Story_01_020703_Doc_1.pdf.

38. *People's Mojahedin Org. of Iran v. United States Dept. of State,* 182 F.3d 17, 23 (D.C. Cir. 1999).

39. The Alien Act, enacted as a two-year measure with the Sedition Act, authorized the president to deport "all such aliens as he shall judge dangerous." Act of June 25, 1798, ch. 58, 1 Stat. 570. It expired in 1800 without having been enforced.

John C. Miller, *Crisis in Freedom: The Alien and Sedition Acts* (Boston: Little, Brown, 1951), 187–93.

40. 8 C.F.R. §241.4 (g)(5)(i) (2002) (authorizing indefinite detention of terrorist aliens).

5. Targeting Citizens

1. Homeland Security Act, Pub. L. No. 107–296, §1514 (codified as 6 U.S.C. §554) (2002)). Richard Armey's role in creating this ban on national identification cards is described in Ellen Sorokin, "Security Bill Loses ID Card, TIPS," *Washington Times,* July 19, 2002, A1.

2. Homeland Security Act, §880 (codified as 6 U.S.C. §460 (2002)). See also Phyllis Schlafly, "Homeland Security or Homeland Spying?," Copley News Service, July 23, 2002; Sorokin, *supra.*

3. See, e.g., *California v. Greenwood,* 486 U.S. 35 (1988).

4. Clyde Wayne Crews, Jr., *The Pentagon's Total Information Awareness Project: Americans Under the Microscope?,* Cato Institute (November 26, 2002), available at http://www.cato.org/tech/tk/021126-tk.html; see also William Safire, "You Are a Suspect," *New York Times,* November 14, 2002, A35; Press Release, ACLU, "ACLU Calls on President Bush to Disavow New Cyber-Spying Scheme that Seeks to Put Every American Under Scrutiny" (November 14, 2002), available at http://www.aclu.org/SafeandFree/SafeandFree.cfm?ID=11309&c=206.

5. Editorial, "Total Information Awareness," *Washington Post,* November 16, 2002, A20 (featuring logo). Poindexter's convictions were overturned on appeal, not on the ground that he did not lie, but only on the ground that the convictions were tainted by his own prior immunized testimony about his lying. *U.S. v. Poindexter,* 951 F.2d 369 (D.C. Cir. 1991).

6. Pub. L. No. 108–7, §111 (2003); Adam Clymer, "Congress Agrees to Bar Pentagon from Terror Watch of Americans," *New York Times,* February 12, 2003, A1.

7. USA PATROIT Act, Pub. L. No. 107–56, 115 Stat. 272 (2001), §215, amending 50 U.S.C. §1861(a)(1)(2001); *id.* at §505(a), amending 1 U.S.C. §2709(b)(2001); *id.* at §507, amending 20 U.S.C. §1232g(j)(1) & (2) (2001).

8. Freedom to Read Protection Act of 2003 (Introduced in House), H.R. 1157, 108th Cong. 1st Sess. (March 6, 2003).

9. See discussion of deportation proceedings against the "LA 8" *infra* Chapter 12.

10. 18 U.S.C. §2339B; 8 U.S.C. §1182(a)(3)(B)(iv)(VI).

11. John Walker Lindh, the so-called "American Taliban," was charged with providing material support to two terrorist organizations by attending their training camps. *United States v. Lindh,* No. CR. 02-37-A (E.D. Va. Oct. 4, 2002), available at http://news.findlaw.com/hdocs/docs/terrorism/uswlindh020502cmp.html. Lynn Stewart, the attorney for Sheikh Omar Abdel Rahman, has been charged with providing material support to an Egyptian terrorist organization by facilitating communications between the sheikh and the group. *United States v. Sattar,* No. CR. 02-395 (S.D.N.Y. Apr. 4, 2002), available at http://news.findlaw.com/ hdocs/docs/terrorism/ussattar040902ind.pdf. Five young men from Lackawanna, New York, have been charged under the material support statute for attending an Al Qaeda training camp. *United States v. Goba,* No. 02-M-107 (W.D.N.Y. Oct. 21, 2002), available at http://news.findlaw.com/hdocs/docs/ terrorism/usgoba102102ind.html. James Ujaama, a Seattle activist, was charged with providing material support by planning to set up a training camp here for Al Qaeda. *United States v. Ujaama* (W.D. Wash. Aug. 28, 2002), available at http://news.findlaw.com/hdocs/docs/terrorism/usujaama82802ind.pdf. A group of men in Detroit has been charged under the same statute for allegedly operating as an underground support unit for terrorist attacks and a "sleeper" operational combat cell. *United States v. Koubriti,* No. 01-80778 (E.D. Mich. Aug. 28, 2002), available at http://news.findlaw.com/hdocs/docs/terrorism/uskoubriti82802ind. pdf. In February 2003, the government indicted Sami Al-Arian, a professor at the University of South Florida, and seven other individuals for a range of crimes, including conspiracy to provide material support to the Palestine Islamic Jihad. *United States v. Al-Arian,* No. 8-03-CR (M.D. Fla. Feb. 20, 2003), available at http://www.usdoj.gov/usao/flm/pr/022003indict.pdf. In March 2003, the United States unsealed arrest warrants for two Yemeni men accused of raising money in Brooklyn for Al Qaeda and Hamas. *United States v. Al-Moayad,* M-03-0016 (E.D. N.Y. 2003) (arrest warrant), available at http://news.findlaw.com/hdocs/docs/ terrorism/usalmoayad10503aff.pdf; *United States v. Zayed* (E.D. N.Y. 2003) (arrest warrant), available at http://news.findlaw.com/hdocs/docs/terrorism/uszayed 10903aff.pdf.

12. International Convention for the Suppression of the Financing of Terrorism (UN, 1999); see, e.g., Jeff Gerth and Judith Miller, "Report Says Saudis Fail to Crack Down on Charities That Finance Terrorists," *New York Times,* October 17, 2002, A20; Serge Schmemann, "U.N. Gets a Litany of Antiterror Plans," *New York Times,* January 12, 2002, A7; Kurt Eichenwald, "Global Plan to Track Terror Funds," *New York Times,* December 19, 2001, B5.

13. *Humanitarian Law Project v. Reno,* 205 F.3d 1130, 1133 (9th Cir. 2000).

14. John Mintz, "Muslim Charity Leader Indicted," *Washington Post,* October 10, 2002, A14; John Mintz, "U.S. Labels Muslim Charity as Terrorist Group," *Washington Post,* October 19, 2002, A2; John Mintz and Neely Tucker, "Judge Backs U.S. on Assets Seizure," *Washington Post,* August 10, 2002, A12.

15. 50 U.S.C. §1701(a).

16. Exec. Order No. 12,947, 3 C.F.R. §319 (1995), reprinted in 50 U.S.C. §1701 (2000). That executive order, which remains in effect, also authorizes the secretary of state to designate additional "Specially Designated Terrorists" if found to be "owned or controlled by, or to act for or on behalf of" an entity designated by the president. *Id.* at §1(a)(iii).

17. Exec. Order No. 13,224 §1(d), 3 C.F.R. §786 (2001), reprinted in 50 U.S.C.A. §1701 (West Supp. 2002).

18. USA PATRIOT Act, §106, amending 50 U.S.C. §1702(a)(1)(B) and adding 50 U.S.C. §1702(c).

19. The Global Relief Foundation, Inc., challenged both the search and seizure of its offices and the freezing of its assets on multiple constitutional grounds. In June 2002, a district court rejected all of the challenges. It found that the freezing order did not constitute punishment, and that therefore protections associated with the criminal process were not applicable. It upheld both the search and seizure and the freezing order on the basis of secret information submitted ex parte and in camera to the court, and not provided to Global Relief Development Foundation or its lawyers. *Global Relief Foundation, Inc. v. O'Neill,* 207 F. Supp. 2d 779 (N.D. Ill. 2002). And it held that IEEPA authorized the freezing of property as long as any foreign national or country had an interest in it, a minimal requirement met by the fact that the foundation had foreign nationals on its board. The U.S. Court of Appeals affirmed that decision in December 2002. *Global Relief Foundation, Inc. v. O'Neill,* 315 F.3d 748 (7th Cir. 2002). The Holy Land Foundation also challenged its designation, and in August 2002, a district court also rejected its challenges, using similar reasoning. *Holy Land Foundation for Relief and Development v. Ashcroft,* 219 F. Supp. 2d 57 (D.D.C. 2002).

20. *Hearing Before the Subcomm. on Int'l Law, Immigration, and Refugees of the House Comm. on the Judiciary,* 103d Cong. 7 (February 23, 1994) (written testimony of Mary A. Ryan, Assistant Secretary for Consular Affairs, U.S. Department of State).

21. List of Specially Designated Terrorists Who Threaten to Disrupt the Middle East Peace Process, 60 Fed. Reg. 41,152 (August 11, 1995).

22. See David Johnston, "U.S. Prosecutors Suspect an American Citizen of Financing Hamas Terror," *New York Times,* June 14, 1998, A20; Ashraf Kalif, "U.S. Citizen Accused by Israel of Having Hamas Ties Becomes Test Case for Arab-Americans and Israeli Justice System," *Cairo Times,* August 6–10, 1998, 11.

23. See *infra* Chapter 10.

24. See David Cole and James X. Dempsey, *Terrorism and the Constitution: Sacrificing Civil Liberties in the Name of National Security* (New York: The New Press, 2002), 79–83.

25. *United States Attorney General Guidelines on General Crimes, Racketeering Enterprise and Domestic Security/Terrorism Investigations* 21–22 (2002), available at http://www.usdoj.gov/olp/generalcrimes2.pdf.

26. *United States Attorney General Guidelines on General Crimes, Racketeering Enterprise and Domestic Security/Terrorism Investigations,* Part II.B (1989), available at http://www.usdoj.gov/ag/readingroom/generalcrimea.htm.

27. *United States Attorney General Guidelines for FBI Foreign Intelligence Collection and Foreign Counterintelligence Investigations* (1983). These guidelines are classified in significant part.

28. Cole and Dempsey, *Terrorism and the Constitution, supra,* 83–86.

29. Special Administrative Measure for the Prevention of Acts of Violence and Terrorism, 66 Fed Reg. 55,062 (October 31, 2001) (amending 2 C.F.R. §501.3(d)).

6. Crossing the Citizen-Noncitizen Divide: An Overview

1. H. Freedman, ed., *Jeremiah, Soncino Books of the Bible* (series ed. A. Cohen) (London: Soncino Books of the Bible, rev. ed. 1985), 52, (quoting Hermann Cohen).

7. Enemy Aliens and Enemy Races

1. Quoted in Peter Irons, *Justice at War* (New York: Oxford University Press, 1983), 83. This account of the treatment of Masuo and Minoru Yasui is drawn from Irons's book, (*id.* at 81–87), and Minoru's own account, told in Bud Schultz and Ruth Schultz, *It Did Happen Here: Recollections of Political Repression in America* (Berkeley: University of California Press, 1989), 347–59.

2. Bonnie Honig, *Democracy and the Foreigner* (Princeton, NJ: Princeton University Press, 2001), 1–14.

3. John Higham, *Strangers in the Land: Patterns of American Nativism 1860–1925* (New York: Atheneum, 1963), 4.

4. James M. Smith, *Freedom's Fetters: The Alien and Sedition Laws and American Civil Liberties* (Ithaca, NY: Cornell University Press, 1956), 12–49.

5. John C. Miller, *Crisis in Freedom: The Alien and Sedition Acts* (Boston: Little, Brown, 1951), 52–53.

6. The Act prohibited "false, scandalous, and malicious writing or writings against the government of the United States, or either house of the Congress . . . or the President . . . with intent to defame [them], or to bring them . . . into con-

tempt or disrepute; or to excite against them . . . the hatred of the good people of the United States. . . ." Act of July 14, 1798, ch. 74, §2, 1 Stat. 596 (1798).

7. 376 U.S. 254, 273–76 (1964).

8. 50 U.S.C. §§21–24 (2002). See generally Gregory Sidak, "War, Liberty, and Enemy Aliens," 67 *New York University Law Review* 1402 (1992).

9. *Ludecke v. Watkins,* 335 U.S. 160, 171–72 (1948).

10. See *Lockington's Case,* Brightly (N.P.) 269 (Pa. 1813) (upholding detention of enemy aliens during War of 1812).

11. 1918 Att'y Gen. Ann. Rep. Exhibit 30, Section 4, pp. 681–82; Richard Gid Powers, *Secrecy and Power: The Life of J. Edgar Hoover* (New York: The Free Press, 1987), 40–55.

12. 1919 Att'y Gen. Ann. Rep. 25.

13. 1942 Att'y Gen. Ann. Rep. 14.

14. See Lawrence DiStasi, ed., *Una Storia Segreta: The Secret History of Italian American Evacuation and Internment During World War II* (Berkeley, CA: Heyday Books, 2001), xviii, 16, 19–20; John Christgau, *"Enemies": World War II Alien Internment* (Ames: Iowa State University Press, 1985).

15. Athan Theoharis, *Spying on Americans: Political Surveillance from Hoover to the Huston Plan* (Philadelphia: Temple University Press, 1978), 41.

16. *Id.* at 12.

17. Memorandum of Attorney General Biddle to Hugh B. Cox. Assistant Attorney General, and J. Edgar Hoover, Director, FBI (July 16, 1943), reprinted in *Wartime Violation of Italian American Civil Liberties Act: Hearing on H.R. 2442 Before the Subcommittee on the Constitution of the House Committee on the Judiciary* 55–56 (October 26, 1999).

18. Supplementary Detailed Staff Reports on Intelligence Activities and the Rights of Americans, Book III, Final Report of the Select Committee to Study Governmental Operations with Respect to Intelligence Activities, S. Rep. No. 94-755, 94th Cong., 2d Sess. 420-21 (1976) (hereinafter Church Committee, Book III).

19. Samuel Hopkins Adams, "Invaded America," *Everybody's Magazine,* v. 37, pp. 55–56 (March 1918), quoted in Higham, *supra,* 214.

20. Final Report of General DeWitt, quoted in Jacobus tenBroek, Edward N. Barnhart and Floyd W. Matson, *Prejudice, War and the Constitution* (Berkeley: University of California Press, 1954), 110.

21. Brief of Japanese American Citizens League, Amicus Curiae at 198, *Korematsu v. United States*, 323 U.S. 214 (1944) (No. 22), reprinted in *Landmark Briefs and Arguments of the Supreme Court of the United States: Constitutional Law*, eds. Philip B. Kurland and Gerhard Casper (Arlington, VA: University Publications of America, 1975), vol. 42, 309–530.

22. James MacGregor Burns, *Roosevelt: The Soldier of Freedom* (New York: Harcourt Brace Jovanovich, 1970), 215, quoted in Michi Weglyn, *Years of Infamy: The Untold Story of America's Concentration Camps* (New York: Morrow, 1976), 43.

23. Some naturalized Italian citizens, for example, were required to leave their homes and move from the West coast. DiStasi, *supra*, 21–22, 139. The naturalized Italian-Americans were not ordered to move en masse, however, but on an individualized basis. *Id.* American citizens were also affected if they were the children or spouses of interned foreign nationals. Arthur Jacobs, a twelve-year-old American of German parents, was interned in the United States along with his father, who was accused of having pro-German sentiments and Nazi connections. The evidence against his father was never revealed, and he was detained despite a unanimous recommendation from his hearing board and a letter from the United States Attorney both recommending against his internment. After the war, Jacobs's father was threatened with deportation, and agreed to return to Germany. His family accompanied him, only to be detained again when they arrived in Germany. See Arthur Jacobs, *The Prison Called Hohenasperg: An American Boy Betrayed by his Government During World War II* (Parkland, FL: Universal Publishers, 1999).

24. tenBroek, Barnhart, and Matson, *supra*, 15–16.

25. *Id.* at 18.

26. *Id.* at 17.

27. Chinese Exclusion Act of 1882, ch. 126, 22 Stat. 58 (1882) (repealed 1943).

28. Geary Act of 1892, ch. 60, §6, 27 Stat. 25 (1892).

29. See *The Chinese Exclusion Case*, 130 U.S. 581 (1889) (affirming constitutionality of Chinese Exclusion Act of 1882); *Fong Yue Ting v. United States* 149 U.S. 698 (1893) (affirming "one white witness" rule of evidence).

30. Thomas Alexander Aleinikoff, David A. Martin, and Hiroshi Motomura, *Immigration and Citizenship: Process and Policy* (St. Paul, MN: West Group, 4th ed. 1998), 165.

31. See generally Irons, *Justice at War, supra*; tenBroek, Barnhart, and Matson, *supra*.

32. tenBroek, Barnhart, and Matson, *supra*, 33–67.

33. *Id.* at 81.

34. *Id.* at 83–84.

35. *Id.* at 110; see also *id.* at 92 ("Local, state, and national officials voiced the conviction that the absence of sabotage in the present makes it all the more certain in the future.").

36. *Korematsu v. United States,* 323 U.S. 214 (1944); *Hirabayashi v. United States,* 320 U.S. 81 (1943); *Yasui v. United States,* 320 U.S. 115 (1943).

37. *Hirabayashi v. United States,* 320 U.S. at 96–97, 101.

38. *Id.* at 101.

39. *Korematsu,* 323 U.S. 214.

40. *Korematsu,* 323 U.S. at 235 (Murphy, J., dissenting); see Jacobus tenBroek, "Wartime Power of the Military Over Citizen Civilians Within the Country," 41 *California Law Review* 167, 206 (1953).

41. *Korematsu v. United States,* 584 F. Supp. 1406, 1417 (N.D. Cal. 1984); *Hirabayashi v. United States,* 828 F.2d 591 (9th Cir. 1987); Civil Liberties Act of 1988, Pub. L. No. 100-383, 102 Stat. 903 (1988) (acknowledging "fundamental injustice" of internment and providing restitution for all persons ordered to leave their homes).

42. *Stenberg v. Carhart,* 530 U.S. 914, 953 (2000) (Scalia, J., dissenting). See also *Adarand Constructors, Inc., v. Peña,* 515 U.S. 200, 236 (1995) (O'Connor, J., joined by Rehnquist, C. J., and Kennedy, Scalia, and Thomas, JJ.) ("*Korematsu* demonstrates vividly that even 'the most rigid scrutiny' can sometimes fail to detect an illegitimate racial classification. . . . Any retreat from the most searching judicial inquiry can only increase the risk of another such error occurring in the future."); *id.* at 244 n. 2 (Stevens, J., dissenting, joined by Ginsburg, J.) (referring to the "shameful" burdens that the government imposed on Japanese Americans during World War II, some of which the Court upheld in *Korematsu*); *id.* at 275 (Ginsburg, J., dissenting, joined by Breyer, J.) ("[T]he enduring lesson one should draw from *Korematsu*" is that "scrutiny the Court described as 'most rigid' nonetheless yielded a pass for an odious, gravely injurious racial classification."); *Metro Broadcasting v. F.C.C.,* 497 U.S. 547, 633 (1990) (Kennedy, J., dissenting, joined by Scalia, J.) ("Even strict scrutiny may not have sufficed to invalidate early race-based laws of most doubtful validity, as we learned in *Korematsu*."). Only Justice Souter has yet to weigh in. I am indebted to Professor Eric Muller for this point.

43. William Rehnquist, *All the Laws but One: Civil Liberties in Wartime* (New York: Alfred A. Knopf, 1998), 208–11.

44. Civil Liberties Act of 1988, 50 U.S.C. §1989 *et seq.* (1988).

45. Eugene V. Rostow, "The Japanese American Cases: A Disaster," 54 *Yale Law Journal* 489, 532 (1945).

46. For an excellent comparison of the treatment of Japanese-Americans during World War II with the treatment of Arabs and Muslims in the United States, even before September 11, see Natsu Taylor Saito, "Symbolism Under Siege: Japanese American Redress and the 'Racing' of Arab Americans as 'Terrorists," 8 *Asian Law Journal* 1 (2001).

47. Church Committee, Book III, *supra,* 438–39. For an excellent summary of the detention program, see Robert Justin Goldstein, "An American Gulag? Summary Arrest and Emergency Detention of Political Dissidents in the United States," 10 *Columbia Human Rights Law Review* 541, 558–61 (1978).

48. Church Committee, Book III, *supra,* 438–41; Hearings Before the Senate Select Committee to Study Governmental Operations with Respect to Intelligence Activities, 94th Cong. 1st Sess., Vol. 6 at 416–26, 657–65 (1975).

49. Church Committee, Book III, *supra,* 440.

50. 64 Stat. 1019, §103(a) (1950), repealed by Act of September 25, 1971, Pub. L. No. 92–128, §2, 85 Stat. 347.

51. Richard Longaker, "Emergency Detention: The Generation Gap 1950–71," 27 *Western Political Quarterly* 395 (1974); see also William M. Wiecek, "The Legal Foundations of Domestic Anticommunism: The Background of *Dennis v. United States,*" 2001 *Supreme Court Review* 375, 426–27; 64 Stat. 1019, §104(d) (providing that "the Attorney General or his representative shall not be required to furnish information the revelation of which would disclose the identity or evidence of Government agents or officers which the Attorney General believes would be dangerous to the national safety and security to divulge").

52. Wiecek, *supra,* 427.

53. Church Committee, Book III, *supra,* 441, 445–46.

54. *Id.* at 87, 509–18.

55. Pub. L. No. 92–128, §2, 85 Stat. 347 (1971), codified at 18 U.S.C. §4001.

56. Immigration and Naturalization Service, *Alien Terrorists and Undesirables: A Contingency Plan* (1986), attached as Exh. 2 to Declaration of Paul Hoffman, filed with Motion for Preliminary Injunction in *American-Arab Anti-Discrimination Comm. v. Meese,* Civ. No. 87-02107 (SVW) (C.D. Cal.) (filed Apr. 6, 1987); see Mary Thornton, "Arab Groups See INS Bias; U.S. Denies Plan to Seek Deportations," *Washington Post,* February 7, 1987, A17; Ronald L. Soble, "INS Labels Terrorist Emergency Proposal Just an 'Option Paper,' " *Los Angeles Times,* February 7, 1987, 31.

8. Alien Radicals and Radical Citizens: From Anarchism to Sedition

1. *Bailey v. Richardson,* 182 F.2d 46 (D.C. Cir. 1950), *aff'd summ.,* 341 U.S. 918 (1951); Laura Kalman, *Abe Fortas: A Biography* (New Haven, CT: Yale University Press, 1990), 137–41; Thurman Arnold, *Fair Fights and Foul: A Dissenting Lawyer's Life* (New York: Harcourt, Brace & World, 1965), 206–08.

2. *Brandenburg v. Ohio,* 395 U.S. 444 (1969).

3. *Scales v. United States,* 367 U.S. 203 (1961); *NAACP v. Claiborne Hardware Co.,* 458 U.S. 886, 932 (1982) (recognizing that "guilt by association is a philosophy alien to the traditions of a free society and the First Amendment itself, we have held that civil or criminal disabilities may not be imposed on one who joins an organization which has among its purposes the violent overthrow of the Government, unless the individual joins knowing of the organization's illegal purposes and with the specific intention to further those purposes.")(citations omitted).

4. *Greene v. McElroy,* 360 U.S. 474 (1959) (holding that government must provide meaningful opportunity to challenge evidence before it can fire employees); *Cole v. Young,* 351 U.S. 536 (1956) (same).

5. Immigration Act of 1903, ch. 1012, §2, 32 Stat. 1213, 1214 (1903), repealed by Immigration Act of February 5, 1917, ch. 29, §38, 39 Stat. 874, 897 (1917). See also William Preston, Jr., *Aliens and Dissenters: Federal Suppression of Radicals, 1903–1933* (Cambridge, MA: Harvard University Press, 1963), 208–37.

6. Preston, *supra,* 31–32.

7. Samuel F. Miller, *The Conflict in This Country Between Socialism and Organized Society* (1888), reprinted in Charles N. Gregory, *Samuel Freeman Miller* (Iowa City: The State Historical Society of Iowa, 1907), 168.

8. William M. Wiecek, "The Legal Foundations of Domestic Anticommunism: The Background of *Dennis v. United States,*" 2001 *Supreme Court Review* 375, 381; see generally John Higham, *Strangers in the Land: Patterns of American Nativism 1860–1925* (New York: Atheneum, 1963).

9. Robert J. Goldstein, *Political Repression in Modern America: From 1870 to the Present* (Cambridge, MA: Schenkman Publishing Co., 1978), 68.

10. *Turner v. United States,* 194 U.S. 279, 292 (1904).

11. Goldstein, *Political Repression, supra,* 78 (quoting *Washington Post*).

12. *Id.* at 79.

13. Immigration Act of February 5, 1917, ch. 29, §19, 39 Stat. 874 (1917).

14. Preston, *supra,* 100.

15. *Id.* at 100, 164–65, 180.

16. *Id.* at 173; see also *id.* at 184 (observing that the INS adopted this argument as official policy in July 1918).

17. Paul L. Murphy, *World War I and the Origins of Civil Liberties in the United States* (New York: W. W. Norton, 1979), 105–06; Louis F. Post, *The Deportations Delirium of Nineteen-Twenty: A Personal Narrative of an Historic Official Experience* (New York: Da Capo Press, 1923), 63.

18. Immigration Act of October 16, 1918, ch. 186, 40 Stat. 1012 (1918); see Murphy, *supra*, 105–06.

19. Wiecek, *supra*, 384; see also Richard G. Powers, *Secrecy and Power: The Life of J. Edgar Hoover* (New York: The Free Press, 1987), 70.

20. R. Baker and W. Dodd, eds., *The Public Papers of Woodrow Wilson: The New Democracy* (New York: Harper and Brothers, 1926), vol. 3, 423.

21. Espionage Act of June 15, 1917, Pub. L. No. 65-24, 40 Stat. 217 (1917).

22. Baker and Dodd, *supra*, vol. 5, 66–67.

23. *New York Times,* November 21, 1917, 3, col. 3.

24. Theodore Roosevelt, *The Foes of Our Own Household* (New York: George H. Doran Company, 1917), 31.

25. William Hornaday, *Awake! America: Object Lessons and Warnings* (New York: Moffat, Yard, and Co., 1918), 106–07.

26. "Addresses Delivered at the Boston Meeting: Address of the President," 5 *American Bar Association Journal* 527, 537 (1919).

27. Sedition Act of 1918, Pub. L. No. 150, 40 Stat. 553 (repealed 1921).

28. Zechariah Chafee, *Free Speech in the United States* (Cambridge, MA: Harvard University Press, 1941), 51.

29. *Gilbert v. Minnesota,* 254 U.S. 325, 325 (1920).

30. *Schenck v. United States,* 249 U.S. 47, 52 (1919).

31. *Frohwerk v. United States,* 249 U.S. 204 (1919).

32. *Abrams v. United States,* 250 U.S. 616 (1920). The trial of the Russian Jews illustrates the kind of justice meted out to dissidents during World War I. The trial judge, Henry Clayton, consistently harangued the defendants, at one point saying to the lead defendant, Jacob Abrams: "You keep talking about producers. Now may I ask why you don't go out and do some producing: There is plenty of untilled land needing attention in this country." During sentencing, Judge Clayton stated that he would brook no arguments "the purpose of which is to give aid and comfort to soap-box orators and to such as these miserable defendants who

stand convicted before the bar of justice." Reprising his oddly agricultural theme, Judge Clayton said of the defendants that "not one of them has ever produced so much as a single potato. The only thing they know how to raise is hell, and to direct it against the government of the United States." Quoted in Thomas A. Lawrence, "Eclipse of Liberty: Civil Liberties in the United States During the First World War," 21 *Wayne Law Review* 33, 91–93 (1974).

33. Goldstein, *Political Repression, supra,* 134–35.

34. "War Resolutions," 3 *American Bar Association Journal* 577 (1919), quoted in Michael Linfield, *Freedom Under Fire: U.S. Civil Liberties in Times of War* (Boston: South End Press, 1990), 39; Murphy, *supra,* 194.

35. Lawrence, *supra,* 78–87 (canvassing articles supportive of the sedition laws by University of Minnesota Professor W. R. Vance, Princeton's Edward Corwin, Northwestern's John Wigmore, Henry Taft, a partner at Cadwalader, Wickersham, and Taft, and several others).

36. John H. Wigmore, *"Abrams v. United States:* Freedom of Speech and Freedom of Thuggery in War-Time and Peace-Time," 14 *Illinois Law Review* 539, 549, 543 (1920).

37. Peter Irons, " 'Fighting Fair': Zechariah Chafee, Jr., the Department of Justice, and the 'Trial at the Harvard Club,' " 94 *Harvard Law Review* 1205 (1981). J. Edgar Hoover appears to have personally ordered that a file be made on Chafee, a file maintained throughout Chafee's career. Donald L. Smith, *Zechariah Chaffee, Jr.: Defender of Liberty and Law* (Cambridge, MA: Harvard University Press, 1986), 40–41.

38. Lawrence, *supra,* 111–12.

39. Higham, *supra,* 6–9 (noting anti-Catholic, antiradical, and racist strains of nativism).

40. *Id.* at 204–09 (discussing "100 percent Americanism" during World War I).

9. "The Course of Least Resistance": J. Edgar Hoover's First Job and the Palmer Raids of 1919–20

1. Richard G. Powers, *Secrecy and Power: The Life of J. Edgar Hoover* (New York: The Free Press, 1987), 40–55.

2. *Id.* at 56–59; William M. Wiecek, "The Legal Foundations of Domestic Anti-communism: The Background of *Dennis v. United States,*" 2001 *Supreme Court Review* 375, 388; Irving Howe and Lewis Coser, *The American Communist Party: A Critical History* (New York: Praeger, 1962), 26.

3. Wiecek, *supra,* 389.

4. Robert K. Murray, *Red Scare: A Study in National Hysteria, 1919–1920* (Minneapolis: University of Minnesota Press, 1955), 69–71.

5. *Id.* at 72.

6. *Id.* at 77–79.

7. William Preston, Jr., *Aliens and Dissenters: Federal Suppression of Radicals, 1903–1933* (Cambridge: Harvard University Press, 1963), 210.

8. Powers, *supra*, 70.

9. Report of the Attorney General of the United States: 1920 (quoted in Louis F. Post, *The Deportations Delirium of Nineteen-Twenty: A Personal Narrative of an Historic Official Experience* (New York: Da Capo Press, 1923), 53–54).

10. Post, *supra*, 307.

11. Regin Schmidt, *Red Scare: FBI and the Origins of Anticommunism in the United States, 1919–1943* (Copenhagen: Museum Tusculanum Press, 2000), 268.

12. *Id.* at 249–50.

13. Post, *supra*, 24.

14. Constantine Panunzio, *The Deportation Cases of 1919–1920* (New York: Commission on the Church and Social Service, Federal Council of the Churches of Christ in America, 1921), 60–62.

15. Quoted in Murray, *supra*, 208.

16. John Higham, *Strangers in the Land: Patterns of American Nativism 1860–1925* (New York: Atheneum, 1963), 228.

17. Richard G. Powers, *Not Without Honor: The History of American Anticommunism* (New York: The Free Press, 1995), 26.

18. Preston, *supra*, 214–18; Murray, *supra*, 211. Prior to December 31, 1919, Rule 22, which governed immigration hearings, provided that:

At the beginning of the hearing under the warrant of arrest the alien shall be allowed to inspect the warrant of arrest and all evidence on which it was issued, and shall be apprised that he may be represented by counsel.

As amended that day, the rule read:

Preferably at the beginning of the hearing under the warrant of arrest *or at any rate as soon as such hearing has proceeded sufficiently in the development of the facts to protect the Government's interests,* the alien shall be allowed to inspect the warrant of arrest and all the evidence on which it was issued and shall be apprised that thereafter he may be represented by counsel.

Panunzio, *supra,* 37 (emphasis added).

19. Preston, *supra,* 219.

20. Panunzio, *supra,* 37.

21. Preston, *supra,* 221; see also Panunzio, *supra,* 94.

22. Panunzio, *supra,* 58–60

23. *Id.* at 44–45.

24. Powers, *Secrecy and Power, supra,* 73.

25. Post, *supra,* 93.

26. Murray, *supra,* 217–18.

27. *Id.* at 217 (quoting *Washington Post,* January 4, 1920).

28. Powers, *Not Without Honor, supra,* 438 n. 46.

29. Post, *supra,* 167–68. Schmidt reports slightly different numbers, maintaining that of 2,435 cases forwarded to Post for deportation, Post cancelled 1,486 and ordered 481 persons deported, with the remainder deferred, reopened, or pending. Schmidt, *supra,* 303.

30. Post, *supra,* 185.

31. Robert D. Warth, "The Palmer Raids," 48 *Southern Atlantic Quarterly.* 1, 18 (1949).

32. Post, *supra,* 192.

33. *Id.* at 255.

34. *Id.* at 272–74.

35. *Culyer v. Skeffington,* 265 F. 17, 32 & 37 n. 2 (D. Mass. 1920).

36. *Id.* at 43.

37. *Skeffington v. Katzeff,* 277 F. 129 (1st Cir. 1922).

38. National Popular Government League, *Report Upon the Illegal Practices of the Department of Justice* (Washington, D.C., 1920).

39. Schmidt, *supra,* 308–09.

40. *Attorney General Palmer on Charges Made Against the Department of Justice by Louis F. Post and Others,* Hearings Before the House Committee on Rules, 66th Cong. 2d Sess. Parts 1–3, pp. 6–10 (June 1, 1920).

41. Schmidt, *supra,* 320–24.

42. Powers, *Secrecy and Power, supra,* 72; Preston, *supra,* 194; *Attorney General Palmer on Charges Made Against Department of Justice by Louis F. Post and Others: Hearings Before the House Committee on Rules,* 66th Cong. 2d Sess. Parts 1–3, pp. 14, 29 (June 1, 1920); State of the Union Address of Woodrow Wilson, 1919, available at http://www.janda.org/politxts/index/html (supporting Attorney General Palmer's measures to address "the widespread condition of political restlessness in our body politic").

43. 66 Cong. Rec. 2d Sess. (1920), appendix, (quoted in Preston, *Aliens and Dissenters, supra,* 227).

44. Post, *supra,* 313–14.

45. *Id.*

10. The Second Red Scare: Targeting Radical Citizens

1. Arthur J. Sabin, *In Calmer Times: The Supreme Court and Red Monday* (Philadelphia: University of Pennsylvania Press, 1999), 27–28.

2. *Id.* at 27.

3. William Preston, Jr., *Aliens and Dissenters: Federal Suppression of Radicals, 1903–1933* (Cambridge: Harvard University Press, 1963), 291.

4. Regin Schmidt, *Red Scare: FBI and the Origins of Anticommunism in the United States, 1919–1943* (Copenhagen: Museum Tusculanum Press, 2000), 366.

5. House Resolution, adopted May 1938, quoted in Alan Barth, *The Loyalty of Free Men* (London: Gollancz, 1951), 51.

6. 53 Stat. 1148, 5 U.S.C. §118j (1939).

7. Civil Service Circular No. 222 (Hatch Act Enforcement Order), June 20, 1940, reprinted in Eleanor Bontecou, *The Federal Loyalty-Security Program* (Ithaca, NY: Cornell University Press, 1953), 285–86.

8. 55 Stat. 5, 6 (1940), reprinted in Bontecou, *supra,* 284.

9. 84 Cong. Rec. 10370, 76th Cong. 1st Sess. 10370 (July 28, 1939) (statement of Representative Thomas F. Ford).

10. Act of June 28, 1940, ch. 439, 54 Stat. 670.

11. The Alien Registration Act of 1940, Pub. L. No. 670, 54 Stat. 670, Title III, §§30–31 (1940).

12. Exec. Order 9835, 12 Fed. Reg. 1935 (Mar. 21, 1947).

13. Internal Security Act of 1950, Pub. L. No. 81-831, §22, 64 Stat. 987, 1006 (1950).

14. Internal Security Act of 1950, §22, 64 Stat. at 1008.

15. Internal Security Act of 1950, 64 Stat. 987, Title I.

16. Stanley Kutler, *The American Inquisition: Justice and Injustice in the Cold War* (New York: Hill and Wang, 1982), 122.

17. *Id.* at 130.

18. *Kessler v. Strecker,* 307 U.S. 22 (1939).

19. Ann Fagan Ginger, *Carol Weiss King: Human Rights Lawyer, 1895–1952* (Niwot, CO: University Press of Colorado, 1993), 301.

20. H.R. 9766, 76th Cong. 3d Sess. (1940).

21. Richard Steele, *Free Speech in the Good War* (New York: St. Martin's Press, 1999), 102.

22. S. Rep. 2031, 76th Cong., 3d Sess. 9–10 (reproducing letter of Attorney General Robert H. Jackson).

23. 54 Stat. 670, §23, overruling *Kessler v. Strecker,* 307 U.S. 22 (1939).

24. 86 Cong. Rec. 9031 (1940).

25. Steele, *supra,* 109.

26. *Id.* at 103.

27. *Bridges v. Wixon,* 326 U.S. 135 (1945).

28. *Id.* at 148 ("Freedom of speech and of press is accorded aliens residing in this country."); *id.* at 153–54 ("So to hold would allow men to be convicted on unsworn testimony of witnesses—a practice which runs counter to the notions of fairness on which our legal system is founded").

29. *Id.* at 161 (Murphy, J., concurring). The Supreme Court majority quoted this statement with approval eight years later in *Kwong Hai Chew v. Colding,* 344 U.S. 590, 596 n.5 (1953).

30. *Bridges v. Wixon,* 326 U.S. at 157 (Murphy, J., concurring).

31. *Bridges v. United States,* 345 U.S. 209 (1953).

32. Robert R. Brunn, "Bridges Trial in Retrospect: Was World Communism Star Witness?" *Christian Science Monitor,* April 1950.

33. *Carlson v. Landon,* 342 U.S. 524 (1952); *Harisiades v. Shaughnessy,* 342 U.S. 580 (1952).

34. *Galvan v. Press,* 347 U.S. 522 (1954).

35. 347 U.S. at 530–31. The Court also found that the law did not violate the Constitution's Ex Post Facto Clause, which bans retroactive imposition of punish-

ment, because it reasoned that deportation did not constitute punishment. *Id.* at 531–32.

36. President's Commission on Immigration and Naturalization, *Whom We Shall Welcome* (Washington: U. S. Govt. Print Off., 1953), 229–30.

37. Presidential Proclamation 2523, 3 C.F.R. §§270, 271 (1938–1943 Compilation); 8 C.F.R. §175. 57 (b) (1950); see *Kwong Hai Chew v. Colding,* 344 U.S. 590, 599–600 (1953).

38. President's Commission, *Whom Shall We Welcome, supra,* 228–30. Edward Ennis, former General Counsel of INS, testified in 1951 that he had taken part in drafting the 1941 regulation authorizing exclusion based on confidential information. He explained that it was intended to be used "perhaps in several years in only two or three cases, a very extraordinary provision in a real shooting war." But, he continued, after the war its use had become almost routine: "In 1948 . . . this provision has come to be used in almost a routine manner, and under its operation people have actually been held at Ellis Island or elsewhere for years and then allowed to enter the United States." *Revision of Immigration, Naturalization, and Nationality Laws: Joint Hearings Before the Subcommittees of the Senate and House Judiciary Committees,* 82nd Cong. 1st Sess. 139 (March 14, 1951) (testimony of Edward J. Ennis).

39. Internal Security Act of 1950, §22, 64 Stat. 987, 1008 (1950).

40. *United States ex rel. Knauff v. Shaughnessy,* 338 U.S. 537 (1950).

41. *Id.* at 544.

42. *Id.* at 551 (Jackson, J., dissenting).

43. Ellen Knauff, *The Ellen Knauff Story* (New York: W. W. Norton, 1952), xv–xvi, 226–27.

44. Niels W. Frenzen, "National Security and Procedural Fairness: Secret Evidence and the Immigration Laws," 76 *Interpreter Releases* 1677, 1678 (November 22, 1999).

45. It is not clear what Mezei's status was during his previous twenty-five-year residence. The government alleged that he had never been admitted for permanent residence, and apparently Mezei admitted that he had not legally entered the United States. Brief for Petitioner in *Mezei,* at 3 n.2.

46. *Mezei,* 345 U.S. at 208; see also Charles Weisselberg, "The Exclusion and Detention of Aliens: Lessons from the Lives of Ellen Knauff and Ignatz Mezei," 143 *University of Pennsylvania Law Review* 933, 965 (1995).

47. *Mezei,* 345 U.S. at 208.

48. *Id.* at 220 (Jackson, J., dissenting).

49. Michal R. Belknap, *Cold War Political Justice: The Smith Act, the Communist Party, and American Civil Liberties* (Westport, CT: Greenwood Press, 1977), 47–50, 82–85.

50. Ralph Brown, Jr., *Loyalty and Security: Employment Tests in the United States* (New Haven, CT: Yale University Press, 1958), 322.

51. See, e.g., *Schenck v. United States,* 249 U.S. 47 (1919).

52. *United States v. Dennis,* 183 F.2d 201, 212 (2d Cir. 1950).

53. *Dennis v. United States,* 341 U.S. 494, 516–17 (1951).

54. Brown, *supra,* 323.

55. Zechariah Chafee, Jr., *The Blessings of Liberty* (Philadelphia: Lippincott, 1956), 85.

56. See *Communist Party v. Subversive Activities Control Board,* 351 U.S. 115 (1956); *Garner v. Board of Public Works,* 341 U.S. 716 (1951); *Gerende v. Board of Supervisors of Elections,* 341 U.S. 56 (1951); *American Communications Ass'n v. Doud,* 339 U.S. 990 (1950).

57. William M. Wiecek, "The Legal Foundations of Domestic Anticommunism: The Background of *Dennis v. United States,*" 2001 *Supreme Court Review* 375, 429.

58. *Id.* at 406.

59. Belknap, *supra,* 156.

60. *Id.* at 190–92.

61. *Id.* at 204–05.

62. *Id.* at 215.

63. I. F. Stone, *The Haunted Fifties* (New York: Random House, 1963), quoted in Sabin, *supra,* 138.

64. *Yates v. United States,* 354 U.S. 298, 324–25 (1957) (emphasis added).

65. *Service v. Dulles,* 354 U.S. 363 (1957); *Watkins v. United States,* 354 U.S. 178 (1957); *Sweezy v. New Hampshire,* 354 U.S. 234 (1957); see generally Sabin, *supra,* 138–72.

66. *Scales v. United States,* 367 U.S. 203, 224 (1961).

67. *Id.* at 229.

68. The Court also rendered the Subversive Activities Control Act unenforceable. In 1961, the Court initially upheld against a First Amendment challenge a requirement that Communist organizations register. *Communist Party v. Subversive Activities Control Board*, 367 U.S. 1 (1961). But in 1965, it ruled that requiring registration violated the Fifth Amendment privilege against compelled self-incrimination. *Albertson v. Subversive Activities Control Board*, 382 U.S. 70 (1965). No group ever registered under the Act.

69. Brown, *supra*, 21.

70. Bontecou, *supra*, 167.

71. Exec. Order 9835, 12 Fed. Reg. 1935 (Mar. 21, 1947).

72. Barth, *supra*, 106.

73. Bontecou, *supra*, 171; see generally *id*. at 157–204 (on the makeup, evolution, and uses of the attorney general's lists).

74. *Id*. at 176–79; Barth, *supra*, 107.

75. Robert J. Goldstein, *Political Repression in Modern America: From 1870 to the Present* (Cambridge, MA: Schenkman Publishing Co., 1978), 302–03; Bontecou, *supra*, 109–10.

76. Goldstein, *supra*, 302–03; Bontecou, *supra*, 111.

77. Quoted in Brown, *supra*, 35–36.

78. Bontecou, *supra*, 108.

79. *Id*. at 140–41.

80. Transcript of loyalty board hearing, quoted in Barth, *supra*, 119–22.

81. Exec. Order 9835, 12 Fed. Reg. 1935 (Mar. 21, 1947).

82. Exec. Order 10241, 16 Fed. Reg. 3690 (Apr. 28, 1951).

83. Exec. Order 10450, 18 Fed. Reg. 2489 (Apr. 27, 1953).

84. Bontecou, *supra*, 70–71.

85. Exec. Order 9835, 12 Fed. Reg. 1935 (Mar. 21, 1947).

86. Statement of Loyalty Review Board, U.S. Civil Service Comm., adopted December 17, 1947 (quoted in Bontecou, *supra*, 206); see also *Bailey v. Richardson*, 182 F.2d 46, 57–58 (D.C. Cir. 1950), *aff'd by an equally divided Court*, 341 U.S. 918 (1951); Wiecek, *supra*, 432 (defenders of the loyalty review boards "relied on the right-privilege distinction, insisted that the administrative hearings provided ad-

equate process, pointed out that no criminal consequences were involved, and that the FBI had to protect the confidentiality of its informants").

87. Goldstein, *supra*, 374–75.

88. Brown, *supra*, 181.

89. HUAC, *Hearings Regarding Communist Espionage in the United States Government* 1310 (1948), quoted in David Caute, *The Great Fear: The Anti-Communist Purge under Truman and Eisenhower* (London: Secker and Warburg, 1978), 97.

90. H.R. Rep. No. 1476, 76th Cong., 3d Sess. 24 (1940).

91. 93 Cong. Rec. A4277 (November 20, 1947).

92. 83 Cong. Rec. 7568, 7586 (1938) (emphasis added).

93. Michael Linfield, *Freedom Under Fire: U.S. Civil Liberties in Times of War* (Boston: South End Press, 1990), 88; Robert K. Carr, *The House Committee on Un-American Activities* (Ithaca, NY: Cornell University Press, 1952), 452.

94. Frank J. Donner, *The Un-Americans* (New York: Ballantine Books, 1961), 142–43.

95. *Id.* at 9.

96. Zechariah Chafee, *The Blessings of Liberty* (Philadelphia: Lippincott, 1956), 91; Carr, *supra* 295–97, 305–06.

97. United States Congress House Committee on Un-American Activities, *Hearings Regarding the Communist Infiltration of the Motion Picture Industry* (Washington, DC: U.S. Government Printing Office, 1947), 118–19.

98. Carr, *supra*, 306.

99. Barth, *supra*, 10–11.

100. Chafee, *supra*, 83, 99.

101. See, e.g., *Barsky v. United States*, 167 F.2d 241 (D.C. Cir. 1948), *cert. denied*, 334 U.S. 843 (1948); *id.* at 252 (Edgerton, J., dissenting); *United States v. Josephson*, 165 F.2d 82 (2d Cir. 1947), *cert. denied*, 333 U.S. 838 (1948); *id.* at 93 (Clark, J., dissenting); see generally, Carr, *supra*, 406–48.

11. Extending the Boundaries: From Martin Luther King, Jr., to Watergate

1. Ellen Schrecker, *Many Are the Crimes: McCarthyism in the United States* (Boston: Little Brown, 1998), 227–28; Robert J. Goldstein, *Political Repression in Modern America: From 1870 to the Present* (Cambridge, MA: Schenkman Publishing Co., 1978), 407; Supplementary Detailed Staff Reports on Intelligence Ac-

tivities and the Rights of Americans, Book III, Final Report of the Select Committee to Study Governmental Operations with Respect to Intelligence Activities, S. Rep. No. 94–755, 94th Cong., 2nd Sess. (1976) (hereinafter, "Church Committee, Book III"); Morton H. Halperin, Jerry J. Berman, Robert L. Borosage, and Christine M. Marwick, *The Lawless State: The Crimes of the U.S. Intelligence Agencies* (New York: Penguin Books, 1976), 126.

2. Church Committee, Book III, *supra,* 420–21.

3. Halperin, et al., *supra,* 8, 109.

4. Goldstein, *supra,* 407.

5. *Id.* at 394; Church Committee, Book III, *supra,* 454–518.

6. Richard Powers, *Secrecy and Power: The Life of J. Edgar Hoover* (New York: The Free Press, 1987), 75.

7. Church Committee, Book III, *supra,* 394.

8. *Id.* at 279.

9. Halperin, et al., *supra,* 99 (quoting Church Committee, Book III, *supra,* 414–15).

10. Goldstein, *supra,* 448.

11. Halperin, et al., *supra,* 99.

12. *Id.* at 99, 120, 136, 139–43.

13. Goldstein, *supra,* 478–79.

14. *Id.* at 457.

15. *Id.* at 478.

16. Halperin, et al., *supra,* 106–07.

17. See generally *id.* at 61–89.

18. Church Committee, Book III, *supra,* 23–27, 507.

19. Goldstein, *supra,* 464.

20. *Id.* at 481–82.

21. *Id.* at 538–45.

12. From Communism to Terrorism: Lessons of a Young Lawyer

1. *Randall v. Meese*, 854 F.2d 472 (D.C. Cir. 1988); David Cole, "What's a Metaphor?: The Deportation of a Poet," 1 *Yale Journal of Law and Liberation* 10 (1989).

2. *In re Randall*, Deportation Hearing Transcript at 165–66 (March 17, 1986), quoted in Cole, "What's a Metaphor," *supra*, 5–6.

3. See Cole, "What's a Metaphor," *supra*, 11–12.

4. Decision of INS District Director A. H. Guigni, October 2, 1985, denying Randall's application for permanent resident status, reprinted in *Randall v. Meese*, 854 F.2d 472, 486–87 (D.C. Cir 1988).

5. Decision of Immigration Judge Martin Spiegel, August 28, 1986, quoted in Cole, "What's a Metaphor," *supra*, 14.

6. *American-Arab Anti-Discrimination Comm. v. Reno*, 70 F.3d 1045, 1053 (9th. Cir. 1995) (quoting *Hearings before the Senate Select Committee on Intelligence on the Nomination of William H. Webster, to be Director of Central Intelligence*, 100th Cong., 1st Sess. 94–95 (April 8, 9, 30, 1987; May 1, 1987)).

7. *Reno v. American-Arab Anti-Discrimination Comm.*, 525 U.S. 471 (1999), Joint Appendix at 93 (Declaration of INS District Director Ernest Gustafson).

8. *Id.* at 94.

9. *Id.* at 150–51, 172–74, 181, 184, 190–91.

10. *Id.* at 165.

11. *Id.* at 142–43.

12. *Id.* at 152.

13. *American-Arab Anti-Discrimination Comm. v. Meese*, 714 F. Supp. 1060 (C.D. Cal. 1989), *aff'd in part and rev'd in part*, 970 F.2d 501 (9th Cir. 1992).

14. See Immigration and Nationality Act of 1990, Pub. L. No. 101–649, 104 Stat. 4978; *American-Arab Anti-Discrimination Comm. v. Thornburgh*, 970 F.2d 501 (9th Cir. 1992) (noting that "Communism" and other advocacy grounds had been repealed and dismissing on that ground).

15. Immigration and Nationality Act of 1990, Pub. L. 101–649, §602(a)(4)(B), 104 Stat. 4978 (amending 8 U.S.C. §1251 (1990)).

16. *American-Arab Anti-Discrimination Comm. v. Reno*, 70 F.3d 1045 (9th Cir. 1995).

17. *American-Arab Anti-Discrimination Comm. v. Reno*, 119 F.3d 1367, 1370 (9th Cir. 1997), *vacated on other grounds*, 525 U.S. 471 (1999).

18. 70 F.3d at 1064–66 (describing government arguments for diminished First Amendment protection for aliens facing deportation).

19. *Id.*

20. *Reno v. American-Arab Anti-Discrimination Comm.*, 525 U.S. 471.

21. *Wayte v. United States*, 470 U.S. 598 (1985) (the decision to prosecute may not be " 'deliberately based upon an unjustifiable standard such as race, religion, or other arbitrary classification,' including the exercise of protected statutory and constitutional rights") (internal citations omitted); *C.E. Carlson v S.E.C.*, 859 F.2d 1429, 1437 (10th Cir. 1988) (setting forth test for First Amendment selective enforcement claim); *United States v. Berrios*, 501 F.2d 1207, 1211 (2d Cir. 1974) (setting forth test for selective enforcement claims generally).

22. *United States v. Robel*, 389 U.S. 258 (1967); *Aptheker v. Secretary of State*, 378 U.S. 500 (1964); *Keyishian v. Board of Regents*, 385 U.S. 589 (1967).

23. As described above, the USA PATRIOT Act expressly makes material support to designated terrorist organizations a deportable offense. See *supra* Chapter 4.

24. "The Ghost of McCarran-Walter," Editorial, *New York Times*, December 9, 1991, A16; "Deport for Acts, Not Speech," Editorial, *Washington Post*, November 30, 1991, A22; "Is That All There Is?" Editorial, *Los Angeles Times*, March 6, 1987, Metro, Part 2, p. 4.

25. This description is drawn largely from David Cole, "Secrecy, Guilt by Association, and the Terrorist Profile," 15 *Journal of Law and Religion* 267 (2001).

26. Verified Petition for Habeas Corpus Relief, Attachment A, *Kiareldeen v. Reno*, 71 F. Supp. 2d 402 (D.N.J. 1999) (No. 99-3925) (hereinafter *"Kiareldeen* Petition") (reproducing INS summary provided at initial bond redetermination hearing).

27. *Kiareldeen v. Reno*, 71 F. Supp. 2d 402, 416 (D.N.J. 1999); *Kiareldeen* Petition, *supra*, Attachment E.

28. *Kiareldeen v. Reno*, 71 F. Supp. 2d at 417–418.

29. *In re Kiareldeen*, No. A77-025-332, slip op. at 13–14 (U.S. Immigration Ct. April 2, 1999).

30. *Id.* at 14–15.

31. *Id.* at 8–9.

32. See *Kiareldeen v. Reno*, 71 F. Supp. 2d at 417; *Kiareldeen* Petition, *supra*, §22–26; *id.* at Attachment F, 2–3 (reproducing decision of immigration judge *In*

re Kiareldeen, No. A77–025–332, slip op. at 13–14 (U.S. Immigration Ct. April 2, 1999)).

33. See *In re Kiareldeen,* No. A77-025-332, (BIA Oct. 20, 1999) (dismissing the government's appeal of the immigration judge's bond order); *In re Kiareldeen,* No. A77-025-332 (BIA October 15, 1999) (dismissing the government's appeal of the immigration judge's decision); *In re Kiareldeen,* No. A77-025-332 (U.S. Immigration Ct. April 2, 1999).

34. *Matter of Kiareldeen,* A77-025-332, slip op. 15 (U.S. Immigration Ct. April 2, 1999) (decision of immigration judge).

35. *Id.* at 12.

36. *Matter of Kiareldeen,* No. A77-025-332, slip dissent 1 (BIA June 29, 1999) (Moscato, J., dissenting from Decision Denying Request to Lift Stay of Release Order).

37. *Id.*

38. *Id.* at 1–2.

39. *Matter of Ahmed,* No. A90-674-228, slip op. at 20 (U.S. Immigration Ct. May 5, 1997) (decision of immigration judge).

40. *Id.,* see also David Cole, "Blind Decisions Come to Court," *The Nation,* June 16, 1997, 21–22.

41. *Id.*

42. See Unclassified Summary of Classified Material Previously Provided to IJ and BIA, filed as Ex. 1 to Reply Declaration of Daniel S. Alter in *Ahmed v. Reno,* 97 Civ. 68729 (TPG) (S.D.N.Y.).

43. E.O. 12958, 60 Fed. Reg. 19825, 19826 (1995).

44. Declassified Version of Classified Attachment to Decision of Immigration Judge 8–9, *Matter of Ahmed,* No. A90-674-28 (Immigration Ct. June 24, 1999); Benjamin Weiser, "F.B.I. Said Freeing Prisoner Would Aid Arab Status," *New York Times,* November 11, 1999, B1.

45. Andrew Cockburn, "The Radicalization of James Woolsey," *New York Times Magazine,* July 23, 2000, 26.

46. Niels W. Frenzen, "National Security and Procedural Fairness: Secret Evidence and the Immigration Laws," 76 *Interpreter Releases* 1677, 1684 (November 22, 1999).

47. Dan Weikel, "INS Judge Frees Iraqi Dissident Held for 4 Years," *Los Angeles Times,* August 19, 2000, B1, B5; Tim Weiner, "At Rehearing, Iraqi Doctor Wins Round in Deportation," *New York Times,* May 7, 2000, A19.

48. *Matter of Kiareldeen*, A77-025-332, slip op. 15–16 (U.S. Immigration Ct. April 2, 1999) (decision of immigration judge); Declassified Version of Classified Attachment to Decision of Immigration Judge 10–11, *Matter of Ahmed*, A90-674-238 (U.S. Immigration Ct. June 24, 1999).

49. Cole, "Secrecy, Guilt by Association," *supra*.

50. See e.g., "Free Nasser Ahmed," Editorial, *Washington Post*, November 23, 1999, A26; "Secret Evidence," Editorial, *Washington Post*, November 3, 1999, A34; "A Blow for Secret Evidence," Editorial, *Washington Post*, August 6, 1999, A20; Anthony Lewis, "Abroad at Home; Kafka in America," *New York Times*, September 26, 1997, A27; David Cole, "If All Don't Have Rights, None of Us Do," *Los Angeles Times*, March 19, 1998, Metro, Part B, 6; Niels W. Frenzen, "Commentary; INS Must Stop Using Secret Evidence," *Los Angeles Times*, December 21, 2000, Metro, Part B, 11; "A Wrongful Detention, Righted: Victory for Justice," Editorial, *Miami Herald*, October 22, 1999, 6B.

51. Secret Evidence Repeal Act of 2000, H.R. 2121, H.R. Rep. No. 106–981, 106th Cong. (2000); Secret Evidence Repeal Act of 2001, H.R. 1266, 107th Cong. (2001).

52. See "The 2000 Campaign; 2nd Presidential Debate Between Gov. Bush and Vice President Gore," *New York Times*, October 12, 2000, A22.

53. *American-Arab Anti-Discrimination Comm. v. Reno*, 70 F.3d at 1070; *Rafeedie v. INS*, 880 F.2d 506, 512–13, 516 (D.C. Cir. 1989); *Al Najjar v. Reno*, 97 F. Supp. 2d 1329, 1356 (S.D. Fla. 2000), *vacated as moot on appeal*, 273 F.3d 1330 (11th Cir. 2001); *Kiareldeen v. Reno*, 71 F. Supp. 2d 402 (D.N.J. 1999); but see *Suciu v. INS*, 755 F.2d 127, 128 (8th Cir. 1985) (holding, without analysis, that use of secret evidence is consistent with due process).

54. *Rafeedie*, 880 F.2d at 516.

55. *American-Arab Anti-Discrimination Comm. v. Reno*, 70 F.3d at 1066–71.

56. *Al Najjar v. Ashcroft*, 273 F.3d 1330, 1340–41 (11th Cir. 2001).

57. *Kiareldeen v. Ashcroft*, 273 F.3d 542, 555 (3d Cir. 2001).

58. Geoff Dougherty and Laurie Cohen, "U.S. Using New Law on Secret Evidence: Patriot Act Invoked to Fight Lawsuit by Muslim Group," *Chicago Tribune*, March 15, 2002, 1.

59. *Padilla ex rel Newman v. Bush*, 233 F. Supp. 2d 564 (S.D.N.Y. 2002); *Padilla v. Rumsfeld*, 243 F. Supp. 2d 42, 54 (S.D.N.Y. 2003).

13. Legitimacy and Double Standards

1. Douglas Farah, "Saudis Face U.S. Demand on Terrorism; Halting Financiers May Be Urged," *Washington Post,* September 26, 2002, A1.

2. Peter Baker, " 'I'll Never Go Back'; Saudis Who Once Embraced America Now Feeling Embittered and Betrayed," *Washington Post,* November 26, 2002, A1.

3. Steven R. Weisman, "Bush Condemns Saudi Blasts; 7 Americans Are Dead," *New York Times,* May 14, 2003, A1; Steven R. Weisman with Douglas Jehl, "Ambassador Says Saudis Didn't Heed Security Request," *New York Times,* May 15, 2003, A1.

4. Bill Dedman, "Memo Warns Against Use of Profiling as Defense," *Boston Globe,* October 12, 2001, A27.

5. Ann Fagan and Patrick Badgley, "Sniper Arrests Show Limits of Profiling," *Washington Times,* October 25, 2002, A15.

6. Dedman, *supra;* David Cole and John Lamberth, "The Fallacy of Racial Profiling," *New York Times,* May 13, 2001, §4, 13; David Harris, *Profiles in Injustice: Why Racial Profiling Cannot Work* (New York: The New Press, 2002), ch. 8.

7. Malcolm Gladwell, "Connecting the Dots," *The New Yorker,* March 10, 2003, 83, 88 (noting risk that false positives inevitably reduce sensitivity); Malcolm Gladwell, "Safety in the Skies; How Far Can Airline Security Go?," *The New Yorker,* October 1, 2001, 50 (making similar arguments about the difficulty of remaining alert when reviewing metal detectors at airports); Richard K. Betts, "Analysis, War, and Decision: Why Intelligence Failures Are Inevitable," 31 *World Politics* 61, 63 (1978) ("Making warning systems more sensitive reduces the risk of surprise, but increases the number of false alarms, which in turn reduces sensitivity.").

8. Supplemental Excerpts of Record, Volume 2, 393, *American-Arab Anti-Discrimination Committee v. Reno,* 70 F.3d 1045 (9th Cir. 1995) (No. 96-55929).

9. Letter from Coleen Rowley, FBI Special Agent, to Robert Mueller, FBI Director (February 26, 2003), available at http://www.nytimes.com/2003/03/05/politics/ROWLEY-LETTER.html?ex=1049885288&ei=1&en=c7721fleb1f719cf.

10. U.S. Department of Justice, Office of the Inspector General, *The September 11 Detainees: A Review of the Treatment of Aliens Held on Immigration Charges in Connection with the Investigation of the September 11 Attacks* (April 2003) (released June 2, 2003).

11. Thomas Ginsberg, "Departing INS Chief Leery of Changes Facing Agency," *Philadelphia Inquirer,* January 5, 2003, B3.

12. Jim McGee, "Ex-FBI Officials Criticize Tactics on Terrorism; Detention of Suspects Not Effective, They Say," *Washington Post,* November 28, 2001, A1.

13. *Id.*

14. *Current and Projected National Security Threats to the United States:* Hearings Before the Senate Intelligence Committee, February 6, 2002 (testimony of former FBI Executive Assistant Director for Counterterrorism and Counterintelligence Dale Watson).

15. GAO Report GAO-03-459, *Homeland Security: Justice Department's Project to Interview Aliens after September 11, 2001* (April 2003), 5.

16. Tom R. Tyler, *Why People Obey the Law* (New Haven, CT: Yale University Press, 1990), 38. As Tyler finds, "[v]iews about authority are strongly connected to judgment of the fairness of the procedures through which authorities make decisions." *Id.* at 102; see generally David Cole, *No Equal Justice: Race and Class in the American Criminal Justice System* (New York: The New Press, 1999), 169–80 (discussing "costs of inequality" in American criminal justice system).

17. Eric Slater and John Beckham, "Response to Terror; The Investigation; U.S. Moves to Question Mideast Men; Law: Local Officials Face Obstacles in Carrying Out an Order to Contact About 5,000 Recent Visitors," *Los Angeles Times,* November 28, 2001, A1 (reporting that "a former counter-terrorism chief for the FBI said that, while he supports Ashcroft's aggressive campaign against terrorism, questioning the thousands of men would be counterproductive because it could breed hostility in Muslim communities in the United States," and also quoting James Zogby as saying, "It compromises what may be the most important aspect of the investigation: Arab-police bonds of trust").

18. Lawyer's Committee for Human Rights, *A Year of Loss: Reexamining Civil Liberties After September 11* (2002) (quoting Cannistraro), available at http://www.lchr.org.

19. Tom Brune and John Riley, "Taking Liberties, Part One: Collateral Damage," *Newsday,* September 15, 2002, A3.

20. Bill Gertz, *Breakdown: How America's Intelligence Failures Led to September 11* (Washington, DC: Regnery, 2002), 28.

21. Conversation with Alia Mekoub, one of the two Civil Rights Division lawyers, March 14, 2003.

22. Neil A. Lewis, "A Nation Challenged: The Informants; Immigrants Offered Incentives to Give Evidence on Terrorists," *New York Times,* November 30, 2001, B7.

23. Ken Fireman and Tom Brune, "Cooperation Deal; Immigrants Helping Terrorism Probe Offered Visa Help," *Newsday,* November 30, 2001, A5.

24. Thomas Ginsberg, "Few Accept Federal Offer of Visas for Terror Tips," *Philadelphia Inquirer,* February 12, 2003.

25. Allan Lengel and Caryle Murphy, "FBI, Arab Community Join Forces With Panel," *Washington Post*, March 29, 2003, B1.

26. Philip B. Heymann, *Terrorism and America: A Commonsense Strategy for a Democratic Society* (Cambridge, MA: MIT Press, 1998), 141–42.

27. See, e.g., Zbigniew Brzezinski, "Confronting Anti-American Grievances," *New York Times*, September 1, 2002, A9; Thomas Friedman, "Tone It Down a Notch," *New York Times*, October 2, 2002, A27; Frank Bruni, "Europe Pauses and Grieves, But Takes Issue With U.S.," *New York Times*, September 12, 2002, B1; Neil MacFarquhar, "Threats and Responses: Security; For Americans in Mideast, Daily Balance of Risk," *New York Times*, October 31, 2002, A12; Raymond Bonner, "Southeast Asia Remains Fertile For Al Qaeda," *New York Times*, October 28, 2002, A1; Craig A. Smith, "Saved by U.S., Kuwait Now Shows Mixed Feelings," *New York Times*, October 12, 2002, A11.

28. Heymann, *Terrorism and America, supra*, 25–26.

29. *Id.* at xix, 27, 47–51.

30. Paul R. Pillar, *Terrorism and American Foreign Policy* (Washington, DC: Brookings Institution Press, 2001), 186–89.

31. Shireen M. Mazari, "Open Season on Muslims," *The News* (Islamabad, Pakistan), April 17, 2002, at http://www.islamabad.com.

32. Zafar Siddiqui, "Terrorism Statistics Just Do Not Add Up," *Middle East Times*, February 15, 2002, at http://metimes.com.

33. George Monbiot, "War on the Third World: A New U.S. Racism Is Branding Those of Asian and Middle Eastern Origin as Terrorists," *The Guardian* (London), March 5, 2002, 15.

34. Bob Marshall-Andrews, "This Is No Way to Lead a Free World," *The Evening Standard* (London), December 6, 2001, 6 (criticizing military tribunal procedures and noting that "[t]hese measures do not, of course, apply to American citizens whose constitutional rights to trial remain unaltered no matter what their complicity in acts of terror and violence."); Herve Bourges and Mahmoud Hussein, "A New American Order?," *Le Monde* (Paris), December 27, 2001 ("These emergency procedures that are worthy of third world dictatorships are all the more deplorable since they are meant for non-US citizens, introducing discrimination between Americans and others."); Tehran Voice of the Islamic Republic of Iran Radio 1, November 29, 2001 ("Bush has in effect drawn a clear line between the rights of American citizens and foreign immigrants. This is a blatant case of discrimination in rights, something which is not practiced anywhere else in the world.").

35. "Legal Double-Standards Are Not the Way to Win a War Against Terrorism," *The Independent* (London), January 14, 2002, 3; see also "Enough Discrimina-

tion and Profiling," *Amman Jordan Times*, November 13, 2001, at http://www.jordantimes.com.

36. Gay Alcorn, "Dragnet Entangles Mystery Australian," *The Age* (Melbourne), November 30, 2001, 9.

37. Shannon McCaffrey, "Foreign Diplomats Complain of Secrecy: U.S. Sharing Few Facts on Detainees," *Chicago Tribune*, January 1, 2002, 10.

38. *Id.*

39. Gregory Boyd Bell, "U.S. Is Playing POW Name Games," *Newsday*, January 25, 2002, A39.

40. *Id.*

41. "A Place in the Sun, Beyond the Law," *Economist*, May 10, 2003, 12.

42. "Bush Administration Clamps Down on Mideast Foreign Visitors," Agence France Presse, June 6, 2002.

43. "US Restrictions Against Muslims Most Humiliating," *Rawalpindi Jang* (Pakistan), June 8, 2002, 10.

44. "U.S. Security Plan," *Arab News* (Saudi Arabia), June 8, 2002, at http://www.arabnews.com/Article.asp?ID=15867&ArY=2002&ArM=6&ArD=8.

45. " 'Combating Terrorism' Could Threaten Civil Liberties," *Amman Al-Ra-y* (Jordan), June 13, 2002, at http://www.alrai.com.

46. See "Ex-PM Bhutto Joins Protests Over New U.S. Controls on Pakistanis," Agence France Presse, January 7, 2003 (reporting on complaints lodged with United States by Foreign Minister Khurshid Mahmud, the Pakistani embassy, and former prime minister Benazir Bhutto); Alan Sobhani, "Sheer Highhandedness," *Tehran Kayhan Int'l in English*, December 23, 2002, 2 (reporting on formal protest lodged by Iranian Foreign Ministry); Anwar Izbal, "Muslims Protest New US Restrictions," *Middle East Times*, November 29, 2002 (reporting "recent statement by the Malaysian Prime Minister Mahatir Muhammad who said targeting Muslims would only encourage people such as Osama Bin Laden who want to prevent the Islamic and the Western worlds from understanding each other"); see generally Sonni Efron, "New U.S. Tracking of Foreign Visitors Angers Muslims," *Pittsburgh Post-Gazette*, September 9, 2002 (reporting that special registration "is prompting an angry outpouring from Muslim nations").

47. Oren Gross, "Cutting Down Trees: Law-Making Under the Shadow of Great Calamities," in eds. Ronald Daniels, Patrick Macklem, and Kent Roach, *The Security of Freedom: Essays on Canada's Anti-Terrorism Bill* (Toronto: University of Toronto Press, 2001), 39; Heymann, *Terrorism and America, supra,* xix (1998) (arguing that targeting minorities in fighting terrorism "in the long run creates

instability and encourages support for violent opposition"); Paddy Hillyard, "In Defense of Civil Liberties," in *Beyond September 11: An Anthology of Dissent,* ed. Phil Scraton (London: Pluto Press, 2002), 107, 111 ("while political violence poses a threat to democracy the more important threat comes from the response to it by attacking the very principles on which it is based").

48. Gross, *supra,* 40–42.

49. See, e.g., Jude McCulloch, " 'Either You Are With Us or You Are With the Terrorists': The War's Home Front," in *Beyond September 11, supra,* 54, 57; Bill Ralston, "Resistance to Terror: Lessons from Ireland," in *Beyond September 11, supra,* 59; Heymann, *Terrorism and America supra,* 114 (arguing that "relaxed arrest policies in Northern Ireland and Israel have at times poured kerosene on the fires of terrorist violence, increasing opposition to the government and expanding the scope of the conflict").

50. President Bush, *Address to a Joint Session of Congress and the American People* (September 20, 2001) (speech available at http://www.whitehouse.gov).

51. Elizabeth Becker, "One Year Later, Ridge Sees a Country Better Prepared," *New York Times,* September 6, 2002, A1.

52. David Carr, "The Futility of 'Homeland Defense,' " *Atlantic Monthly,* January 2002, available at http://www.theatlantic.com/issues/2002/01/carr.htm.

53. *Id.*

54. *Id.*

55. Mike Gray, *Drug Crazy: How We Got Into This Mess and How We Can Get Out* (New York: Random House, 1998), 148–49.

56. Daniel Benjamin and Steven Simon, *The Age of Sacred Terror* (New York: Random House, 2002), 403.

57. Bill Gertz reports that at a meeting in March 2002 of the National Military Intelligence Association, "[t]he main problem identified by intelligence officials was the failure to share intelligence information among agencies of the United States government." Gertz, *Breakdown, supra,* 157.

58. Benjamin and Simon, *supra,* 226–27, 302–03 (describing turf battles between FBI and other federal agencies, and its reluctance to share information); see also *Protecting America's Freedom in the Information Age: A Report of the Markle Foundation Task Force* (2002), 21.

59. Eric Lichtblau, "Aftereffects: Intelligence; Agencies Still Fail to Share Information, Reports Say," *New York Times,* April 30, 2003, A16; GAO Report GAO-03-322, *Information Technology: Terrorist Watch Lists Should Be Considered to Promote Better Integration and Sharing* (2003).

60. Benjamin and Simon, *supra*, 300.

61. On the advantages of competition over coordination in intelligence gathering and analysis, see Gladwell, "Connecting the Dots," *supra*, 87–88.

62. *The Intelligence Community's Knowledge of the September 11 Hijackers Prior to September 11, 2001: Hearing Before the Joint Committees on Intelligence,* 107th Cong. 2, 21 (September 20, 2002) (testimony of Eleanor Hill, Joint Staff Director).

63. See *Joint Inquiry Staff Statement, Part I: Hearing Before the Joint Committees on Intelligence,* 107th Cong. (September 18, 2002), available at http://intelligence. senate.gov/0209hrg/020918/hill.pdf; Dana Priest, "9/11 Report Says Agencies Received Credible Clues," *Washington Post,* September 18, 2002, A12; Gertz, *Breakdown, supra,* 73 (analysis is "considered the weakest part of American intelligence"); Jessica Stern, *The Ultimate Terrorists* (Cambridge, MA: Harvard University Press, 1999), 13 (stressing need for better analysis of information gathered by intelligence).

64. *Protecting America's Freedom in the Information Age, supra,* 2.

65. David Cole and James X. Dempsey, *Terrorism and the Constitution: Sacrificing Civil Liberties in the Name of National Security* (New York: The New Press, 2002), 79–86.

66. See Stern, *supra,* 128–48.

67. See generally Cole, *No Equal Justice, supra,* 158–61 (discussing difficulties of prevailing on selective prosecution claim in criminal context).

68. *Reno v. American-Arab Anti-Discrimination Comm.,* 525 U.S. 471 (1999).

69. Avishai Margalit, "The Wrong War," *New York Review of Books,* March 13, 2003, 5.

70. See "Ranking the Rich," *Foreign Policy,* May/June 2003, 56 (ranking the United States last in foreign aid as a percentage of gross domestic product, and second to last on a multi-factor Commitment to Development Index); Organization for Economic Cooperation and Development, Table 1: Net Official Development Assistance in 2001 (ranking United States last in official development assistance as a percentage of gross national income), available at http://www.oecd.org/pdf/ M00029000/M00029445.pdf.

71. *Department of Justice Oversight: Preserving Our Freedoms While Defending Against Terrorism: Hearings Before the Senate Committee on the Judiciary,* 107th Cong. 313 (2001) (testimony of Attorney General John Ashcroft).

14. The Bill of Rights as Human Rights

1. *Mathews v. Diaz,* 426 U.S. 67, 80 (1976).

2. *The Japanese Immigrant Case (Yamataya v. Fisher),* 189 U.S. 861 (1903); *The Chinese Exclusion Case (Chae Chan Ping v. United States),* 130 U.S. 581 (1889).

3. *Galvan v. Press,* 347 U.S. 522 (1954).

4. *Porterfield v. Webb,* 263 U.S. 225 (1923) (upholding Washington's alien land law); *Terrace v. Thompson,* 263 U.S. 197 (1923) (upholding California's alien land law). In 1948, the Court invalidated California's law as applied to a U.S. *citizen* child of a Japanese national. *Oyama v. California,* 332 U.S. 633 (1948). And in *Takahashi v. Fish & Game Comm'n,* 334 U.S. 410 (1948), the Court invalidated a California law barring issuance of commercial fishing licenses to Japanese resident aliens, but expressly distinguished the alien land laws. 334 U.S. at 422. Thus, "the U.S. Supreme Court technically never found the [alien land] laws unconstitutional." Brant T. Lee, "A Racial Trust: The Japanese YWCA and the Alien Land Law," 7 *Asian Pacific American Law Journal* 1, 28 (2001).

5. *Shaughnessy v. United States ex rel. Mezei,* 345 U.S. 206 (1953).

6. *Foley v. Connelie,* 435 U.S. 291 (1978) (permitting states to require citizenship in hiring state troopers); *Ambach v. Norwick,* 441 U.S. 68 (1979) (permitting states to require citizenship in hiring public school teachers); *Cabell v. Chavez-Salido,* 454 U.S. 432 (1982) (permitting states to require citizenship in hiring of deputy probation officers).

7. A November 2001 poll conducted by National Public Radio, Harvard University's John F. Kennedy School of Government, and the Kaiser Family Foundation found that 56 percent of those surveyed said that noncitizens visiting or living legally in the United States should have different rights than U.S. citizens. The question specifically excepted the right to vote or hold public office. Deborah L. Acomb, "Poll Track for December 15, 2001," *National Journal,* December 15, 2001.

8. U.S. Constitution, Art. I, §§2, 3; Art. II, §1, Amend. 15. The Constitution's limitation to citizens of the right against discriminatory denial of the vote does not mean that noncitizens cannot vote. If a state or locality chooses to enfranchise its noncitizen residents, it may do so. Indeed, until the early twentieth century, noncitizens routinely enjoyed the right to vote as a matter of state and local law. By contrast, the Constitution expressly restricts to citizens the right to hold federal elective office.

9. *Kwong Hai Chew v. Colding,* 344 U.S. 590, 596 n.5 (1953) (construing immigration regulation permitting exclusion of aliens based on secret evidence not to apply to a returning permanent resident alien because of the substantial constitutional concerns that such an application would present).

10. *Yick Wo v. Hopkins*, 118 U.S. 356, 369 (1886).

11. *Zadvydas v. Davis*, 533 U.S. 678, 693 (2001); see also *Mathews v. Diaz*, 426 U.S. 67, 77 (1976) (holding that due process applies to all aliens in the United States, even those whose presence is "unlawful, involuntary, or transitory").

12. *Almeida-Sanchez v. United States*, 413 U.S. 266 (1973). See also *Bridges v. Wixon*, 326 U.S. 135, 161 (1945) (Murphy. J., concurring) (arguing that non-citizens are protected by the First, Fifth, and Fourteenth Amendments); *Wong Wing v. United States*, 163 U.S. 228 (1896) (holding that noncitizens charged with crimes are protected by the Fifth, Sixth, and Fourteenth Amendments); *Fong Yue Ting v. United States*, 149 U.S. 698, 724 (1893) (observing that foreign nationals are entitled to all "the safeguards of the Constitution, and to the protection of the laws, in regard to their rights of person of property, and to their civil and criminal responsibility"); *Nishimura Ekiu v. United States*, 142 U.S. 651, 660 (1892) (noting that foreign nationals incarcerated here have a constitutional right to invoke habeas corpus). Chief Justice Rehnquist suggested some limitation on the rights of some foreign nationals in the United States in his plurality opinion in *United States v. Verdugo-Urquidez*, 494 U.S. 259, 271 (1990), in which he suggested that a Mexican citizen who had been involuntarily brought into this country for criminal prosecution was not part of "the people" eligible to invoke the Fourth Amendment. However, he was unable to garner a majority for that view, and Justice Kennedy, whose vote was necessary to the majority in that case, expressly rejected Rehnquist's suggestion that the Fourth Amendment did not extend to all persons present in the United States. 494 U.S. at 276-77 (Kennedy, J., concurring). Justice Kennedy rested instead on the fact that the search took place beyond our borders, a factor also relied upon by Chief Justice Rehnquist. *Id.* at 278.

13. Jonathan Elliot, *The Debates in the Several State Conventions on the Adoption of the Federal Constitution* (Philadelphia: J. B. Lippincott, 1836), v. 4, 556.

14. The debate that accompanied the enactment and ultimate demise of the Alien and Sedition Acts suggests that there was in fact substantial disagreement about the status of foreign nationals' rights in the early years of the republic, at least in a time of crisis. Opponents of the Alien Act, mostly Republicans, pointed to the broad language of the Bill of Rights and the legal obligations imposed on all persons residing within our territory as support for the notion that foreign nationals were entitled to the protection of the Bill of Rights. Others, mostly Federalists, maintained that the Constitution was a more limited social compact that protected only "we the people." See Gerald L. Neuman, *Strangers to the Constitution: Immigrants, Borders, and Fundamental Law* (Princeton, NJ: Princeton University Press, 1996), 52–63. But as with the Sedition Act, so with the Alien Act, those espousing the more inclusive, rights-protective views ultimately prevailed. Cf. *New York Times Co. v. Sullivan*, 376 U.S. 254, 273–76 (1964) (relying on history of repudiation of

Sedition Act as evidence for importance of protecting political dissent under First Amendment).

15. See generally Suzanna Sherry, "The Founders' Unwritten Constitution," 54 *University of Chicago Law Review* 1127 (1987).

16. Richard B. Lillich, *The Human Rights of Aliens in Contemporary International Law* (Manchester, England: Manchester University Press, 1984), 41; Universal Declaration of Human Rights, G.A. Res. 217A(III), U.N. GAOR, 3d. Sess., Supp. No. 13, at 71, U.N. Doc. A/810 (1948).

17. Lillich, *supra,* 43; Baroness Elles, *International Provisions Protecting the Human Rights of Non-Citizens* at para. 45, U.N. Doc. E/CN.4/Sub.2/392/Rev.1, U.N. Sales No. E.80.XIV.2 (1980); David Weissbrodt, *Prevention of Discrimination and Protection of Indigenous Peoples and Minorities: The Rights of Non-Citizens* at para. 30, U.N. Doc E/CN.4/Sub.2/2001/20 (2001); Carmen Tiburcio, *The Human Rights of Aliens Under International and Comparative Law* (The Hague, Netherlands: Martinus Nijhoff Publishers, 2001).

18. Universal Declaration of Human Rights, pmbl., art. 7–11, 19, 20(1), G.A. Res. 217 A (III), U.N. GAOR, 3d Sess., at 71, U.N. Doc. A/810 (1948).

19. General Comment 15, *The Position of Aliens Under the Covenant,* Human Rights Committee, U.N. Doc. HRI/GEN/I/Rev. 1, at 18 (1994), 27th Sess., 1986, at para. 7; Lillich, *supra,* 46; Weissbrodt, *supra,* para. 38–43.

20. U.N. GAOR, 40th Sess., Supp. No. 53, at 252, U.N. Doc. 40/144 (December 13, 1985). Interestingly, while international instruments generally prohibit discrimination on a number of grounds, including national origin, they generally do not expressly prohibit discrimination on grounds of nationality. " '[N]ational origin' refers to a person's descent, not to his juridical nationality." Lillich, *supra,* 46. However, international scholars have nonetheless generally interpreted human rights treaties to bar nationality-based discrimination, except pursuant to otherwise lawful immigration restrictions, or in times of war, where necessary to defend the nation. See Weissbrodt, *supra,* paras. 30, 37; Baroness Elles, *supra,* §299.

21. B. G. Ramcharan, "Equality and Nondiscrimination," in Louis Henkin, ed., *The International Bill of Rights: The Covenant on Civil and Political Rights* (New York: Columbia University Press, 1981), 246, 263.

22. Peter Nobel, "The Alien Under Swedish Law," 11 *Comparative Law Yearbook* 165, 168 (1992) (noting that "as far as constitutional rights and freedoms are concerned, the alien lawfully staying in Sweden is equal to the national in respect of the freedoms of expression, information, congregation, political and religious opinions, association, demonstration and all rules to protect integrity and rule of law as well as protection of property, material as well as immaterial").

23. See, e.g., *Yamani v. Canada,* [1995] 1 F.C. 174.

24. Constitution of Italy, Arts. 13, 14, 17–21, 24; see Bruno Nascimbene, *Lo Straniero Nel Diritto Italiano* (Milano, Italy: Giuffrè Ed., 1988); Cass., sez. un., 21 Feb. 2002, n.2513 ("citizens of a country other than the EU ones do not only enjoy the fundamental human rights as provided for by national law, international conventions and common principles of international law, but also the principle of equal treatment as Italian citizens with respect to judicial guarantees and due process of law"), available at http://www.cittadinolex.kataweb.it/article/0.1519.181051137.00.html.

25. Ruth Rubio-Marín, *Immigration as a Democratic Challenge: Citizenship and Inclusion in Germany and the United States* (Cambridge, England: Cambridge University Press, 2000), 187–88 & n.16.

26. See Lillich, *supra,* 94; Weissbrodt, *supra,* para. 124 (quoting Exclusion, Equality Before the Law and Non-Discrimination, Proceedings of a seminar organized by the Secretariat General of the Council of Europe in cooperation with the International Center for Sociological, Criminal and Penitential Research and Studies [INTERCENTER] of Messina, Italy [Taormina Mare, Italy, 29 September–1 October 1994], 135).

27. David Feldman, "Human Dignity as a Legal Value—Part I," 1999 *Public Law* 682, 690–91.

28. *Palko v. Connecticut,* 302 U.S. 319, 325 (1937).

29. Alexander M. Bickel, *The Morality of Consent* (New Haven, CT: Yale University Press, 1975), 33–54.

30. *Dred Scott v. Sandford,* 60 U.S. (19 How.) 393 (1856).

31. *Id.* at 403.

32. *Id.* at 404–05. This is almost the same language the Supreme Court used nearly one hundred years later when it held that Ellen Knauff, a German citizen seeking admission to the country, could assert no constitutional objection to the fact that she was being excluded on the basis of secret evidence because "[w]hatever the procedure authorized by Congress is, it is due process as far as an alien denied entry is concerned." *United States ex rel. Knauff v. Shaughnessy,* 338 U.S. 537, 544 (1950). See *supra,* Chapter 10.

33. Civil Rights Act of 1866, Ch. 31, §1, 14 Stat. 27.

34. Bickel, *supra,* 53.

35. David A. Martin, "Graduated Application of Constitutional Protections for Aliens: The Real Meaning of *Zadvydas v. Davis,*" 2001 *Supreme Court Review* 47, 93–94.

36. John Hart Ely, *Democracy and Distrust: A Theory of Judicial Review* (Cambridge, MA: Harvard University Press, 1980), 161–62. Ely notes that "[a]liens cannot vote in any state, which means that any representation they receive will be exclusively 'virtual,' " that aliens have been the subject of substantial prejudice throughout our history, that recent immigrants in particular tend to live fairly discrete and unassimilated lives, and that "our legislatures are composed almost entirely of citizens who have always been such."

37. Interestingly, while citizenship is a prerequisite to running for president or Congress, the political branches, it is not a requirement for appointment to the federal judiciary, which is responsible for enforcing constitutional rights.

38. *Graham v. Richardson,* 403 U.S. 365, 372 (1971).

39. *First National Bank of Boston v. Bellotti,* 435 U.S. 765 (1978).

40. *American-Arab Anti-Discrimination Comm. v. Meese,* 714 F. Supp. 1060 (C.D. Cal. 1989) ("it is impossible to adopt for aliens a lower degree of First Amendment protection solely in the deportation setting without seriously affecting their First Amendment rights outside that setting"), *aff'd in part and rev'd in part on other grounds,* 970 F.2d 501 (9th Cir. 1992).

41. See, e.g., Testimony of Larry Parkinson, Deputy General Counsel, FBI, Before House of Representatives Subcommittee on Immigration of the Judiciary Committee, *The Secret Evidence Repeal Act, Hearings on H.R. 2121,* 106th Cong. 18, 36 (February 10, 2000) (arguing that foreign nationals are entitled to diminished due process protection).

42. *Mathews v. Eldridge,* 424 U.S. 319 (1976) (establishing balancing test for determining what process is due); *Landon v. Plasencia,* 459 U.S. 21 (1982) (holding that *Mathews* balancing also governs what process is due in immigration proceedings).

43. See, e.g., *Kiareldeen v. Reno,* 71 F. Supp. 2d. 402, 410 (D.N.J. 1999) (rejecting government's "keys to cell" argument).

44. *Yick Wo v. Hopkins,* 118 U.S. 356, 369 (1886).

45. *Plyler v. Doe,* 457 U.S. 202 (1982).

46. *Graham v. Richardson,* 403 U.S. 365 (1971) (striking down under "strict scrutiny" a state statute denying welfare benefits to certain persons based on their immigration status). A distinction based on *alienage* differentiates between citizens and noncitizens generally; all of immigration law has at least this feature. A classification based on *nationality* treats nationals of particular countries differently, as in laws currently on the books treating Cuban nationals more favorably than other immigrants. And discrimination on the basis of *national origin* is

predicated on the individual's country of birth, regardless of current citizenship (as in the Japanese internment laws). All three are presumptively suspect when adopted by states.

47. *Mathews v. Diaz,* 426 U.S. 67, 90 (1976).

48. T. Alexander Aleinikoff, *Semblances of Sovereignty: The Constitution, the State, and American Citizenship* (Cambridge, MA: Harvard University Press, 2002), 156.

49. See *supra* note 6.

50. See *Cabell v. Chavez-Salido,* 454 U.S. at 438 (citizenship is "not a relevant ground for [state] distribution of economic benefits [but] it is for determining membership in the political community").

51. The notion that noncitizens are entitled to the same constitutional protection for their basic human rights as citizens must be qualified in at least one respect. The Supreme Court has historically treated foreign nationals outside our border very differently from those within our jurisdiction. As the Court recently noted, "it is well established that certain constitutional protections available to persons inside the United States are unavailable to aliens outside of our geographic borders. But once an alien enters the country, the legal circumstance changes, for the Due Process Clause applies to all 'persons' within the United States. . . ." *Zadvydas v. Davis,* 533 U.S. at 693. Like plenary power, however, the notion that foreign nationals outside our borders enjoy no constitutional protection has often been overstated. The case most often cited for the proposition, *United States ex. rel Knauff v. Shaughnessy,* 338 U.S. 537 (1950), discussed in Chapter 10, involved a challenge to the procedures used to decide an initial entrant's request for admission. The Court reasoned that noncitizens seeking initial entry have no right to enter, and therefore may not object on due process grounds to the procedures used to determine whether they may enter.

That result, however, does not compel the much more sweeping conclusion that foreign nationals outside our borders have no constitutional rights whatsoever. Rather, it may simply reflect the proposition—equally applicable to citizens—that where a statute does not create an entitlement, no "liberty" or "property" interest is implicated by the denial of the gratuitous benefit it offers, and therefore due process does not attach. See, e.g., *Olim v. Wakinekona,* 461 U.S. 238, 248–49 (1983) (holding that state prison regulations did not create a liberty interest implicated by a transfer to another state, and therefore due process was not triggered); *Board of Regents of State Colleges v. Roth,* 408 U.S. 564, 578 (1972) (holding that an untenured professor had no property interest in being rehired and therefore no due process objection to the procedures used to reach that decision). Since the Court treated Knauff as having no entitlement to enter, but as merely seeking a benefit, she had neither a liberty nor a property interest sufficient to trigger due process protection, just as a convicted prisoner has no liberty or property interest in a discretionary pardon from the governor, and therefore may not challenge the procedures by which pardons are granted. Where, by contrast, the government is not merely denying foreign nationals outside of our borders a gratuitous benefit, but affirmatively subjecting them to the obligations of our legal system, they should reciprocally receive the protection of the constitutional limits on such government action. See Neuman, *Strangers to the Constitution, supra,* 108–17 (arguing that aliens should have constitutional rights abroad where the United States imposes its sovereign legal obligations on them). On this view, while a decision to deny initial entry to a foreign national might not trigger due process, because he has no independent right to enter, a decision to *detain* an entering non-national would trigger due process, because detention affirmatively deprives the person of physical liberty, and "[f]reedom from imprisonment . . . lies at the heart of the liberty that [the Due Process] Clause protects." *Zadvydas,* 533 U.S. at 690; see also *Foucha v. Louisiana,* 504 U.S. 71, 80 (1992) ("[C]ommitment for any purpose constitutes a significant deprivation of liberty that requires due process protection") (internal citations omitted); *Meyer v. Nebraska,* 262 U.S. 390, 399 (1923) ("Without doubt, [liberty] denotes . . . freedom from bodily restraint."). Admittedly, *Knauff* and *Shaughnessy v. United States ex rel. Mezei,* 345 U.S. 206 (1953), suggest that detention of arriving foreign visitors does not change the constitutional calculus, but in that respect they are wrongly decided, because detention cannot be equated with the mere denial of a benefit. See David Cole, "In Aid of Removal: Due Process Limits on Immigration Detention," 51 *Emory Law Journal* 1003, 1031–37 (2002).

52. *Brandenburg v. Ohio,* 395 U.S. 444 (1969).

53. The issue here is not whether it makes sense to focus on Arab and Muslim foreign nationals in the search for Al Qaeda operatives. I address that argument in Chapters 3 and 13, and maintain that ethnic profiling is not justified as a legal matter or as a matter of sound security policy. The question posed here is broader: Are noncitizens living in the United States, or otherwise subjected to American legal obligations, entitled to the same basic constitutional protection as citizens, or do they deserve only diminished constitutional safeguards?

54. Rubio-Marín, *supra,* 52.

55. See, e.g., *Fiallo v. Bell,* 430 U.S. 787, 796 (1977) (quoting *Mathews v. Diaz,* 426 U.S. at 81–82); *The Chinese Exclusion Case (Chae Chan Ping v. United States),* 130 U.S. at 603–06. The plenary power doctrine has been subject to widespread criticism. See Stephen Legomsky, *Immigration and the Judiciary* (Oxford, England: Oxford University Press, 1987), 177–222; Neuman, *Strangers to the Constitution, supra,* 118–38; Louis Henkin, "The Constitution and United States Sovereignty: A Century of Chinese Exclusion and its Progeny," 100 *Harvard Law Review* 853 (1987).

56. *Zadvydas v. Davis*, 533 U.S. at 695; see also *Carlson v. Landon*, 342 U.S. 524, 537 (1952) ("the power to expel aliens . . . is, of course, subject to judicial intervention under the 'paramount law of the Constitution.' ") (internal citations omitted)).

57. *Kwong Hai Chew v. Colding*, 344 U.S. at 596 n.5.

58. *Harisiades v. Shaughnessy*, 342 U.S. 936 (1952); *Dennis v. United States*, 341 U.S. 494 (1951); see *American-Arab Anti-Discrimination Comm. v. Meese*, 714 F. Supp. at 1077–78; see also T. Alexander Aleinikoff, "Federal Regulation of Aliens and the Constitution," 83 *American Journal of International Law* 862, 869 (1989).

59. See, e.g., *Zadvydas*, 533 U.S. at 690 (relying on *United States v. Salerno*, 481 U.S. 739 (1987), involving the preventive detention of a citizen in criminal proceedings, and *Foucha v. Louisiana*, 504 U.S. 71 (1992), involving preventive detention of a citizen in civil commitment proceedings); see also *United States v. Salerno*, 481 U.S. 739, 748 (1987) (citing *Carlson v. Landon*, 342 U.S. 524 (1952), as support for permitting preventive detention in some circumstances in criminal cases). See generally Cole, "In Aid of Removal," *supra*.

60. *Demore v. Kim*, 123 S. Ct. 1708 (2003).

61. *Mathews v. Diaz*, 426 U.S. at 80.

62. *Carlson v. Landon*, 342 U.S. at 534.

63. *Bugajewitz v. Adams*, 228 U.S. 585, 591 (1913).

64. *Graham v. Richardson*, 403 U.S. at 374.

65. See, e.g., *Rust v. Sullivan*, 500 U.S. 173, 197 (1991) (characterizing "unconstitutional condition" cases as involving "situations in which the Government has placed a condition on the recipient of the subsidy rather than on a particular program or service, thus effectively prohibiting the recipient from engaging in the protected conduct outside the scope of the federally funded program"); *Connick v. Myers*, 461 U.S. 138, 142 (1983) ("For at least fifteen years, it has been settled that a State cannot condition public employment on a basis that infringes the employee's constitutionally protected interest in freedom of expression.").

66. See, e.g., Peter Schuck, *Citizens, Strangers, and In-Betweens: Essays on Immigration and Citizenship* (Boulder, CO: Westview Press, 1998), 163–75.

Conclusion: Breaking the Cycle

1. Francis Biddle, *In Brief Authority* (Garden City, NY.: Doubleday, 1962), 219.

2. *Congressional Globe*, April 11, 1871, at 574.

3. William J. Brennan, Jr., "The Quest to Develop a Jurisprudence of Civil Liberties in Times of Security Crises," 18 *Israel Yearbook of Human Rights* 11, 11 (1988).

4. 18 U.S.C. §4001(a); Stephen I. Vladeck, "A Small Problem of Precedent: 18 U.S.C. §4001(a) and the Detention of U.S. Citizen 'Enemy Combatants,' " 112 *Yale Law Journal* 961 (2003).

5. The Privacy Act of 1974, 5 U.S.C. §552(a), Pub. L. No. 93-579 (1974); Foreign Intelligence Surveillance Act, 50 U.S.C. §§1801-1808, Pub. L. No. 95-511 (1978); Freedom of Information Act, Pub. L. No. 93-502, §§1–3, 88 Stat. 1561 (codified as amended at 5 U.S.C. §552) (1974).

6. *Railway Express Agency, Inc. v. New York,* 336 U.S. 106, 112 (1949) (Jackson J., concurring).

7. Oren Gross, "Chaos and Rules: Should Responses to Violent Crises Always Be Constitutional?," 112 *Yale Law Journal* 1011, 1031–43 (2003).

8. *Railway Express Agency, Inc. v. New York,* 336 U.S. at 112 (Jackson, J., concurring).

9. H. Freedman, ed., *Jeremiah, Soncino Books of the Bible* (series ed. A. Cohen) (London: Soncino Books of the Bible, rev. ed. 1985), 52 (quoting Hermann Cohen).

INDEX

Daughtery, Harry, 125
Debs, Eugene Victor, 105, 106
Declaration on the Human Rights
    of Individuals Who are Not
    Nationals of the Country in
    which They Live, 214–15
Dedman, Bill, 184
Defense Advance Research Projects
    Agency (DARPA), 18, 73–74,
    232
Demore v. Kim, 224
Dennis v. United States, 139–41, 147
deportation
    Bill of Rights as irrelevant for,
        164, 167
    Communist Party association
        and, 119–20, 121, 122–24,
        132–36
    detention without bond and,
        19–21
    expatriated citizens and, 69–70
    fear of, and freedom of speech,
        218
    plenary power doctrine and,
        224–25
    political dissent in World War I
        and, 109–11
    targeting of Arab and Muslim
        community and, 19–21, 50,
        191–92
    for terrorist activity, 165–66
    for visa violations, 165–66, 168
    voluntary departure and, 33–34,
        38–39, 122
DESA. *See* Domestic Security
    Enhancement Act (DSEA)

detention as security measure. *See
    also* Japanese internment;
    preventive detention campaign
    Congressional repudiation of,
        102, 103
    "Contingency Plan" of 1986 and,
        102, 103
    extension to citizens, 7
    plenary power and, 225
    post-Cold War programs and,
        101–2
Detroit, Michigan, 256n.11
De Witt, John L., 95, 97, 141
Doctorow, E. L., 162
Domestic Security Enhancement
    Act (DSEA), 69–71
domestic security investigations,
    effective techniques for,
    188
domestic spying
    FBI and, 18, 79–81, 156–58,
        164–65, 186, 201, 231
    guidelines for, 79–81, 201, 231
    "Palmer Raids" and, 125, 128
double standard. *See also* citizen-
    noncitizen rights distinction
    as constitutionally wrong, 11–13,
        90–91, 152–53, 211–27
    as counterproductive, 9–10,
        184–89, 226
    as detrimental to citizen's
        interests, 5, 7–9, 226
    flaws in arguments for, 7–13,
        222–26
    international cooperation and,
        9–10, 183, 194–97